Ethical Encounters

ELORA HALIM CHOWDHURY

Ethical Encounters

Transnational Feminism, Human Rights,
and War Cinema in Bangladesh

TEMPLE UNIVERSITY PRESS
Philadelphia • Rome • Tokyo

TEMPLE UNIVERSITY PRESS
Philadelphia, Pennsylvania 19122
tupress.temple.edu

Library of Congress Cataloging-in-Publication Data

Names: Chowdhury, Elora Halim, author.
Title: Ethical encounters : transnational feminism, human rights, and war
   cinema in Bangladesh / Elora Halim Chowdhury.
Description: Philadelphia : Temple University Press, 2022. | Includes
   bibliographical references and index. | Summary: "Reading national
   cinema made by and centrally about women in Bangladesh, this book is an
   exploration of the intersection of feminism, human rights, and memory"—
   Provided by publisher.
Identifiers: LCCN 2021046377 (print) | LCCN 2021046378 (ebook) | ISBN
   9781439922248 (cloth) | ISBN 9781439922255 (paperback) | ISBN
   9781439922262 (pdf)
Subjects: LCSH: Human rights in motion pictures. | National characteristics
   in motion pictures. | Women in motion pictures. | Feminism and motion
   pictures. | Feminist film criticism. | Bangladesh—History—Revolution,
   1971—Motion pictures and the revolution. |
   Bangladesh—History—Revolution, 1971—Women. |
   Bangladesh—History—Revolution, 1971—Women—Personal narratives. |
   Bangladesh—In motion pictures.
Classification: LCC PN1993.5.B3 C48 2022 (print) | LCC PN1993.5.B3
   (ebook) | DDC 791.43082/095492—dc23/eng/20220111
LC record available at https://lccn.loc.gov/2021046377
LC ebook record available at https://lccn.loc.gov/2021046378

Printed in the United States of America

9 8 7 6 5 4 3 2 1

This book is dedicated to my parents,

FAZLUL HALIM CHOWDHURY *(1930–1996) and*

SHAMSUN NAHAR CHOWDHURY,

for their unwavering and principled commitment to justice.

My mother's art of storytelling about 1971

inspired the aesthetic and feminist imaginings

in this book.

Contents

Acknowledgments

This book has taken me on a decade-long exploration, leading me to unexpected spaces, archives, collaborations, and conversations. An incredible journey, it has taught me to see differently, look at marginal narratives, and peel away at familiar and cherished truths. In so doing, this research has opened up possibilities for more capacious imaginings of women's agencies, desires, and survival, centering on justice and responsibility.

A book is always a collaborative undertaking, spanning multiple personal and professional trajectories of one's life. My curiosity about Bangladesh's Liberation War has its roots in my family's experiences and encounters during that tumultuous time. I grew up hearing gendered stories of anticolonial and national liberation struggles from my father, who was an academic and an activist, and my mother, who endured many losses during the war and was a passionate supporter of the freedom struggle. Their community of friends, colleagues, and various associates over the years shared the inspiration and experience of the Liberation War, continuing to relive the trauma of the birth of Bangladesh yet instilling in us—myself, my siblings, and many others who were in our circle of kin, family, and nation—an enduring sense of ethical citizenship. My heartfelt gratitude to this community of elders and multigenerational survivors for the hardship and wisdom borne of that experience that they have passed on to so many.

In the deeply intimate realm of women's cinema about the liberation struggle—*Muktijuddho*—I found powerful stories of compassion, healing, and a sensibility for justice. Immense gratitude to all the filmmakers and storytellers who have helped create this imaginative genre, filled as it may be with contradictions yet rife with aesthetic and political possibilities. Each and every film speaks of the courage of everyday people who fought for and believed in an alternative world of gendered peace and justice. Respect and admiration for Shameem Akhtar, Farzana Boby, Shabnam Ferdousi, Leesa Gazi, Rubaiyat Hossain, Yasmine Kabir, Tareque and Catherine Masud, and Nasiruddin Yousuff for their incredible talent and ethical commitment. I hope that this book does justice to their vision in even small ways.

Along the way, as a student of cinema studies, I was fortunate to have met Esha Niyogi De, who has been a friend and mentor. I owe much gratitude to her brilliant vision and expansive thinking about cross-border women's cinema, which enabled me to participate in several workshops, in Bangladesh, India, and Pakistan, that strengthened my understanding about the intricacies of filmmaking, industry, and regional connectivities. I am deeply grateful to all the South Asia Regional Media Scholars Network (SARMSNet) participants, and, especially, to Nasreen Rehman, whose sharp insights about Bangladesh-Pakistan history, and personal experiences of feminist activism, greatly enriched my own thinking about war and its various untold stories.

This book would not have been possible without the generous and thoughtful readings by friends and colleagues. Azza Basarudin, Alka Kurian, Sharmila Lodhia, Liz Philipose, Khanum Shaikh—thank you for the loving friendships, encouragement, and critical suggestions over many years. I am endlessly grateful for my writing group in Boston for reading numerous chapters through various stages and offering insightful comments. Ayesha Irani, Sarah Pinto, Jyoti Puri, and Banu Subramaniam—I am so inspired by your tireless engagements. A very special thanks to Rahnuma Ahmed, Tina Beyene, Deepti Misri, Nadine Shaanta Murshid, and Catherine Sameh, who read numerous chapters carefully and offered steadfast encouragement and astute comments. In this vein, I am also indebted to Cynthia Enloe, Wendy Hesford, Chandra Talpade Mohanty, and Jennifer Nash, who have charted new terrains in feminist thought and whose work has been enormously inspirational for my own.

To Shaun Vigil, my editor at Temple University Press, I am most grateful for his support and respectful investment in this interdisciplinary work. It is rare to come across a reader who unreservedly embraces feminist work that spans so many genres, histories, and regions; I am truly appreciative of his keen understanding and interest. The external reviewers provided insightful suggestions to improve the breadth and scope of the work, and I am enormously appreciative for their generosity and contributions. An earlier version of Chapter 1 first appeared as "War Healing and Trauma: Reading the Feminine Aesthetics and Politics in Rubaiyat Hossain's Meherjaan" in *Feminist Formations*, Volume 28, Issue 3, January 2016, pages 27–45. Published by Johns Hopkins University Press. Copyright © 2016 Feminist Formations. An earlier version of Chapter 2 was published in 2021 as "Ethical Reckoning: Human Rights and National Cinema in Bangladesh" in *Meridians: Feminism, Race, Transnationalism*, Vol. 20, No. 1, 151–173. An earlier version of Chapter 4 appeared in 2020 as "Muktijuddho Film as Disruptive Archive, Filmmaker as Witness" in *South Asia Chronicle*, Vol. 10, 59–95. I am grateful for the productive feedback by the reviewers and editors of these volumes.

This research has benefited from the generous support of University of Massachusetts Boston College of Liberal Arts Deans Office, Labor Resource Center, and the Office of Global Programs. Numerous grants from these units enabled me to travel, do archival research in South Asia, and participate in important regional conferences. I am forever indebted to the excellent research assistants who have helped me along the way: Ria Goveas, Sara Monami Hossain, Riva Pearson, Sumiya Shimu, and Shilpi Suneja. Incredible interlocutors without whom I would have been lost, they helped me find resources, contributed to myriad aspects of the scholarship, assisted with copyediting, formatting, and various painstaking and unglamorous chores that go into the making of a book project. I have been fortunate to work with superbly talented copyeditors, Anna Alves and Perri Schenker, whose magic helped transform words to prose. A warm thanks to Fakhrul Alam Shohag at the Bangladesh Film Archive for his encyclopedic knowledge about the industry and cinematic history of Bangladesh and for the invigorating conversations. I am so grateful to Aedyn Downey, the hidden treasure of UMass Boston, the fabulously talented department manager of Women's, Gender, and Sexuality Studies, for helping acquire films otherwise difficult to find. I want to thank the students of my seminars, "Human Rights Cinema" and "Advanced Topics in Human Rights," for their spirited reflections and conversations that greatly enriched my thinking. My department colleagues have provided me with an intellectually rigorous community to further my work over the years and the wider network of colleagues at UMass Boston has provided valuable dialogists. Thank you for your friendship and collegiality: Nada Ali, Chris Bobel, Maria Brincker, Carol Cohn, Shoshanna Ehrlich, Amani El Jack, Leila Farsakh, Sana Haroon, Andrés Fabian Henao-Castro, Jean Humez, Ayesha Irani, Aparna Mujumdar, Louise Penner, Pratima Prasad, and Rajini Srikanth. I am incredibly blessed to be in the sisterhood of Nafisa Halim, Nazli Kibria, Marisol Negrón, Isis Nusair, Mickaella Perina, Bandana Purkayastha, Michelle Rowley, Faith Smith, Nafisa Tanjeem, and Lynnell Thomas, who have taught me, cared for and supported me, and inspired me in more ways than I can count. In addition, I have learned so much from and with feminist researchers and comrades whose contributions have enriched the fields of transnational feminisms and Bangladesh

Studies: Rahnuma Ahmed, Kiran Asher, Srimati Basu, Kabita Chakma, Piya Chatterjee, Sushmita Chatterjee, Bina D'Costa, Sylvanna Falcón, Kaberi Gayen, Meghna Guhathakurta, Lamia Karim, Farida Khan, Shenila Khoja-Moolji, Viviana MacManus, Nadine Murshid, Navine Murshid, Richa Nagar, Rachel Afi Quinn, Seuty Sabur, Yasmin Saikia, Elora Shehabuddin, and Dina Siddiqi. My neighborhood friends Suha Abu-Amara, Ken and Christine Baily, Kristin Butcher, Kate Carpenter-Bernier, Desmond Hall, Toni Hicks, Anu Medappa Jayanth, Inci Kaya, Felicia Khan, Shruti Mandana, Charlotte Rice, and Tripti Thomas have provided nourishment and illuminating conversations. Their camaraderie, especially as I completed book revisions during the isolating conditions of a global pandemic, provided enduring enrichment for the soul and mind.

It has been a privilege to be in residence at the Newhouse Humanities Center at Wellesley College to further my work in conversation with a brilliant group of Fellow-Fellows. I am so enlivened by this community of scholars who pushed me to think beyond my own interdisciplinary and transnational boundaries. This work was enhanced greatly by the commentaries and suggestions of peers and colleagues gleaned over numerous presentations, including at Syracuse University; Northwestern University; Dhaka University, Bangladesh; Lahore University of Management Sciences (LUMS), Pakistan; Jadavpur University, India; University of California Los Angeles (UCLA); Cornell University; and at several National Women's Studies Association (NWSA) conferences.

Last but certainly not least, thank you: To my life companion, Alok Kapoor, who has supported me, encouraged me, and ensured me unencumbered time and space to write and think. Even though we work in seemingly divergent fields, his critical skills have been essential for my scholarly growth, and his technical expertise has helped immeasurably in getting the nitty-gritty of this project completed. My mother-out-law, Sheela Kapoor, who always cheered on my scholarly endeavors and proudly displayed my books on her coffee table. My eldest sister, Sadeka Halim, who believed in me, even when at times I felt doubtful; her—as well as that of my siblings Zakia Chowdhury and Enamul Aziz Chowdhury, and a host of aunties, uncles, cousins, nephews, and nieces—pride and joy in my work and success is heartwarming. My children, Zain and Zahin, are the light and joy of my life, my biggest fans, who give me the strength and inspiration to imagine and carry on!

Ethical Encounters

Prologue

Shameem Akhtar's film *Rina Brown* (2017) is about unfulfilled dreams of love and freedom. Akhtar, one of only a few independent women filmmakers in Bangladesh, sets the story in contemporary Bangladesh tracing the return of Rina, an Anglo-Christian, to the independent nation of Bangladesh, which she had left decades earlier, during the turbulence of the Bangladesh Liberation War, or *Muktijuddho*. She returns to Dhaka as a participant in a seminar about women in conflict. There, forty years after the war's end, she searches for her adolescent love, Darashiko, a Bengali Muslim freedom fighter turned business executive. Over the course of a long afternoon, the two reminisce about the fading aspirations of the nationalist struggle and the attendant unreconciled trauma. As the freedom struggle had gained momentum, Dara had introduced Rina to Bengali literature, history, and music, and she had shared with him her faith in the church as an anchor to her vision for love and freedom. It had been an interfaith union against the backdrop of the leftist secular leanings of the Bengali intelligentsia, with the families of the two star-crossed lovers remaining fearful and suspicious of each other. A modern remake of Ajoy Kar's 1961 film *Saptapadi*, *Rina Brown* unfolds the intimate geographies of love and loss among individuals from India and then West and East Pakistan. *Saptapadi* was set amid the rising agitations for India's independence in the 1940s, and the youthful romance between a Bengali Hindu and an Anglo-Christian etches the many intimate divides of religion, ethnicity, and culture. In a similar format, Akhtar's film relies on flashbacks, documentary footage, and play-

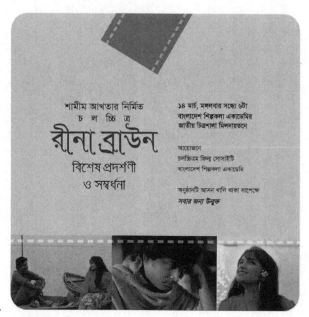

Figure P.1 Film poster for *Rina Brown* (dir. Shameem Akhtar, 2017).

back singing to foreground the conflicted legacy of the Muktijuddho told through the unfulfilled romance between a Bengali Muslim and an Anglo-Christian. As the couple look out on the sweeping urban landscape of the city of Dhaka and think about what could have been, the vacant footbridge, bereft of pedestrians, stands as a metaphor to all that the war tore asunder and to the imaginary borders that became intractably entrenched. War changed everything, yet, as Dara expresses forlornly, "We could not change the country." Rina's past is indelibly linked to the history of Bangladesh, but she is now a stranger whose suffering is incomprehensible to the postwar generation.

I begin with this vignette from Akhtar's film—a woman-centered Muktijuddho film—because it shines light on what the set of essays in this book strives to do: reimagine a Muktijuddho gender ideology in and through visual culture that engages with yet ruptures and incites a new imaginary for gender justice. Organized as a set of essays, each chapter in this book sheds light on women-centric cinema in Bangladesh and the ways in which these defy conventional readings of aesthetics and politics of the Muktijuddho filmic narrative. They tell the stories of the birth of a nation from the margins.

Historian Willem Van Schendel (2015) argues that in the aftermath of the Bangladesh Liberation War in 1971, three competing genres of historiography emerged: one that memorializes the war as a national triumph, one that frames it as a betrayal to Pakistan, and one that recounts a benevolent intervention by India.[1] In more recent years, Van Schendel further argues, a more complex historiography has begun to unfold that reads nuance into such reductive and monolithic renditions. These second-generation narratives complicate victims and aggressors, loss and triumph, and villains and heroes, and they simultaneously strive for more ethical recognitions drawing on the multiplicity of experiences. A new wave of critical feminist scholarship has emerged around the nexus of gender, violence, war crimes, reconciliation, and the Bangladesh War of Independence. In *The Spectral Wound* (2015), for instance, a groundbreaking book on this topic, Nayanika Mookherjee cogently argues that the Muktijuddho functions as a metanarrative in Bangladesh and that gender violence is continually invoked in state speeches, policies, and public discourse to the extent that it has become eulogized and normalized. At the same time, even as her work brings a multilayered analysis to a gendered narrative of the war, Mookherjee points out that the Pakistani account of 1971 is absent from her study. This is not a limitation, as accounts of the war and its memorialization vary according to the geopolitical context, but it goes to emphasize how it has been predominantly studied within the integrity of national borders. Additionally, it hints at the way the historiography of the emergence of Bangladesh has been scribed, reified, and imagined, to the obfuscation of its transregional and cross-border intricacies and implications.

Those growing up in postindependence Bangladesh have been steeped in the idea that the liberation struggle was the beginning of our nationalist history, but beyond its national borders that struggle and its legacy remains lesser known. Bangladesh was carved into the Eastern Wing of Pakistan in the 1947 partition of the Indian subcontinent at the end of British colonial rule. Separated by a thousand miles of Indian territory, the two wings shared a religion and were meant to be a Muslim homeland, even while a substantial Muslim population remained in India. However, while they were followers of a common faith, the populations of the two wings of Pakistan were divided by language, culture, and, ultimately, political representation. East Pakistan was more populous yet lesser represented in the central government, and the economic and political relation between the two wings took on colonial dimensions of resource extraction and uneven development that favored West Pakistan. Bengali discontent with the regime culminated in 1970, when the Awami League of East Pakistan won the majority of seats to form a national government with Sheikh Mujibur Rahman[2] as the rightful prime minister. Pakistan's military leader, General Yahya Khan, and his administration stalled and then followed with military intervention to crush the Bengali nationalist movement. The planned military crackdown—centered around Rajarbag Police Line, former East Pakistan Rifles Barracks of Pilkhana, Bongsal, Dhamondi, Mohammadpur, and Dhaka University—came to a head on March 25, 1971, the night known as Operation Searchlight.

The event is memorialized in multiple films—most prominently in Kawsar Chowdhury's *Shei Rater Kotha Bolte Eshechi* (*Tales of the Darkest Night*, 2002)—novels, and memoirs. Nadeem Zaman's debut novel, *In the Time of the Others*, set in Dhaka during the tumult of 1971, depicts that fateful night:

> Besides the university, the East Pakistan Rifles constabulary was also shelled and partially set ablaze. Punjabi and Baluchi soldiers marched in to finish killing the remaining Bengali officers. The Rajarbagh Police Line was defended in the face of tanks, bazookas and automatic rifles, leaving even the attacking soldiers talking about the standoff for days afterward. Captain Shaukat [the West Pakistani commanding officer] as he commanded his company to enter the dormitories of Jagannath Hall[3] and Iqbal Hall, and shoot their occupants where they found them alive, including those still, astonishingly, asleep, heard the reports of the EPR and Rajarbagh incidents in the following days, and wished he had been at one of those. A real fight was one where fire was returned for fire. The students at the dorms had old bolt-action rifles, which they had used. But to take them as a match for the firepower they were facing was a joke. Shaukat saw their feeble efforts blasted through with machine guns and semi-automatics, before being marched outside to face firing squads. (2018, 52–53)

In a recent article commemorating Bangladesh's fiftieth year of independence, British journalist Simon Dring, who was among a small group of foreign correspondents sheltered by Bengali staff and present at the Intercontinental Hotel (now renamed Ruposhi Bangla), describes what he witnessed on the morning of March 27:

> The truth was indeed impossible to hide and to be told by those who survived. At Dhaka University, I saw the bodies of some 30 students in and around Iqbal Hall; an art student was sprawled across his easel; bodies floated in a nearby lake; others near Jagannath Hall had been thrown into hastily dug graves and bulldozed over by a tank. Seven teachers had been gunned down in their quarters and a family of 12 killed in an outhouse. At least 200 students had died at the university—and other teachers, we were told, had been murdered in their homes.
>   In the sprawling, narrow streets of the old city—like Tanti Bazaar and Niar Bazaar—many areas had been burnt to the ground;

people dragged from their houses and shot; a police inspector wandering among the ruins was looking for his constables: "I've found only 30—all of them dead."

At the Rajarbagh Police Lines, tanks had been used to support troops firing incendiary rounds into the men's sleeping quarters. More than 1,100 police officers were based here—many died. (*Daily Star* 2021)

Dring also writes that on the afternoon of March 25, President Yahya Khan had flown back to West Pakistan following the talks between the political leaders of the two wings of Pakistan. The talks were meant to find a solution to the crisis in East Pakistan but had come to an abrupt end.

Historians and journalists have written about the massive atrocities committed against the Hindu minority, Bengali academics and intelligentsia, and women, among others in the following months. Tensions rose between Bengalis and Urdu-speaking minorities, leading to attacks on this community that had migrated to East Pakistan from India after partition and was known as Biharis and pro-Pakistani. Official Bangladesh government figures suggest three million deaths in 1971. Sexual violence was deployed as a systematic tool of war, resulting in two hundred thousand to four hundred thousand rapes and twenty-five thousand pregnancies. The Muktijuddho, referred to as another, although lesser-known, partition of the Indian subcontinent, has been recorded in history—mostly in Bangladesh and the surrounding region—as an eruption of what has been an ongoing dispute over "religious essentialism versus inclusive secularism" (Tripathi 2016, xiii). The seeming conflict over the religious and ethnic identity of Bengali Muslims and the threat it posed to the Pakistani state are poignantly depicted in Zaman's novel through the rationalizations of an officer, Shaukat, of the West Pakistani army:

What he had done during the night [of Operation Searchlight], shooting the six Muslim students, had clarified in his mind. If they were true Muslims they would have fought on the right side. Instead, they had joined forces with the enemy. Hiding behind being Muslim was as heinous an act as maligning the Prophet (Peace be upon Him). His father would agree. Shaukat had done his duty, to his uniform, to his country, and to his faith. (2018, 63–64)

Two days later, after Sheikh Mujib[4] had been arrested by the order of President Yahya Khan and flown to West Pakistan where he remained imprisoned during the war, General Ziaur Rahman, sector commander of the East

Bengal Regiment, declared the independence of Bangladesh in an announce-
ment in the Free Bangla Radio from Chittagong:

> *The Government of the Sovereign State of Bangladesh, on behalf of our
> great national leader, the supreme commander of Bangladesh, Sheikh
> Mujibur Rahman, do hereby proclaim the independence of Bangla-
> desh. It is further proclaimed that Sheikh Mujibur Rahman is the sole
> leader of the elected representatives of the 75 million people of Ban-
> gladesh. I therefore appeal on behalf of our great leader Sheikh Muji-
> bur Rahman to the governments of all the democratic countries of the
> world, especially the big world powers, and the neighboring countries,
> to take effective steps to stop immediately the awful genocide that has
> been carried out by the army of occupation from Pakistan. To dub us,
> the legally elected representatives of the majority of the people, as re-
> pressionist is a cruel joke and contradiction in terms which should be-
> fool none. The guiding principle of the new state will be first, neutral-
> ity, second, peace, and third, friendship to all and enmity to none. May
> Allah help us. Joy Bangla.* (Zaman 2018, 69–70; italics in the original)

These founding principles were later translated into the constitution of Bangladesh in the form of nationalism, socialism, democracy, and secularism.
It is noteworthy that Sheikh Mujib's declaration, as enunciated by General
Ziaur Rahman, ended with references to faith in God (Allah) and to the
nationalist slogan "Joy Bangla." These foundational elements to the Bengali
nationalist identity—the religious and the ethnic—were the cause for military retaliation by the Western Wing of the nation. In one poignant scene of
his novel, Zaman showcases this conflict as a Pakistani soldier harasses four
Bengali Muslim men to prove their legitimacy to the nation. The soldier, aptly
named Bismillah,[5] stops the car in which the men are traveling after curfew
and commands that they produce their curfew passes. He then proceeds to
rough them up and orders them to recite the *qalma*[6] or "your Jai Bungla"
(the Punjabi-Urdu pronunciation of the Bengali nationalist slogan "Joy Bangla," indicating allegiance to the geopolitical and cultural entity of Bengal
and the erstwhile nation of Bangladesh). Bismillah goads the Bengalis:

> "Say, say, my proud countrymen, say it, 'Jai Bungla.'" The rifle swung
> back and forth like he was watering plants. "'Jai Bungla,' say it." When
> one of the Bengali men recites the *qalma* in English, "There is no
> God but God, and Muhammad is His Messenger" Bismillah retorts,
> "Not like a whitey, asshole, say it like a true Muslim." In response,
> the Bengali man recites the *qalma* in Arabic to prove his authentic

Muslim identity: "La-ilaha-il-Allah-Muhammad-ar-Rasul-Allah."
(2018, 89–90)

The religious divisions between West Pakistanis and Bengalis that Zaman spotlights were not new to the region. Bengal was first partitioned by the British in 1905 but reunited in 1911. It was partitioned again in 1947 with the formation of India and Pakistan. For those separated into Muslim East Pakistan and Hindu West Bengal in India, this partition cut at the heart of the centuries-long sociocultural history of Bengal. At the same time, the partition divided East and West Pakistan not only geographically and along religious lines but also across economic, political, cultural, and historic regional conflicts. The colonial relation between the two wings resulted in East Pakistan's exploitation by West Pakistan, whereby the former generated more revenue yet received a smaller allocation and investment of resources toward national development. The West Pakistani ruling elite formed the central government, while Bengalis were deemed a lesser, smaller, darker race, with pagan influences closer to their Hindu West Bengali neighbors (Akram). According to the "Women of 1971" campaign report from the human rights organization Drishtipat, the mass killings of Bengalis in 1971 were characterized in the following way:

> The genocide and gendercidal atrocities were also perpetrated by lower-ranking officers and ordinary soldiers. These "willing executioners" were fueled by an abiding anti-Bengali racism, especially against the Hindu minority. "Bengalis were often compared with monkeys and chickens," said Pakistan General Niazi. "It was a low-lying land of low-lying people." The Hindus among the Bengalis were as Jews to the Nazis: scum and vermin that [should] best be exterminated. As to the Moslem Bengalis, they were to live only on the sufferance of the soldiers: any infraction, any suspicion cast on them, any need for reprisal, could mean their death. And the soldiers were free to kill at will. The journalist Dan Coggin quoted one Punjabi captain as telling him, "We can kill anyone for anything. We are accountable to no one." This is the arrogance of power. (Rummel 1997, 335)

Tripathi writes: "The roots of the Bangladesh War of 1971 lay in this simple fact, which neither Pakistan, nor India understood fully—that Bangladeshis saw themselves as Bengali and Muslim" (2016, 4). Bangladeshi independence from Pakistan in 1971, celebrated as the victory of a linguistic and secular nationalism over religious identity, does not suggest that it drifted into a closer relationship with West Bengal, India, a dimension of the

Bengali identity that West Pakistan held in suspicion. While it has been argued that Bangladeshis are closer to West Bengalis culturally than to Pakistanis, and they do share a language, this argument does not take into consideration the intracultural variations of a nation based on space, time, or economic class. Zeeshan Rahman Khan (2006) argues:

> Muslim Bangalis historically defined their political orientation neither through language nor through culture as is testified to by their separation from West Bengal. Also, that the creation of Bangladesh has little to do with language and culture and much more to do with tangible factors such as economics and social justice is evidenced by the fact that Bangali was established as an official language of Pakistan. Therefore, the fight on the language front had already been fought and won—years before the need for separation became a reality.

Lamia Karim (2004) has argued that in postindependence Bangladesh, subsequent ruling parties have further constructed a Bangladeshi identity with a specific Islamic wedge as a political move to garner support of Islamic parties. Set within this historical background, what it means to be a Bangladeshi—a Bengali yet Muslim—is an assertion of many different intersecting layers of history and experience.

The idea of a shared regional history yet a distinct ethnic and cultural history—that is, the distinguishing features of a Bengali, Bangladeshi, yet Muslim identity—is beautifully articulated in Tareque Masud's classic film *The Clay Bird* (*Matir Moina* 2002), which reflects a version of Bangladeshi Islam shaped by the region's specific social and historical forces. Masud describes this in a 2004 interview with Sandip Roy of *India Currents*:

> Sufi *baul* tradition [mystic minstrels] is a combination of Vaishnav mysticism and Iranian sufism. . . . [This] popular Islam is more inclusive, more pluralistic, more diverse and syncretic in nature, based on wisdom and common sense. This is in sharp contrast with what I call "scholastic" Islam, a bookish and modernist Islam. . . . The modernists are using this scholastic Islam for their own ends. They are trying to impose a creed and not the culture, even though clearly Islam is not just a creed; it is a culture like any other.

This version of Islam challenges the view of a unitary Islam; it challenges ideas about a monolithic Muslim world. *The Clay Bird* is set in Bangladesh in the 1960s on the eve of the Liberation War. It portrays the fragile ties holding together the two Muslim-majority populations of West and East

Figure P.2 Baul singers (*The Clay Bird* [dir. Tareque Masud, 2002]).

Pakistan. In his review of the film, Roy (2004) writes, "The heart of the film is the struggle between two definitions of Islam—one more secular and rooted in the music of the wandering *baul* folk singers, the other more orthodox and rigid." In a 2002 interview with *Le Monde*, Masud says:

> For [Bangladeshis], Islam is rooted in our own soil, it has evolved and adapted to our own traditions, including Hinduism. It has thus become our own form of Islam, a popular Islam. This is expressed through the "bahas" songs that we hear in the film. These mystical songs are still very popular, and serve to transmit much of our knowledge and heritage. They are a means of meditation and prayer.

A powerful scene is set under a tree where the baul singers debate the meaning of God in the context of competing social forces of nationalism, gender, and Islamist ideologies. The scene follows:

> *Female baul: If you want to go to heaven, keep fear of Allah in your*
>   *heart*
> *Male baul: If you want to be close to Allah keep love within your*
>   *heart*
> *Female baul: I'm just your daughter's age*
> *I'll assume the side of Sharia*
> *To take an anti-Sufi stance*

Don't take what I say to heart
You ignore the holy scriptures
What kind of Muslims are you?
Why are the Mullahs always angry with you?
Keep fear of Allah in your heart
Male baul: You need wisdom to grasp the Qur'an
How can half-read Mullahs interpret intricate scriptures?
Without knowing the text they preach to others
The dogmatic Mullahs make a living from deception
We don't lust for heaven
We have no fear of hell
If you want to be close to Allah
Keep love within your heart

In another scene in *The Clay Bird*, two teachers in a madrassa debate the merit of religious education in preserving the unity of Pakistan on the basis of one religion and in the face of perceived communist and secularist threats. One of the more progressive teachers says: "Islam didn't spread here [in Bengal] through the sword. It was the selfless Sufis who went to low caste Hindus to spread Islam's message of peace and equality. The kings of Iran and Arabia conquered land but not peoples' hearts. It was thanks to the Sufis that people embraced Islam. The truth is: you cannot make Islam flourish with politics or arms. It is by speaking the Islamic knowledge that Islam will prosper." He goes on to pose the illuminating question, "If Pakistan collapses why would Islam be endangered? Did Pakistan establish Islam or rather enforce military rule [in then-East Pakistan]?" A similar question could be posed of the political attempts by some postindependence parties in Bangladesh to create an Islamic wedge to garner support for Islamic parties (Karim 2004). Karim argues that this nationalist identity is in contrast to earlier versions, which embraced the ethnolinguistic Bengali identity.

Meghna Guhathakurta (2005) describes how earlier social movements in Bangladesh relied on literary and folk traditions of Bengal as opposed to Islamist politics. She contrasts this to recent moves by the Islamist-aligned Bangladeshi government to quash the efforts of Dhaka University students who have embraced similar commemorations of nationalist struggles. According to Guhathakurta, "Cultural activism or the cultivation of secular and progressive ideals through various art forms have had a significant contribution toward the practice of democracy and free thinking in Bangladesh." Students and young people responded by ever-more-enthusiastic celebrations of *Pohela Boishakh* (the Bengali New Year) and *Boshonto Utshob* (the first day of spring), both deemed un-Islamic by the Islamists. Students of the Fine Arts Department protested on campus with a spontaneous street theater performance that invoked the liberation struggle. Guha-thakurta further notes, "They were drawing satirical portraits of the power relations between the University administration and the ruling party cad-res. [One student] later admitted that she had felt she had been transported to a 'muktanchal' [free zone] of the Liberation War, i.e., the areas which were liberated of Pakistani army occupation by the Muktibahinis (the free-dom fighters)." These contemporary protests are reminiscent of not only the Bengali resistance against Pakistani repression but also the deeply cultural spirit of democratic struggles against power etched in the consciousness of the younger generations through family storytelling: "A connection with a period of history which [the younger generation] had not witnessed but was engraved deep in the collective unconscious mind of an oppressed people" (Guhathakurta 2005). Oral history, film, literature, and memoirs have con-tinued to shape this collective consciousness and identity of the liberation struggle.

Raised in postwar Bangladesh in a family and community with strong an-ticolonial and nationalist political leanings, I grew up—as did most of my generation—under the shadow of the ubiquitous and defining narrative of the Bangladesh Liberation War. Yet, I had limited understanding of how the same war was understood and remembered in Pakistan. It is not a stretch to say that many of us grew up cultivating a heavy dose of outrage and ha-tred toward what we had come to define as our former oppressors. The story of 1971 continues to be deeply personal, intimate, and political for Bangla-deshis across generations. Even as a scholar-teacher in the field of South Asian Studies, I have found it limiting to discuss among colleagues and students the conflicted histories and legacies of the partition and the Lib-eration War, and not least because of the knowledge gaps that still persist and hinder meaningful and trusting alliances. As Van Schendel (2015) and many others have noted, the voluminous literature about the struggle for self-determination comprises memoirs, personal essays, media commentar-ies, and scholarly, literary, and filmic representations; and perhaps these provide a richer and more intimate window into the human relations sev-ered, lost, and only tentatively resewn. Stories as they are narrated in film or literary forms are a powerful mode of passing on and re-creating family, community, and national knowledge about the self and the collective. They not only make visible the visceral social injustices but also offer ways for audi-ences to act and connect to movements they may not have access to otherwise.

My own consciousness was formed by the stories told and retold by my family and the larger community, stories that espoused strong nationalist, secular, and liberatory politics. As a Bangladeshi, I was raised with an enduring sense of nationalist identity and rage against the legacies of both Pakistani and British colonialism. My father, an academic and political activist deeply invested in the national development of Bangladesh, was among the people whose lives were at risk of the Pakistani army's systematic killings to crush the intellectual force of the erstwhile East Pakistan. During the war, like many of their academic friends and political allies, my parents had to flee their home on the campus of Rajshahi University—a hotbed of student insurgency—and take shelter in a remote village in Northern Bangladesh.

Later, nearly two months into the war, my family had to return to their home on campus, in part because the Pakistani government had issued an order for all academics to resume teaching. The more pressing reason for their return, however, was because they got news that the Pakistani army had been tipped off to their hiding place. Another professor at the university, my father's colleague and a known *razakar* (war collaborator), had told the army, *"chiria to bhaag giyaa"* (the bird has flown), describing my family's flight to the village. Collaborators can work on both sides, however, and a different collaborator, on a separate occasion, actually saved my father. On one occasion during the war, on a road trip to Dhaka from Rajshahi, my family was stopped at an army roadblock. Pakistani soldiers asked my father to step out of the car and show his identification papers. One member of the cadre happened to be a Bihari, a non-Bengali Muslim. As a community, Biharis sided with West Pakistan in the war. But this soldier had ties to Rajshahi University. Upon recognizing my father, he convinced the others in the regimen to let him go.

Many a night during my childhood, and even now, my mother and aunts would regale my siblings and me with memories of the hardship and fear they endured in those nine months of war and the incredible kindness and generosity of the people who saved their lives. Those stories, learned through the memories of the generation who lived it, instilled in me—as well as many of my generation—a sense of responsibility, awe, and respect for those whose struggles had ensured us the gift of Bangladeshi citizenship. Growing up in a nationalist household, I absorbed multiple narratives of the memory of 1971. Among them were the narratives I learned from cinema, which was a way to visualize the stories told within family and community. Every Independence Day, March 26, and Victory Day, December 16, would be commemorated by Bangladesh Television's screening of a war film bound to pull at our heartstrings. All members of the household would sit around our twenty-inch Philips black-and-white television set. My mother would ensure that the household chores of the domestic staff be completed on time so that all were free to enjoy these screenings. Such emphasis on films as a way to engage in family and national conversations in my upbringing perhaps explains my ongoing interest in the genre of Muktijuddho cinema and how it

dramatized the memorialization and mourning borne of the freedom struggle. Indelibly emotive, and intersubjective, it is constitutive of historical identity—one that I cannot claim to be objective, rather interested and contingent. I offer a reading of Bangladeshi national cinema after 1971 organized
around the historic event of Muktijuddho and how it functions as the struc-
turing principle for identity, trauma, reconciliation, and justice. Not exhaus-
tive by any means, this book engages with select women-centric films to illuminate a subjugated film historiography that disrupts the entrenchment
of a tenuous yet hegemonic nationalist representation and experience.

I absorbed the prevailing narratives of 1971 through gatherings of mostly male intellectuals of my father's generation. They unfolded eloquent discussions on nation building, the political and strategic decisions of the nationalist leaders in the region, the government of the Awami League political
party, and the legendary Father of the Nation, Sheikh Mujib. My education
about the war, however, also came from those stories of my mother, her younger sister, and the wives of my father's friends and colleagues. It is their stories—lesser known in official narratives of war—that depicted the more vivid
images of "living under occupation."

It was my mother who described how her family home was destroyed in
a routine raid by the Pakistani army in North Bengal. Her father, my grandfather, was a civil surgeon who had to go into hiding in Dhaka because he had
served the freedom fighters as the leader of the local chapter of the Awami
League party. His eldest son, my *boromama* (eldest maternal uncle)—also a
physician serving in the army—was stationed in a prison camp in West Pakistan. My grandmother, aunt, and two younger uncles—both students at Dhaka
University—shuttled back and forth between their home in a village of Shirajganj to Rajshahi city and my parents' home on the campus. On one occasion, fearing an impending raid, my grandfather, his sons and youngest
daughter, members of the extended family who lived in the same household,
and the servants took shelter in the woods behind the family homestead in
Shirajganj. My grandmother was ill and did not have the strength to flee
with the rest of the family. The soldiers kicked down the front door and
searched every corner of the house. Unable to find anyone other than my
grandmother, they started to interrogate her in Urdu. She did not understand
their questions, which enraged them all the more. One of them dragged her
out of the house by the arm, after which she lost consciousness. She was later
found by neighbors after the army had left. The army had destroyed the
furniture, looted the valuables including cash, silver and gold jewelry, and
any other items they were able to carry with them in their trucks, and set fire
to the homestead where my grandmother lay unconscious on the floor.

My mother also told stories of how Bengalis looted one another's homes
and collaborated with the Pakistani army in identifying households harbor-

ing freedom fighters. After the raid, for instance, her cousins went scavenging in neighbors' homes to salvage some of their looted belongings. My mother's youngest sister was seventeen at the time. She told me about many of her male cousins and acquaintances who were freedom fighters. My aunt, against the wishes of her parents, harbored weapons for them and provided them with food and supplies. She spoke of the special hiding place she had behind their house, under the bushes by the bank of the pond. "I know how to fire a rifle," she would tell me with pride. I learned from her that lights would go out every night as a measure of precaution against the air raids, and she and her brothers would play games by candlelight. "You were not even born then," she would remind me. That would be my mother's cue to remind me that she was pregnant with me in 1971.

I was born one month before Bangladesh was liberated in 1971. The night before I was born in Rajshahi Medical Hospital, my father's older brother, an engineer who worked for Radio Bangladesh, was fatally shot in Dhaka in an apparent case of mistaken identity. He left behind his wife, my *chachi* (aunt), and three children, aged fifteen, twelve, and four. My cousin recalled the thoughts running through her mind when she saw her father's dead body: "I kept wondering what was to become of us. My father was the only earning member of the family; my mother had never worked. I felt as though time had stopped and my life was over. Who was going to take care of us?" As the eldest daughter, she had to assume responsibility. She started tutoring classes for school children to supplement the family income. "I used to cry by myself when no one was watching," she said. Her mother, my aunt, took on two jobs: as a Bangla language teacher in a local school and a staff artist at Radio Bangladesh. Indeed, every family in Bangladesh has stories to tell about the trauma of 1971, which is inextricably linked with our national consciousness and identity as Bengali and Bangladeshi. It is this common thread of national memory that makes the cinematic narratives—produced and reproduced as they are aurally, visually, and structurally through tropes, signifiers, and repetitions—all the more relevant and powerful in a collective memorialization of a liberatory history. For me, personally, the stories told to me by my mother are etched in my memory alongside the historical memoirs, essays, and fiction I read and with the films about the war I grew up watching. The plotlines they narrate are so intimately familiar to the stories I grew up with, they often merge in my imagination, the putative cohesion of which I aim to put into question in this book.

According to feminist scholar Bina D'Costa (2005), 1971 has been preserved in statist narratives as a war of liberation, emerging out of a terrible and stunning violence, and has experienced ongoing processes of realignment of its nationalist and masculinist identity. These narratives have been actively constructed through ideology and practice—particularly emphatically by means of visual narratives—as gendered memories where women have been rendered victim/plundered and men war heroes/martyrs. In actuality, societal norms of seclusion and the separation of private and public spaces broke down in 1971, and Bengali men could not live up to the role of women's "protectors." The post-1971 narrative of the state as protector was a response to the gendercidal/genocidal practices of the war, which targeted Bengali soldiers, Hindus, women, Awami League political figures, students, intellectuals, and cultural activists.[7] Although women participated in the war and had diverse roles—in active combat, political and cultural activism, caring for the wounded, transporting and hiding weapons, sheltering freedom fighters—these statist histories have represented them predominantly as victims of sexual violence by the Pakistani army and as mothers of freedom fighters and the nation. The Bangladesh government made a significant gesture in recognizing women survivors of sexual violence following independence by bestowing on them the honorific *Birangona* (brave woman, or, alternatively, war heroine). The title, proclaimed by Father of the Nation, Sheikh Mujibur Rahman, purported to honor the women for their role in the freedom struggle. However, the label frequently served to further ostracize the women as their reintegration into society remained incomplete. On October 23, 2015, the Bangladesh government for the first time declared forty-three *Birangona* as freedom fighters; the Bangladesh parliament previously recognized the proposal in January 2015. The depiction of Birangona women in cinema is taken up at length in the following chapters of the book.

D'Costa (2005) has argued that women have been important in national image making yet excluded from its official history. On the one hand, the Pakistani army operated under orders to teach the "lesser breed" of Bengalis a lesson by impregnating the women in an effort to create a new and compliant race or to dilute Bengali nationalism. It was implied that good Muslims would not defy their fathers, or a compliant Bengali race subjugated by military and sexual domination of the paternalist Pakistani state would not rise up and challenge it (Brownmiller 1975; D'Costa 2004). On the other hand, in postliberation Bangladesh, the government responded to the Pakistani-sponsored campaign of rape with state-sponsored abortion and foreign adoption programs to cleanse the nation of Pakistani blood. While purity for Pakistan meant diluting the Bengali race, for Bangladesh it meant cleansing it of all traces of Pakistan. In both contexts, women's bodies became the site of violence; in neither were women's experiences adequately documented or recognized.

This lesser-told story of women's diverse participation in 1971 is the subject of Tareque and Catherine Masud's important short film, *Narir Kotha*

(*Women and War*, 2000), which opens with the following script in black and white:

> Bangladesh gained its independence from Pakistan in 1971 through a war of liberation. Millions of people, mostly unarmed civilians, were killed by the Pakistani Army and their collaborators; millions of women were systematically raped and maimed. The story of women in the war and their roles, not just as victims of sexual violence, but as fighters and martyrs has mostly remained untold. Internationally, the brutality suffered by Bangladeshis is yet to be acknowledged as genocide, and the cruelty suffered by women in '71 is yet to be recognized as a war crime.

The opening and closing scenes of the film draw from historical black-and-white footage of the war, in particular, the many facets of women's roles therein including combat training, nursing, and caregiving in rehabilitation centers. One striking shot shows women donating their gold bangles and earrings along with grains for the war fund. These scenes are accompanied by the voice of acclaimed folk singer Momtaz Begum singing baul music composed by Shah Alam Boyati:

> *No one talks about the role of women*
> *Everyone sings the praise of men*
> *Didn't women contribute to the cause of Independence?*
> *Nine months of grief and pain*
> *Does the father have the only claim of parentage?*
> *Have we all forgotten the sacrifice*
> *Of millions of mothers and sisters?*
> *Didn't women contribute to the cause of Independence?*

The attention to diverse women's myriad roles in war is highlighted in the film through interviews including one with sculptor Ferdousi Priyobhashini, the first survivor to speak publicly of her experiences of rape and torture in 1971. Additional interviewees include Sritirekha Biswas, another war survivor, who was twelve years old in 1971 and among the millions who crossed over to India as refugees, and Mazlibala, an indigenous woman who speaks of her community fighting the Pakistani army with bows and arrows, as well as men and women from Choto Paitkandi village who also took part in guerilla resistance against the Pakistani army. The attention to intersectionality in the film disrupts the Bengali and Muslim as well as masculinist hegemonic representational politics of contemporary Bangladeshi cinema about 1971. The picture that emerges in this film is that of a peoples'

Figure P.3 Interview with Ferdousi Priyobhashini (*Narir Kotha* [dir. Catherine and Tareque Masud, 2000]).

war fought across class, gender, religious, and ethnic lines and in various roles by the people of then East Pakistan. Importantly, the film raises two critical points especially relevant for representation of women and violence: one raised by Mazlibala when she poses the question, "Is it just a matter of physical 'dishonor'?" when recounting the trauma of 1971; and another by Priyobhashini commenting on the continuing and multifaceted violence against women, "The situation has not really changed, even today in 1999. Rather all over the world, killing and rape of women has increased." She reads off the headlines in the Bengali-language daily *Ittefaq*, "Refugee Exodus: Kosovo to Become Empty Wasteland." Broadening the relegation of women's roles to sexual victimization and locating the Bengali struggle for self-determination within a global, transcultural, and transhistorical context of conflict and gender violence, the Masuds' film—indeed, filmography of this leading filmmaking duo in Bangladeshi nationalist cinema, as *Narir Kotha* is part of a trilogy along with *Muktir Gaan* (*Songs of Freedom*, 1995) and *Muktir Kotha* (*Words of Freedom*, 1999)—opens up significant questions to grapple with regarding the past and continuing encounters between war, women, and cinema.

These narratives, literature, and films about the liberation struggle are etched into the consciousness of my own and subsequent generations. This book emerges out of my investment in making meaning from the complex and tortured history of Bangladeshi identity, representation, and gender justice. This book also turns a feminist critical eye to contemporary, woman-centered Muktijuddho films coming out of Bangladesh and how these cultural texts imagine, disrupt, and reinscribe a gendered nationalist landscape of trauma, freedom, and justice. I draw inspiration, especially, from critical Black and transnational feminist traditions that highlight global and multiple structures of domination—in troubling the structures of conventional narratives and ways of seeing that are often circumscribed by a racialized and sexualized grid (Hartman 2008; Fleetwood 2011). In encouraging critical modes of viewing, Nicole Fleetwood reminds us of the complexities in desiring "the cultural product [to] solve the very problem that it represents: that seeing black is always a problem in a visual field that structures the troubling presence of blackness" (3). In *Troubling Vision* (2011), Fleetwood asserts, "Blackness and black life become intelligible and valued, as well as consumable and disposable through racial discourse"—that is, through circulating blackness, which "fills in the void and is the void," also as it "attaches to bodies and narratives coded as such but it always exceeds these attachments" (6). While Fleetwood refers to Black cultural production and its narrative power within a racialized and bounded location, in this book, I draw from this critical Black feminist tradition to trouble the possibility and problematic gendering practices of Muktijuddho ideology as represented in Muktijuddho cinema. An engagement with the cinematic traditions of telling women's narratives of the war elucidates gendered/sexualized coding of women's bodies even as these codings fleetingly exceed such nationalist framings. I draw on Alexander Weheliye's argument that the conceptual and pedagogical tenets of Black Studies, like no other theoretical or methodological tradition, has illuminated the technologies of domination and articulations of the human (4).

In that vein, seen through the lens of Black feminism, human rights cinema can illuminate local and global injustices, shedding light on the interconnected ways such histories of oppression manifest. The woman-centered Muktijuddho films I examine in this book claim a particular aesthetic that transcends the dominant nationalist history and sentiment and lay claim to an alternative politics. The paramount sentiment in Muktijuddho cinema is in a vein similar to what Hamid Dabashi describes as a defining feature of Palestinian cinema: "a subdued anger, a perturbed pride, a sublated violence" (2006, 11). He goes on to suggest that Palestinian cinema is "the mutation of that repressed anger into an aestheticized violence—the aesthetic presence of a political absence." It is "an aesthetic under duress"; and by calling attention to the cinematic impulse to building an awareness and counterhistory, the films I draw attention to in this book, simultaneously induce a quest for gender justice akin to the genre of human rights cinema. Dabashi aptly points out that structural to this genre of cinema is a sensibility of "traumatic realism" (21). Indeed, it is this aesthetic more so than a categorization of national cinema that underscores the potential of Palestinian cultural productions. Jankovic (2014) writes about the possibilities offered by rubrics such as women's and Palestinian cinema even as these might be limiting considering the ghettoization or essentialist risks entailed by the former and the contested notion of Palestine in geopolitical terms by the latter. National cinema can be a confining rubric precisely because there might be less room for contestation of the ideas of the nation, which might be revered as sacrosanct. Despite its potentially unifying impulse, women's cinema can offer a unique form of political expression and agency and push against notions that political unity or national unity is more important than gender and sexual justice. Drawing on claims made by women's cinema as a genre enables an inward- and outward-looking critique challenging both patriarchal nationalism and national liberation. Moreover, Black and transnational feminist critiques help lay claim to social and political issues affecting Bangladeshi society at large and not prescriptive and presumptuous feminist issues imposed on the global South context by neoliberal or Western humanitarian concerns. Thus, a braiding of these three analytical threads in this book—national cinema, human rights cinema, and Black and transnational feminist critiques—in critical dialogue yields a new feminist politics, a new aspiration and desire for gender justice.

Human rights cinema in this sense goes even beyond attesting to history; it also troubles historical evidence and gestures toward an endangered memory, thereby creating a form of alternative visual record of a "silenced crime" (Dabashi 2006, 11). With regard to Palestinian women's and human rights cinema, Jankovic poses the important question, "Why, how, and in what forms does and/or might cinema become a locus of struggle and protest in the global cinema context?" (Jankovic 2014, 11). This is a critical question to pose regarding the emergence, infrastructure, and circulation of Muktijuddho cinema in Bangladesh. In fact, from its beginning, when the erstwhile government of Bangladesh (then East Pakistan) commissioned cultural artists and activists like Alamgir Kabir and Zahir Raihan to make documentaries such as *Stop Genocide* (1971)—a history that I elaborate on in the Introduction—to record and make known to a global audience the atrocities of the war, Muktijuddho cinema continues the historic struggle to document the untold stories of a colonial occupation, a struggle for self-determination, and the complexities of narrating and bearing witness to women's stories, goals which I share in writing this book.

By showing larger and more far-reaching relations of oppression, cinema of this genre brings into focus the effects on the marginalized communities represented and, at the same time, brings the stories to a transnational audience. In so doing, they can engender a more self-reflexive dialogue as well as aid in the mobilization of transnational solidarity. This model of solidarity is akin to Sara Ahmed's definition: "Solidarity does not assume that our struggles are the same struggles, or that our pain is the same pain, or that our hope is for the same future. Solidarity involves commitment, and work, as well as the recognition that even if we do not have the same feelings, or the same lives, or the same bodies, we do live on common ground" (2004, 189). At the same time, however, such cultural productions illuminated through filmic rubrics like national, human rights, or women's cinema can allude to a grounding across temporal and spatial landscapes as they illuminate and seek to challenge regulatory and asymmetrical power relations. They gesture toward a desire for healing and justice as a direction not fully arrived at.

In the case of Muktijuddho cinema, which has remained largely within the purview of a national context in Bangladesh, the newer productions I draw attention to disrupt conventional masculinist nationalist approaches at a number of levels. First, these are predominantly directed by women and feature women's narratives—itself a rare occurrence within national cinema. These films launch a transnational conversation around gender, sexual oppression, and racial oppression by bringing the Bengali struggle for emancipation to life for many who did not witness the struggle or would otherwise not have access to such stories. Second, my reading of these films draws from a long and rich tradition of transnational and Black feminism that enable the visibilization of such stories of oppression while at the same time cautioning about the impossibility of fully narrating these stories. Black feminist scholarly tradition like no other theoretical tradition has illuminated the contested notion of the human, its gendering practices, its occlusions, its original and enduring violences, and even its glimmers of possibilities (Weheliye 2014; Perry 2018). Weheliye argues that, historically, distinctions have been and continue to be made among different categories of humans based on race, nationality, or religion, whereupon values are assigned through racializing assemblages and discursively etched in and through visual phenomena (6)—that is, visual modalities can become a privileged site of the apparatus of racializing dehumanization processes. Black feminist theories of the human offer critical conceptual tools to tease out the "nexus of differentiation, hierarchy, and the human, and ultimately on devising new forms of human life that are not constructed from the noxious concoction of racialization and/as political violence" (6). Imani Perry also takes up the rethinking of humanity and its gendering practices beyond that of the liberal humanist subject as she explores historical and philosophical connections between cultures not as mere comparison but rather to illuminate how multiple forms of domination under patriarchal structures took shape within a global colonial power structure (6). She posits that while multiple iterations of patriarchy took shape in a global age of modernity, it is nevertheless imperative to follow these seemingly disparate "portraits of gender and gendering, ones that reveal both rules and exceptions, and states of exception" to complicate the picture and also to invite multiple layers of readings, viewings, and ongoing dialogue (6). Like Perry, I read stories and narratives in and through film as models to unpack layers of domination and invitations for alternative viewing practices in artistic imagination to usher in more ethical reckonings with past and present.

As the following chapters show, visibilization is bound up with various historical, surveillance, and masculinized/racialized politics, which lends itself to sensationalize as well as provoke critical analysis. Co-optation and appropriation are layered on to the perhaps glimmers of assertion, agency, and fragmented recuperation. Put in relation to each other, or juxtaposed with each other, and using the instruments of transnational and Black feminist theoretical approaches, this book attempts to see interconnected regional and even global power dynamics as they play out in the lives of women in disparate locations. This approach of juxtaposing disparate matrixes of subjugation and agency allows a powerful correspondence in differing localities and histories subjected to similar (but not the same) instances of domination associated with colonial, racialized, and sexualized oppression. While these are not shared experiences—rather, instances in which national memorialization projects organize the suffering and redress of violence—they can incite ethical readings of multiple renderings of colonial violence. In fact, as these cultural critics point out, looking for shared experiences might itself be a colonizing move, but juxtaposing or putting in relation to each other global matrixes of historical oppression can elicit a kind of decolonization.

Film scholar Patricia White (2015) asks the question in the context of socially engaged cinema: What is the "cultural work that concepts and institutions of 'women's cinema' or 'cinema about women' perform and project?" (3). White goes on to contend, "as a transnational formation, contemporary women's cinema draws on many other histories—those of art cinema; national media industries; and a range of aesthetic, intellectual, and political movements, including feminisms, . . . to evaluate how the axes of gender and sexuality can remap its concerns" (8). As such, drawing from a long history of women's cinema and cinema about women as countercinema, White posits it as announcing an oppositional position as well as a political imaginary (9). Certainly, the films in this book are examples of cinema emerging from a marginalized viewpoint—that of women cultural activists, featuring submerged histories of women in the war—and thereby addressing/redressing questions of authorship, exclusion, historical retrieval, and equity (3). Coupled with the transnational and Black feminist political vision as described above, cinema by and about women challenge assumptions about war, and approaches to war cinema as well as question what these films mean for the future of gender justice and representational politics of Muktijuddho cinema. As White surmises, cinema about and by women is part of the feminist film genre that pushes a feminist film critique to step outside of a restrictive "nation-state" framework and urges a reassignment of gender examination of power and knowledge among and within cultures (13). Citing the work of Deleuze and Guattari, White states that women's cinema is pluralistic in form and is not "at home" within conventional cinematic or national discourses.

I embrace White's account that the ability of cinema by and about women to contend with the concept of gender justice remains an aspiration, glimpses of which are visible in the plural, unconventional, oppositional, and transnational stances of Muktijuddho cinema in this book. Drawing on a transnational and woman-of-color theoretical repertoire enables us to shed light on far-reaching cross-border relations of domination and racialized and sexual oppression and to contribute to the feminist analysis of gender violence and gender justice—a conversation I extend to the realm of the nationalist and humanistic cinema of Bangladesh. White posits that a feminist orientation to women's films prioritizes discourses of agency (authorship) and aesthetics (representational schemes) in terms of the politics of location (asymmetries in power). While a critical element of women's cinema is to disentangle women from nationalist ideologies, the national does not simply disappear in transnational cinematic considerations; instead, one might think about how gender influences nationalist projects of memorializations, including cinematic ones. Priya Jaikumar (2007) names this as a conscious consideration of the national and cultural where neither are taken for granted (208). She illustrates how *women* as an optic of the national—both its constitution and its documentation—is a category of analysis in women's cinema. This genre interrogates the political encounters and theories permitted within such an optic: How is the birth of a nation relayed by this optic? How are women constituted as subjects within it? Silence, co-optation, and counterpossibilities are all embedded considerations within a feminist orientation to women's cinema such as the one this book sets out to unfold. Socially oriented human rights cinema might even disentangle the national from "place"-based analysis and display the border-crossing visual tropes that are often associated with such analytics. Women directors and cinema about women have specific contributions to offer through oppositional, counter, and minor narratives in the conjunctures of feminist, human rights, and transnational aspirations.

The ensuing chapters are inspired by myriad border-crossing cinematic productions as they strive for connective understanding of gender justice in a transnational context. At the same time, they reinforce both the realities of geopolitical policing by the nation-states and, hand in hand, the gaps and erasures in mutual knowledge that can undermine trusting cross-border alliances. We can begin to account for our present-day experiences of borders in the subcontinent by turning to Ayesha Jalal's interview in the *Daily Star* and her observation about the division of India and Pakistan, globally conditioned as it was by British colonization. In Jalal's words, "Partition is not just an event that occurred in 1947 . . . as the founding myth of the postcolonial nation-states of India, Pakistan, and Bangladesh. . . . [It] is a way of seeing and being that separates what were once historically indivisible people"—the "innumerable slippages, elisions, and contestations in narratives" about nations and divides are daily, often violently, reenacted in the countries (*Daily Star* 2017). That being noted, we also need a different frame to understand the vicissitudes reverberating from the multiple partitions of the subcontinent, the meaning of Pakistan as an "essentially/exclusively Muslim place" and the question of Bengal's Muslims. In the words of Dina Siddiqi (2017), the Liberation War, seen in the longer trajectory of partition violence, "disrupted, displaced and reconstituted older meanings of partition . . . [by brutally exposing] the irresolution of the Muslim question." Drawing from the work of historian Irfan Ahmed (2012), Siddiqi emphatically proposes that rather than a solution, partition was an "escape" and 1971 a "temporary reprieve" from "the Muslim question." This need to reframe and rethink the divides within the subcontinent, within and against a Muktijuddho gender ideology and, more specifically, in a new era of regional/global hierarchies, is demonstrated by the filmic narrations in this book.

Cinematic representations illuminate the trauma, justice, and healing in relation to the Bangladesh War of Independence and the many conflicts that continue to divide the nation, the region, and interpersonal and political relations within. Deploying a transnational feminist analysis, I examine the films *Meherjaan* (2011) and *Itihaash Konna* (*Daughters of History*, 2000)—by Bangladeshi feminist directors Rubaiyat Hossain and Shameem Akhtar, respectively—which are the subjects of Chapters 1 and 3 in this volume. In Chapter 2, I engage Black feminist theory to unpack the containment of women within a Muktijuddho gender ideology, sexuality and vulnerability by engaging with Nasiruddin Yousuff's *Guerilla* (2011), the first commercial film to center on a woman combatant in 1971. I deploy a critical transnational and woman-of-color feminist approach to friendship politics to further a discussion on solidarity among women across borders in Chapter 3. Chapters 4, 5, and the Epilogue examine socially engaged films such as *Rising Silence*, *Bish Kanta* (*The Poison Thorn*), *Jonmo Shathi* (*Born Together*), and *Shadhinota* (*A Certain Liberation*), all directed by activist-filmmakers. These justice-driven films are critical to understanding and negotiating the layered meanings and consequences of catastrophic human suffering yet at the same time they hint at subjectivities and identities that are not reducible to that suffering only. They are key to creating an alternative and disruptive archive of feminist knowledge—a sensitive witnessing, responsible spectatorship, and just responsibility across time, space, and politics.

I offer in this book a collection of essays emerging out of such cross-border thinking: engaging with shared histories, experiences, and identities in the region. Undoubtedly, scholarly texts and research projects serve the communities that suffered unspeakable trauma in anticolonial and nationalist struggles for self-determination and in the momentous birthing of postcolonial nation states. I believe this analysis can raise awareness and foster much-needed dialogue among ordinary citizens who have grown up with that legacy of liberty and violence of nationalist and anticolonial struggles. This book is an attempt to create that imaginary and intertwined conversation, by engaging with Muktijuddho cinema and its erasures and excesses, aberrations, and promises. It is an engagement of cross-border exchanges, solidarity, and reckoning through woman-centered Bangladeshi films, a critical endeavor of memorializing turbulent times and their ongoing refractions. I maintain that the cinematic representations this book evokes—the power and lasting impact of narrating women's stories and the way their legacies emanate from past connections and constitutive traumas—cannot be overstated.

Introduction

National Cinema and Its Absences

Whereas the prologue mapped my historical and methodological— feminist, human rights, cinematic—approaches to Muktijuddho cinema's investment in identity, gender justice, and healing, this introductory chapter offers an engagement with the Bangladesh postindependent film industry, and its evolving preoccupation with and (de)centering of nationalism, women, and war. Bangladeshi films about the Muktijuddho quite unequivocally form the genre known as "national cinema." These films that depict the defining event for the nation's self-determination have often represented the struggle for independence through a gendered and sexualized lens of male valor and female shame—the heroism of freedom fighters and the sacrifices of women. The Muktijuddho has not been adequately recognized, nor has its impact been assessed globally, or even regionally, for its genocidal violence. Despite some guilty verdicts from the Bangladesh war crimes tribunals in 2011 and onward, state-level negotiations involving India, Pakistan, and Bangladesh have failed to bring about a resolution for the crimes against humanity; instead, political parties in Bangladesh have instrumentalized *shadhinotar chetona* (the spirit of 1971) to advance their varied agendas. In this context, film and literature have been critical mediums through which a collective memory and national solidarity have been shaped.

The films I focus on in this book represent a shift away from the binary of oppression/resistance and victimhood/agency, especially with regard to the depiction of women's experiences. By no means comprehensive of the Muktijuddho genre, the films I chose to examine are mostly by and centrally

Figure I.1 Film poster for *Jibon Theke Neya* (dir. Zahir Raihan, 1970).

about women. Further, the attempt to memorialize the varied experiences of women in the Liberation War is a way to write their complex and agential roles into the national history as well as advocate for recognition, responsibility, and justice. Notably, instead of primarily focusing on state-level negotiations or masculine combat, each film equally highlights the intimate, domestic, or "feminine" sphere as the site of struggle and meaning. By a feminine sphere, I mean those spaces that are relegated to the feminized in dominant patriarchal ideology; however, they can also be read as the source and portrayal of nonconformity, mutuality, and solidarity. By allowing the viewer to remember, imagine, and work through traumatic events such as war and conflict through a feminine aesthetic, cinema can help us appreciate the moral choices and interpretive acts of women, consigned to the feminine sphere and cast as passive victims or witnesses. Women in these films, as we see later in this chapter and in the subsequent chapters, make unexpected and sometimes jarring choices: nursing a wounded soldier from the enemy side, seeking the assistance of a sympathetic Pakistani soldier after having been raped by others like him, and embracing a child of rape even when the nation rejects them. The recognition of these moral choices is a legacy of the war that viewers learn to appreciate through the medium of cinema as an archive where diverse women's stories are memorialized, just as the state erects memorials and museums to commemorate martyrs.

In this chapter, I investigate the role of national cinema in documenting and engendering a conversation about nation, history, identity, healing, and reconciliation. The Introduction has two sections: The first provides a historical context for Muktijuddho films as the genre emerged within the film industry, and the second analyzes war themes among three recent and divergent films that expose the elisions around national identity, gender, and healing. The three films—Munsur Ali's *Shongram 71* (*The Struggle for Love and Survival*, 2014), Shameem Akhtar's *Itihaash Konna* (*Daughters of History*, 2000), and Rubaiyat Hossain's *Meherjaan* (2011)—grapple with contested and difficult questions that push the contours of historical memory. These films engage critically with the multifaceted narratives of the birth of a nation, the foundational struggle over identity, the intimate relations between gender, nation, and sexuality, the legacy of war, and the ethical reckoning with trauma. All three films narrate these themes through the lens of human suffering and the intimate, affective, and interpersonal relationships involving women. Finally, I offer comments about national cinema as an advocacy tool—to generate conversations about history and memory, social as well as political recognition of justice, and human rights—within an increasingly transnational space.

The History of Muktijuddho Cinema

Muktijuddho cinema emerged as a tool, the camera as a weapon, the filmmakers as witness, to narrate the suffering and sacrifice of the Bengali nation and its violent birth. It has evolved out of the experience of a war that is frequently cast as an "Indo-Pak" war, where the role of Indian intervention is seen as both decisive and heroic. In the subcontinent, the Muktijuddho is either erased as a shameful past, as is the case in Pakistan, or is subsumed under the better-known "Indo-Pak" war, in which India plays the hero in bringing liberation to Bengalis, as is the case in India. Other accounts cast it as a "secession" and a betrayal by East Pakistan of West Pakistan. In these views, East Pakistan divested from an Islamic identity to embrace its more Hinduized culture. A racially tinted discourse, ethnic Bengalis—a darker and smaller people—were seen as inferior to the Punjabis of the west. This divestment is traced back to the cruel politics of dividing Bengal, most emphatically in 1947, when an arbitrary line was carved through the region separating the Muslim majority east from the Hindu majority west despite shared culture, language, and history. Internally, the struggle is remembered as a glorious one that brought freedom to its oppressed peoples through revolution. Official figures suggest staggering loss and sacrifice: up to three million died, and sexual violence against women was an organized tool to subdue the Bengali population. This history has figured prominently in films produced both in and out of the commercial film industry in Bangladesh. Although these films vary widely in terms of originality and quality, the liberatory inspiration of 1971 is the main identifiable characteristic that sets this cinema apart as a national phenomenon.

The Bangladesh (previously East Pakistan) Film Development Corporation (FDC) was established in 1957. Tanvir Mokammel, a leading filmmaker in Bangladesh, reflects that in newly created Pakistan, most of the country's resources were channeled into the economic and social development of its Western Wing, where the general sentiment was that the humid, swampy lowlands of the East were not conducive for celluloid. Lahore and Karachi were the main sites for cultural development despite the fact that West Bengal[1]—with geographic temperament similar to those cities—had its own thriving film scene that included the likes of renowned Bengali filmmaker Satyajit Ray. After the Bengali leaders Hoque, Bhashani, and Sorwardy formed the United Front political coalition in 1967, cultural development of East Pakistan gained some momentum. Sheikh Mujibur Rahman, who would later become Bangladesh's first president, was then the minister of industries and commerce under the United Front, and he took the initiative to establish the Eastern Wing of the FDC. Although the first full-length East Pakistani Bengali language film—Abdul Jabbar Khan's *Mukh-O-Mukhosh* (*The Face and the Mask*)—was released in 1956, prior to the establishment of the FDC, it was only after the corporation's establishment that full-length cinema production in East Pakistan started in earnest. From 1956 to 2016 at least 3,300 full-length films were made in East Pakistan/Bangladesh, 3,000 of which were made between 1972 and 2016. Apon Chowdhury (2017) estimates that at least 50 of these are about the Liberation War. Additionally, 140-plus short films and documentaries about the war have been produced.

Chowdhury categorizes war cinema—both feature and documentary—into three groups: those films based directly on the experience of 1971, those that focused on postindependence, and those that integrated the war into the story line through flashbacks, fragments, or as side plot or backdrop. The first category comprises films that were actually made during the war, including the acclaimed documentaries *Liberation Fighters* (1971) and *Stop Genocide* (1971), as well as Chashi Nazrul Islam's *Ora Egaro Jon* (*Eleven Freedom Fighters*, 1972), the first feature film to be released in independent Bangladesh. Interestingly, while many countries with more specialized film industries have taken decades to make films about their own civil wars, four major feature films were released within months of the war's end in Bangladesh—a country whose film history is frequently referred to as "young." This point is important because, as Chowdhury says, after the war many freedom fighters put down their firearms and picked up their cameras for the ongoing battle over nation building. Since early years, Muktijuddho cinema undertook the work of the "archeological method" of intervention (Stillman 2007) claiming and reclaiming a traumatic history frequently through the inclusion of historical footage as well as portraying the lush and fertile landscape of rural Bangladesh—alluding to the sacrifice to emancipate the golden motherland (*shonar Bangla²*). In 1972, four full-length features based on the Liberation War were released: In addition to *Ora Egaro Jon*, these include *Orunodoyer Ognishakkhi* (*Witness to the Rising Sun*), by Shubhash Dotto; *Bagha Bangali* (*The Fierce Bengali*), by Anondo; and *Roktakto Bangla* (*Blood-Stained Bengal*), by Momtaz Ali.

Zahir Raihan, leftist revolutionary writer, thinker, and activist, was already an acclaimed filmmaker in his own right in preindependence Bangladesh, having made the classic nationalist satire *Jibon Theke Neya* (*A Glimpse of Life*), in 1970, and *Behula*, in 1966. In June 1971, as the war raged, the provisional government invited Raihan to make a series of documentaries about the bloody struggle that was erupting in South Asia, about which the global community knew little. The main purpose of the documentaries would be to raise consciousness and spur international intervention. Raihan was already at work on *Stop Genocide*, which documented the terrible violence of the war as it was unfolding and that too with sparse technical and financial resources. Importantly, this film put the Bengali struggle for self-determination within a global context of anticolonial and anti-imperial struggles including critiques of the United States in aiding West Pakistan, and the United Nations for its failure to protect human rights. Archiving the traumatic history meant bringing to light the little known, disappeared stories and thereby reclaiming a particular memory from the vantage point of the marginalized, the invisibilized (Stillman 2007, 498). Charged with this monumental task, Raihan created an advisory board composed of prominent intellectuals, artists, and filmmakers, including Syed Hasan Imam, Alamgir Kabir, and Babul Chowdhury. The result was four critical documentaries: *Stop Genocide* and *Liberation Fighters*, mentioned above, and *A State Is Born* and *Innocent Millions*, all with English subtitles. Together these films aspired to educate the world about the inspiration for and the horrors of 1971. To do so, they employed genocide, destruction, rape, looting, and guerilla warfare as the primary plot points. These films had the effect of canonizing 1971 as an event encapsulated by key motifs—mass murder, rape, arson, and the righteous guerilla insurgence—that over time concretized as tropes. Most important, these films strived to capture the war as it was experienced by the "people of Bangladesh," and the authenticity was rubber-stamped by filmmakers who were also freedom fighters

Figure I.2 Acclaimed director, writer, freedom fighter Zahir Raihan (Credit: Bipul Raihan).

themselves (Hayat 2011). In turn, these documentaries set the context and the ideal for a Muktijuddho ideology for subsequent films.

At the very outset, the creation of FDC in the Eastern Wing of Pakistan was motivated by the desire for self-representation in the face of grave social and political inequality and subjugation by West Pakistan. Rubaiyat Ahmed (2012) posits, however, that the nationalist ideology and inspiration of the Liberation War as it was imagined by these founding freedom fighters and filmmakers was never quite captured in subsequent films—documentary or otherwise, but particularly in feature films, as they became increasingly commercialized. Ahmed sees a shift in Liberation War cinema between 1973 and 1976 that he characterizes depicting a moral decay among freedom fighters, many of whom abused their newfound "freedom" and were seen to have gone astray; this was sensitively portrayed in Alamgir Kabir's *Dhire Bohe Meghna* (*Quiet Flows the Meghna*, 1973). Films such as Khan Ataur Rahman's *Abar Tora Manush Ho* (*Regain Your Humanity*, 1973), Alamgir Kumkum's *Amar Jonmobhumi* (*My Birth Place*, 1973), Narayan Ghosh Mita's *Alor Michil* (*Procession of Lights*, 1974), and Chashi Nazrul Islam's *Shongram* (*The Struggle*, 1974) are significant in grappling with some of the unintended consequences of the war. Harunur Rashid's *Megher Onek Rong* (*Many Colors of Clouds*, 1976) as well as Kabir's *Dhire Bohe Meghna* were two critically acclaimed films that also diverged from some of the formative motifs of this genre. Kabir has written extensively about the social and political landscapes of the years leading up to the war as well as its aftermath, drawing attention to the failure of a nuanced cinematic treatment of the Liberation War. *Dhire Bohe Meghna* is the only feature film he made about the Liberation War—a surprising choice, given his role as a film critic, filmmaker, freedom fighter, journalist for the *Shadhin Bangla Betar Kendro*, and important figure in Bangladesh's nationalist movement. He expressed his disillusionment with Liberation War cinema in the following quote:

One of the obstacles I faced as a filmmaker was that I was a film critic first. Therefore, I could not make a film in the same format that I had critiqued for so long. I decided to make *Dhire Bohe Meghna* in a collage format drawing from real life stories. This film was the product of great respect for our Liberation War. Yet, this was also my last film about the War. In retrospect, I can say now that I did not fully understand the War at the time. I knew the difference between what was real and what was imagined. However, back then I did not realize the difference between villains and heroes in the War. I did not understand who was a *razakar*, and who was a freedom fighter. I had not come to understand these differences immediately after the War ended. (Alamgir Kabir quoted in Khan 2018, 29; translation mine)

Importantly, Kabir in his later writings asserts that the roles of women have been grossly inadequate in Liberation War cinema. Writing about the films that were released in the aftermath of the war, *Ora Egaro Jon* and *Dhire Bohe Meghna* notwithstanding, he says: "Instead of representing the Liberation War, these films exploited one aspect of it, that of the rape of our mothers and sisters. The rape of women was used to titillate the viewers in the increasing commercialization of the film industry. Women's sexuality was objectified for consumption and for profit" (Atikuzzaman and Paul, 202). Kabir points out that these films were, ultimately, "not successful" economically or in establishing a kind of a moral compass regarding the war. In fact, he points out the filmmakers' lack of knowledge about the actualities of the war. Specifically, he criticizes Ali's *Roktakto Bangla* (*Blood-Stained Bengal*), where the map of Bangladesh is literally etched with the blood of a raped woman. Even the iconic *Orunodoyer Ognishakkhi*, according to Kabir, could not escape this propensity to entrench women in the role of victim, thereby "bypassing the grave problems facing the nation and making a minor issue— that of the Birangona[3] women—into a major one" (202). Notably, the Bangladeshi government bestowed on women survivors of sexual violence the honorific Birangona, meaning war heroine, in a gesture to recognize their role in the war. Kabir goes on to make a rather cryptic comment in the same essay: "One of the reasons for the lack of films about the Liberation War is those who experienced it do not feel passionately about it. And those who feel it in their heart, did not experience the War." He goes so far as to suggest that the government should establish rules about the way the war should be memorialized. He also hints at the shifting priorities and political agendas of changing regimes, expressing skepticism about sustained government support for Liberation War memory projects.

Nevertheless, it is curious that a leading figure in the Muktijuddho and its cinema sees the problem of the Birangona as a "minor issue," a topic unworthy of filmic representation. Granted, Kabir rightly takes issue with the angle in which women entered the discourse of 1971 in this genre; however, he simultaneously describes an authentic representation of 1971 as being one in which women are neither major nor minor participants. To bring clarity to Kabir's cryptic comment, Salimullah Khan cites Ahmed Sofa, another prominent Bengali intellectual, who claims that the Liberation War has been memorialized in postindependence literature in a "ritualistic fashion" (2018, 30; translation mine); that is, the war is presented as if the mass murder and rape, the grotesque atrocities that the Pakistani soldiers committed, were the singular representation of the war. Such singular and trope-driven plots, while effective in visibilizing systemic violence, nevertheless omit the multifaceted Bengali struggle for self-determination. That grand narrative, with its intense pain, celebration, and insurgence, remains submerged by the blunt instrumentalization of rape and mass murder.

This desire for a more authentic representation of the revolutionary politics underscoring the Bengali struggle for self-determination was perhaps a central inspiration for the reinvigoration of the film society movement from the earlier preindependence period to the 1980s in Bangladesh. The assassination of Sheikh Mujib, along with eighteen members of his family at his Dhanmondi residence in August 1975, was a turning point for culture and politics in Bangladesh. Muktijuddho-centric films dwindled in quantity and quality, and critics lamented that history was being remade by the army-led governments, which made light of Bengali nationalism and, in fact, joined with antiliberation forces, namely Islamist leadership that had collaborated with the West Pakistani army during the liberation movement.

The founders and prominent contributors of Bangladesh's film society movement—also later known as the parallel cinema movement, highlighting *Bikalpa Dhara* (alternative cinema)—were fresh graduates of Dhaka University who were involved in leftist politics. The group was composed of cultural activists, artists, writers, and filmmakers disheartened by the decline in the film industry. As part of the film society, they organized workshops and published newsletters. These filmmakers, including Tanvir Mokammel, Morshedul Islam, and Tareque Masud, among others, shaped parallel cinema with their 16 mm cameras and modest budgets. According to Maswood (2019), Morshedul Islam feels that "the theme of the liberation war in Bangladeshi films can only be defined as inadequate. The stories are simply absent in the most modern genre that is cinema, though the spirit of liberation war soaks the cultural core of the mainstream life in Bangladesh." In Islam's words, "The film industry helps build a nation" (quoted in Maswood).

Artists such as Raihan and Kabir were the inspiration and mentors for this younger generation. In a tribute to Kabir, Ananta Yusuf writes:

In the early 80s, along with a group of youngsters, Kabir initiated the film society movement. He was considered a mentor because of his refreshing perspective of films. Late Tareq Masud in his memoir, *Cholochitrajatra*, admits that Kabir's contribution to his journey as a filmmaker was immense. When Tareq was making *Adam Surat*, Kabir stood beside him with all his resources. He gladly gave his 16 mm camera to shoot the documentary on SM Sultan. According to Tareq, Kabir was always sympathetic to the filmmakers who didn't have money in their pockets to make a film. He wrote in his book, "He helped me in every way. To pay my gratitude I dedicated 'Adam Surat' to him." (Yusuf 2014)

Kabir's coworkers, admirers, and students aptly call him *Cholochitracharya* (learned person and advocate of cinema). According to documentary filmmaker and activist Manjare Hasin Murad, Kabir was swept away by the massive social, economic, and cultural developments that were profoundly transforming people in the postwar society and was able to perfectly capture it in his cinema. Moreover, he played a crucial role as a social reformist, which is why Murad believes that "the word Cholochitracharya goes well with him" (quoted in Yusuf 2014).

Muktijuddho filmmakers are frequently noted to have used their cameras as "rifles" in the face of colonial occupation. According to film critic Rukhsana Karim Kanon:

After the partition of the Indian subcontinent in 1947, public life was engulfed in turmoil. The impassioned consciousness of the Language Movement was transformed into reality with the War of Liberation that began and ended in 1971. Thousands of innocent freedom loving Bengalis took up arms to fight for their motherland. There was one group of soldiers who fought the war not with arms and munitions. Their weapons were their writings and their photography through which they exposed to the world the bloody massacre of the Bengalis by the barbarous Pakistani military. Likewise, a few courageous filmmakers immortalized the glorious Liberation War through light-camera-action. (2015, 75)

Kanon's observations reemphasize the intricate relationship between Muktijuddho aesthetics, politics, and infrastructure—that it purports to raise awareness about human rights and to simultaneously mobilize for justice.

Because infrastructure has been instrumental in shaping the evolution of Muktijuddho film, it is helpful to consider here the work of critical film theorist Brian Larkin, whose studies in postcolonial African cinema demonstrate the importance of filmic infrastructures, whether technical or financial—that they determine the contours of film aesthetically, socially, and politically (2019). Larkin traces how biennials, film festivals, digital infrastructures, and videos shape viewing practices and distribution as well as mediate cultural production. He probes the distinction between textual readings and an emphasis on material and cultural infrastructures that organize the scope of film. He also illuminates a more blurred inception in African cinema that goes back to the "moment of high nationalism," a point that is certainly instructive to *Muktijuddho* cinema's trajectory. He says, "African film and media have a peculiar ontology because filmmakers producing them and scholars analyzing them have always focused beyond the film text itself and paid attention to how that text exists within a broader technical, economic, and political environment" (106). Larkin argues for a "single cinematic ecology" that is composite and encompasses film festivals, popular film theater, and the newer "enclave cinema"[4] comprising the layered landscape of African cinema. He takes issue with scholarly discussions that undermine the less luminous productions to privilege the newer and more technically sophisticated films (i.e., New Nollywood), asserting that these contemporary international standards are complicit in the embrace of neoliberalism. He shows how high- or low-quality films are not simply an aesthetic choice of filmmakers but actually the technical aftereffect of systems of distribution. Popular cinema is often cast as technically poor, but because these films are distributed across wide strata of audiences, the poor images in some cases are "a material embodiment of their egalitarianism and accessibility" (108). Enclave cinema, on the other hand, in addition to targeting more elite audiences, is also about filmmakers trying to push African cultural production into newer terrains. Yet, Larkin argues that the older structures of open-air markets, film festivals, and biennials "comprise the infrastructure allowing images to circulate and which draw together technical, economic, institutional, and cultural forces to make the movement of images possible." The compound effect here emphasizes that infrastructure both enables and determines culture. This is evident "in the relations between informal marketers, multiplex cinema operators, festival programmers, and art gallery curators all of whom have sophisticated ideas of the sorts of cultural forms relevant to the publics they are addressing and constituting" (115–116). This complex dimension of cinematic form and circulation is also evident in the production of Palestinian cinema, which is also seen, as discussed in the Prologue, as a site of struggle and meaning making in the face of erasure and occupation (Jankovic 2014). Drawing on the work of Tawil-Souri (2005), Jankovic characterizes the exceptional status of Palestinian cinema as it adapts according to the beleaguered struggles it faces, its goal to illuminate significant histories otherwise absent in global or regional discourses, and the ways in which it takes shape through a range of styles, genres, funding, and production modes.

This postcolonial evolution of African cinema loosely parallels the postindependent evolution of cinema industries in Bangladesh. Lotte Hoek (2014), for instance, traces how the introduction of the capacity tax on cinema halls in 1983 had a major impact on shaping audiences across the rural/urban divide in Bangladesh. Instead of placing a tax on individual ticket sales, halls were charged a flat rate based on capacity, location, and amenities. This led to an unprecedented rise in numbers of cinema halls: 350 new halls were built between 1983 to 1988. Moreover, halls in the rural areas were subjected to a 5 percent tax in comparison to the 50 percent for urban cinema halls. The profitability occurring as a result led to wider distribution of films in the rural areas. At the same time, entertainment habits were changing and audiences—especially middle-class women—shifted more and more to home viewing.

These changes in audience were accompanied by parallel cinematic transformations as well. Hoek studies noted film critics of the 1960s and 1970s who wrote about the glory days of Bengali/Bangladeshi cinema, which hearkens back to the aesthetic project of the vernacular elite that came to life in productions such as Khan's *Mukh-O-Mukhosh* (1956) and Kabir's *Shimana Periye* (*Beyond the Horizon*, 1977). Drawing on the work of film historian Zakir Hossain Raju (2002), Hoek surmises, "The cinema emerged as an artistic endeavor and a tool for the production of a national modernity for the Bengali middle class in East Pakistan" (2014, 19), and postindependence Muktijuddho cinema became the grounds on which this national modernity was etched and re-etched. The aesthetic and political style of this genre took on hegemonic standards that reified cultural codes and came to symbolize an "absent fullness"—a term Hoek borrows from Laclau (2006) to denote its ubiquitous yet ephemeral quality (19). Derived from folklore, literature, and fine arts, the aesthetics of the nationalist genre rely on a "vernacular cultural model" and denote a genteel Bengali sensibility, which can be traced to the colonial period (19). In postindependent popular cinema, however, that vernacular elite cultural content gave way to what critics term "obscenity," mainly to draw in the so-called masses. So, in post-1980s cinema, Bangladesh has witnessed not only the disappearance of the urban intelligentsia from the film industry but also an attendant sense of loss over the political project by the very same group (Hoek 2014, 24), a condition frequently lamented by the cultural critics.

The infrastructural influences on cinematic production and exhibition are evident in the art cinema landscape in Bangladesh's own layered film ecology. A reviewer attending the Sixteenth Dhaka International Film Festival, titled "Bangladesh: The Rising National Cinema," conveys these assumptions about the quality of Bangladeshi film by expressing surprise at the volume of films produced in Bangladesh, and describing Bangladeshi cinema in general as "dwarfed by the monumental Indian film industry." According to this reviewer, "To turn to the films about the dramatic history of Bangladesh is to experience less successful productions which pointed out the fact that local directors, as well as scriptwriters, have problems with the building of story arcs and dealing with time shifts and side stories" (Langerova 2018). This interpretation demonstrates the admittedly smaller scale of cinema production in Bangladesh; however, perhaps by misreading the quality as inferior it misses the nuances Larkin articulates regarding postcolonial, nationalist, and socially engaged cinema pushing newer terrains. Applying a mainstream filter and benchmark to assess Muktijuddho cinema is to miss the critical contributions of these films, whose productions are enabled by the seemingly patched-together infrastructures. Nevertheless, these films help build an archive—moreover, a disruptive archive—of Bangladesh's independence struggle from the marginal spaces and positionalities. They enrich the Muktijuddho cinema genre, in which important films such as Yasmine Kabir's *A Certain Liberation* (*Shadhinota*, 2003), Akhtar's *Itihaash Konna* (*Daughters of History*, 2000), Farzana Boby's *Bish Kanta* (*The Poison Thorn*, 2015), and Shabnam Ferdousi's *Jonmo Shathi* (*Born Together*, 2016) are produced.

Mokammel (2017) notes the significance of this cinema in three parts: First, the stories have rarely been told and are often about marginalized people, such as in *Chitra Nodir Paare* (*Quiet Flows the River Chitra*, 1999), which tells the story of a Hindu family living in postindependent Bangladesh. Second, these films are low budget and rely on private donations. Third, they are formatted in 16 mm, which, in addition to being cost efficient, offers other benefits, including the relative freedom from government-controlled FDC policies and the flexibility of holding screenings at film festivals, where audiences can dialogue with the filmmaker and cultural critics. These films did not rely on star power; in fact, in Masud's films ordinary folks were enlisted as actors, which added to their popular appeal. Copyrights remained with the filmmakers, and many went on to win national awards, proving that there is a hunger for realist cinema with plots that are out of the ordinary. That these films were so successful, even achieving recognition exceeding that of Bangladesh's commercial cinema, is particularly significant, according to Mokammel.

The Absent-Present Woman in Muktijuddho Cinema

Despite the widespread recognition of many postindependence films, the absence of women as complex subjects in them—whether commercial or parallel—is glaring. Women's presence in this genre of film can be characterized as a "ghostly presence"—appearing in roles that serve the overarching masculinist narrative, frequently disappeared through tragic death, and haunted by sexual violation and madness. A review of extant literature on Liberation War cinema seems to unravel conversations among men, with only occasional references to women—as either exploited objects or as side characters who make gratuitous, supplementary, or typecast appearances. Rubaiyat Ahmed (2012) criticizes the industry as male dominated in every aspect. She points out that while the film society movement refrained from gratuitous roles for or the objectification of women, it nevertheless failed to create woman-centered films, let alone complex or diverse roles for women in war. The film society movement was mostly limited to an educated middle-class community—an extension of the Bengali intelligentsia who also did not portray the Liberation War in all its complexity or more explicitly beyond a middle-class cultural lens. In an article listing sixty-nine Liberation War films produced between 1971 and 2015, Kanon (2015) includes only five that are under the solo direction of a woman and three that are co-directed by a woman. These are: one commercial feature film, *Meherjaan* (2011) by Hossain; two independent feature films, *Itihaash Konna* (2000) and *Shilalipi* (*The Inscription*, 2004) by Shameem Akhtar; two documentaries, *Shadhinota* (*A Certain Liberation*, 2003) by Yasmine Kabir and *Ekattorer Michil* (*The Struggle of 1971*, 2001) by Kabori Sarwar; and three documentaries, *Narir Kotha* (*Women and War*, 2000), *Muktir Gaan* (*Song of Freedom*, 1995), and *Muktir Kotha* (*Words of Freedom*, 1999), codirected by Tareque and Catherine Masud. The Masuds' filmography, in particular, is considered to be foundational to the historiography of Muktijuddho and national cinema in Bangladesh and has been the subject of several critical scholarly inquiries (Haq and Bhowmick 2014; Rubaiyat Ahmed 2013). While acknowledging their highly acclaimed oeuvre, in this book, I focus on lesser-discussed and -studied films, primarily by and about women, in the interest of amplifying nondominant narratives. Since the publication of Rukhsana Kanon's Karim's 2015 article, at least three new documentaries by women have been released: *Rising Silence* (2019) by Leesa Gazi, *Bish Kanta* (*The Poison Thorn*, 2015) by Farzana Boby, and *Jonmo Shathi* (*Born Together*, 2016) by Shabnam Ferdousi. (These are the focus of Chapters 4 and 5 in this book.) In East Pakistan, the first-ever woman-directed film was *Bindu theke Britto* (*An Unending Circle*, 1970) by Rebeka; even today there are still few women directors of industry-oriented films, but noteworthy ones include Nargis Akhtar, Kohinoor Akhter Suchanda, and Roji (Bhowmick 2009).

Raju argues that national cinema in Third World contexts are vehicles to engage with the predicaments of nationhood and identity within colonial and postcolonial conditions. In Bangladesh, cinema as an institution has grown during a period of debates about nationhood, modernity, and cultural identity. Categories such as Bengalis, Bengali-Muslims, and Bangladeshis have been shaped over the past century in different social, economic, and political circumstances and interacted "with and upon the roles and functions of the cinema. . . . So this cinema, by constructing 'Bangladeshi' identity as the one-size-fits-all umbrella for all Bengali Muslims as well as non-Muslims and non-Bengalis living in Bangladesh, worked toward imagining the sense of a Bangladeshi modernity" (2015, 3). Relatedly, Glen Hill and Kabita Chakma (2020) argue that the reification of Bengali as the dominant ethnicity, culture, and language of Bangladesh and Islam as the dominant religion serves to further marginalize attention to the diversity of the country's ethnically distinct minorities (Hill and Chakma 2020, 77). In the Muktijuddho film genre, only one significant commercial-release film even attempts to portray the indigenous inhabitants of the Chittagong Hill Tracts (CHT) region of Bangladesh, home to the minority ethnic communities. *Megher Onek Rong* (*Many Colors of Clouds*, 1976) directed by Bengali filmmaker Harunur Rashid is set in the CHT and features an indigenous woman, Mathin (Rina Sarki) as married to a Bengali doctor Omor (Omor Elahi). Unlike the earlier practice of casting Bengali actors in the roles of indigenous characters, the film includes a number of actors from the CHT in addition to Mathin who is in one of the leading roles. The film visually portrays the landscape, agrarian life, and cultural practices of the community respectfully and with sensitivity. Nevertheless, the film also raises the question of who has the right to belong to the new nation by contesting Mathin's allegiance to it, thereby reaffirming the central Bengali-Muslim account of nationalism.

Historical events such as the partition of the Indian subcontinent and the Muktijuddho have become touchstones in the region against which the magnitude of postcolonial suffering and loss of human life tend to be measured. Literature, memoir, and film in Bangladesh have become an appendage to the project of nation building and deeply influence how, as witnesses far removed from the time of these events, we access the attempts at eyewitness memorialization. It is important to question how national cinema about the liberation struggle—arguably the quintessential theme of national cinema in Bangladesh—has evolved in representations of gender roles and identity, particularly in times of war. In turning to films about 1971, a close viewing highlights the instability of paternalist postwar nationalism that lies at the heart of nationalist cinema and how, in remembering the war and serving as memorials to it, films also retain the ambiguity of the nationalist project.

In a study mapping a comprehensive log of Liberation War films, Kaberi Gayen (2013) looks at twenty-six full-length and seven key telefilms and, like Apon Chowdhury, categorizes them into three camps, hers being films that are set prewar, during war, and postwar. She further categorizes the films by each decade following national independence as well as by industrial versus alternative film. She draws on alternative filmmaker Catherine Masud's definition of "national cinema" and its quality as an authentic reflection of a country's tradition, society, history, and culture, in all its diversity and richness. Gayen studies these films in both world cinema and Bangladesh national cinema contexts and shows that in prewar films, with few exceptions, women appear in marginal, fragmented, or supporting roles..Even though postindependence films have featured women more centrally, their representational range is limited. In broad strokes, the abject sexual victimization of women leading to loss of life (suicide or otherwise) and harm to mental stability appear to set the stage for most mainstream and even some alternative war cinema.

Nayanika Mookherjee (2015) argues that women's wartime experiences have been memorialized in the Bangladesh public discourse in certain elite-coded ways. For instance, secular Bengali resistance has been signified by women in sari and teep participating in nationalist song and theater, a particular aesthetic that implies ethnically Bengali yet Muslim. While this is a source of pride, women's sexual suffering is met with shameful silence or metaphorized as the plunder of the motherland. Mookherjee points out that women speaking about sexual violence in Bangladesh challenges both the aesthetic and political memorializations of the war. She documents how the narrative of the Birangona's horrific rape is told, not forgotten or silenced, even as the complexities of her life story are occluded from the prevalent discourse of the war. It is not the knowledge of rape that brings social sanction but the speaking of it in public.

Mookherjee's analysis of the representation of sexual violence in wartime is supported in a study by Muhammed Shahriar Haque (2015) about the discursive legitimization of rape discourse in popular cinema of Bangladesh. Haque surmises that both in popular Bollywood Hindi cinema and in the Bangladeshi film industry, popularly referred to as Dhallywood films, rape is deployed through a revenge motif (where the victim/protagonist is acted on) enacted by the male villain. He points out that in Muktijuddho-related films, as well as action-based films, although rape may not be the main theme, nevertheless it occupies a consistent subtheme (15). While a deeper and layered exploration of different facets of rape is rare in subcontinental films because of social taboo (and film censorship codes[5]), it is seen as morally reprehensible, leading to the shame and ostracism of the victim. According to Haque, such portrayal reflects the polarized attitudes in society toward rape, victims of rape, and the rapist. This is affirmed in the acclaimed Muktijuddho cinema *Guerilla* (2011), which I write about in Chapter 2, where the protagonist kills herself rather than be raped by a Pakistani soldier, thus affirming the notion that death is preferable to rape. Haque goes on to conduct a language analysis of rape, especially in Muktijuddho but also other commercial films and identifies commonly used expressions of rape denoting strong stigma: "opobitro (impure), olokkhi (bad omen), noshto (ruined), nichu (low), joghonno (disgusting), jaroj shontan (illegitimate child), upojukto noy (unworthy), choritro hina (characterless), kolongko (stigma), lanchhito (abused), opoya (unlucky), kolongkini bou (stained bride/wife)." Further, the meaning of rape is constructed through the use of the sound of loud diabolical laughter (of a Pakistani soldier) or pleas by the victim: "'no, no, noooooooooo,' 'save me, save me,' 'don't ruin me,'" as well as "intense music, pathetic music, sombre grave music, shrill heart wrenching music, crying weeping, sobbing, screaming or screams, grunts of struggle, grunts of protest" (17). Together the language and sound work to project rape through a myopic lens. Bangladesh Film Censor Board prohibits explicit sexual scenes yet a cinematic discourse operates in Muktijuddho and other popular cinema "within the cultural and censor-regulatory norms of our society, which has a deeper connotative representation" (18).

Although scholarship about film and gender/sexuality in Bangladesh remains quite thin, most comprehensive studies, Gayen's included, draw on Raihan's aforementioned 1970 film *Jibon Theke Neya* (*A Glimpse of Life*), one of the first and most critical representations of national cinema. The film, a political satire based on the Bengali language movement under the rule of Pakistan, represents the myriad struggles leading up to the Liberation War—labor and language, to name only two. It features a calculating autocratic woman who symbolizes the political dictatorship of Ayub Khan in East Pakistan (now Bangladesh). Her control of family members—her husband, two brothers, and the servants—reflects the dynamic of Ayub Khan's rule. The film depicts two stories, running parallel to each other: As the people of East Pakistan rise in political protest in public spaces, the family members raise their voices in the domestic space against the tyrannical woman heading the household. The two brothers in the family get married, but their wives vie for the keys to the house—symbolizing control of the household. Despite several substantial roles, the women in the film are portrayed as either tyrannical and conniving or docile and self-sacrificing. Men's and women's roles are also starkly aligned along domestic and public spaces, with the struggle for women's power focused on control of the home. Ultimately, the film sets up a negative relationship between women and power, where the head of the household—the tyrannical woman—is finally brought to justice in a public court by the oppressed men in the family.

Another of the first noteworthy films about the Muktijuddho is the aforementioned *Ora Egaro Jon* (1972), by director Chashi Nazrul Islam. Unlike some others in the national cinema genre, this highly successful film is set apart because of its multiple and diverse female characters, five of whom have a range of significant roles. Keya is a freedom fighter and the daughter of the leader of the Peace Committee who kills her father to protect freedom fighters from Pakistani soldiers. She is eventually captured, raped, and killed. Mita is a medical student who cares for wounded freedom fighters. She too is raped and attempts suicide. Sheela is a student who is captured for information and tortured. Shabur Ma is an elderly widow who lost a son in the war. There is also an unnamed village woman who provides care and food to freedom fighters. Even though the film highlights multiple female roles, the prominent themes remain sexual victimization and shame resulting in suicide. In addition, women's honor as well as their rehabilitation are viewed as squarely a male responsibility, and women's suffering and shame is only recognized through validation by men. Even Mita, who is a medical student, deems her own contributions to the freedom struggle as meaningless in comparison to her lover, a freedom fighter who is seen as the worthy hero. The film raises the question of social recognition and acceptance of Birangona women despite the Bangladesh government's recognition of women's suffering and provision of financial and social security to them.

In analyzing that category of critical films made in the early years after the war, Gayen argues that those films made tropes of sexual violence against women. Specifically, she refers to films such as Islam's *Shongram* (1974), Ali's *Roktakto Bangla* (1972), Fakhrul Alam's *Joy Bangla* (*Victorious Bangla*, 1972), and Dotto's *Orunodoyer Ognishakkhi* (1972). Women's roles in these films are inevitably tied to sacrifice or loss of innocence leading to the loss of societal respect. Muktijuddho films were fewer in number in the post-1975 era during the period of military dictatorships, a time Gayen claims produced films less critical of the liberation movement. In the 1980s, the influence of Bombay cinema became more pervasive, as dancing and singing sequences featuring women in provocative dress in Pakistani army camps added to their sexualization. At the same time, Pakistani army officers in these films were caricatured as drunk and lascivious. In *Orunodoyer Ognishakkhi*, for instance, Gayen points out that one-third of the film constitutes rape scenes. This is also one of the handful of films that takes up the issue of the *Juddhoshishu* (war child) as the male protagonist, Anwar Hossain, appeals to the nation to accept the child of rape. Harunur Rashid's *Megher Onek Rong* (1976), too, raises the issue of the war child when the mother commits suicide and the child is returned to his father. Other noteworthy films of this era are Khan Ataur Rahman's *Abaar Tora Manush Ho* (1973) and Narayan Ghosh Mita's *Alor Michil* (1974), both of which depict the postwar devastation, disappointment, and chaos. In these films, women are squarely returned to the domestic space as side characters.

Several alternative films have probed the association between woman and nation whereby the rape of women and plunder of a nation are intricately connected. For instance, Morshedul Islam's *Agami* (*The Next*, 1984) and Tanvir Mokammel's *Hooliya* (*Wanted*, 1983) present sexual violence against women as a national humiliation. Women's domestic roles are also increasingly portrayed as holding up the home space, as in Morshedul Islam's *Shorot '71* (*Autumn '71*, 2000) and Humayun Ahmed's popular *Aguner Poroshmoni* (1994). A more recent film, Nasiruddin Yousuff's *Guerilla* (2011), the subject of Chapter 2, is the first to center around a woman as a freedom fighter. Winner of the National Film Award, *Guerilla* traces the story of Bilqis Banu, a middle-class Bengali woman, whose awakening and involvement allows us the window into the unfolding freedom struggle. The film ends, however, with Bilqis's suicide after she avenges the death of her brother and prevents her own sexual assault by a Pakistani army officer. The film's ending—with the woman's annihilation—is seen as preferable to rape, which is perceived as surrender to the oppressor. Throughout the film, we see a play on the title *Guerilla*, where presumably an innocent and docile Bengali woman is capable of acting as an insurgent in the face of personal, communal, and national threat. The motifs of women's sacrifice and agency in death are ultimately embraced, while the question of women's place and integration in the independent nation remains unclear.

Feminist filmmakers and scholars have long engaged with this anomalous relationship of woman to nation. Kathleen McHugh (2009) and Ella Shohat (2003) shine light on how women are both insiders and outsiders to nationalist and colonialist struggles and how a layered perspective is necessary to mount a deeper understanding of this complex and contradictory location. They broaden the discussion by placing women's struggles within the legacy of colonial processes and the realities of globalization while also shedding light on cross-border connections in feminist film representations and interpretations. Seen within a transnational framework, women's wartime experiences are placed at once within a national and global movement for justice that can be instrumental in mobilizing awareness, collective critique, and advocacy. However, in addition to insisting on visibility and positive representations, feminist cinema insists on the political necessity for rejecting tropes through a portrayal of diversity of experiences, and interrogating gender as a regulatory norm. Further, feminist critics bring to light the inward- and outward-looking conversations that engage not only state and military occupation but also family, kin, and community norms and strive for "an ideal of being free from scripts that define what counts as a legitimate life . . . defined here as freedom from norms" (Sara Ahmed, 2004, 151).

Feminist scholar Cynthia Enloe alerts us to the masculinist tendency of the discourses of war to generalize women as victims (and men as the militia), which diverts the gaze from exactly the "conditions and decisions" that turned them into casualties in the service of nationalist mobilization (2004,

104). In contrast to Enloe's critique, which posits war as gendered in its constitution and legacy, Bangladesh film criticism has centered around the portrayal of women as victims of war. This singular focus forecloses alternative narratives to nationalistic ones; women are seen as containers of trauma with a reification of an honor-shame complex. To focus on the gendered constitution and legacy of war, however, and to interrogate the regulatory norms of gender reminds us not only that these are the result of human agency but that women had also participated as combatants—that the very term "combatants"—ought to be expanded from an exclusively militarized notion to include women who tended to wounded soldiers, served refugees, ran programs on *Swadhin Bangla Betar* (Free Bengal Radio Station), provided shelter, food, and clothes to the guerillas, and sent their loved ones to war. Film, then, can be an avenue for arguing against the gendered silences in the memorial process and for demystifying the normative scripts of what constitutes freedom.

Ananya Jahanara Kabir has argued that, as a genre, film functions as "testimonial narratives for survivors" (2005, 178). She suggests that films based on the partition of the Indian subcontinent provide a means for narrative integration of traumatic memory and thereby open up possibilities for mourning and reconciliation. Gayen's study (2013) on representations of women in Muktijuddho films is one such attempt to investigate the role of national films in recuperating, creating, and engendering a sense of national history as well as looking at the diverse and important roles women have played in it. In Gayen's book, commissioned by the Bangladesh Film Archive, she asserts that one has to ask three critical questions to assess whether films about the Muktijuddho present a *shothik dharona* (correct understanding), specifically around women's diverse roles and contributions:

1. What social roles do women occupy in Liberation War films?
2. What do these cinematic representations imply about women's place in society?
3. What modes of participation in the liberation struggle are available to women?

To this list, I add a fourth question: What are the terms through which subjects can become visible as victims/survivors of violence and agents of nation?

In the past two decades, key texts and films have appeared that disrupt the earlier narratives of suffering and bereavement and have begun to lay out a response to these questions. Among the texts are Tahmima Anam's novel *A Golden Age* (2007) and its sequel *The Good Muslim* (2011), Nadeem Zaman's *In the Time of the Others* (2018), Shaheen Akhtar's novel *The Search* (2011), Bina D'Costa's *Nationbuilding, Gender and War Crimes in South Asia*

(2010), Mookherjee's *The Spectral Wound: Sexual Violence, Public Memories, and the Bangladesh War of 1971* (2015), and Yasmin Saikia's *Women, War, and the Making of Bangladesh: Remembering 1971* (2011). Noteworthy films that have contributed to this new genre of cultural production—and that build from Tareque and Catherine Masud's groundbreaking documentaries of the 1990s—include the aforementioned *Guerilla* as well as the three films under discussion in this chapter: *Itihaash Konna*, *Shongram 71*, and *Meherjaan*. Together, these add to a growing tradition of writing, filmmaking, theater, and television drama about the Muktijuddho in mainstream Bangladesh media—a tradition that seeks to illuminate internal and external tensions surrounding the representation of war, gender, memory, and justice for a wider regional and global audience. While it is beyond the scope of this chapter to explore the multigenre investigation of gendered experiences of 1971 initiated by these texts and films, I suggest that together they attempt to restore an ethical dimension to history and to decolonize subjectivity and personal identity as well as illuminate intimate/interpersonal reckonings (Saikia 2011, 9). The ethical encounters staged in these films hearken to a healing and reconciliation, especially of the contested terrain of memorializing a gendered war. Like other texts I mentioned in this genre, these films challenge a number of cherished and inherited "truths" regarding the Bangladesh Liberation War. These texts and films, to different degrees, are groundbreaking. They enlighten a regional and global audience on a conflict almost entirely missing or forgotten outside of Bangladesh. In the fields of genocide and trauma studies, very few know or discuss the history from a Bangladeshi point of view.

Some of these texts are also provocative because they debunk a number of national myths that have shaped the consciousness of the post-1971 nation of Bangladesh. The abundance of literature generated in Bangladesh about the war, published as memoirs, novels, district-level reports, and accounts of war crimes, have narrated the war as a triumph of masculinist liberation, by and large through stories of male valor and female victimization—often represented as the plunder of a nation and its women. This is true in both commercial and art films that depict the war. Thus, women's wartime experiences and struggles in these narratives are reduced to sexual victimization and relegated as a private suffering and rendered as shameful (Saikia 2011, 54).[6] In contrast, this new genre of texts prioritizes women's narratives as the primary vehicle for reconstructing this forgotten history. Unlike the predominant masculinist narratives, the female characters in these films are agentic and project what Janell Hobson calls "embodied resistance" (2008, 232). Even so, none of them represent the "emblematic survivor" of 1971 (Rothe 2011, 36). In challenging women's representations, these films push against masculinist visions of national cinema and broaden the narrativization to a more global genre of human rights.

War Themes in *Shongram 71, Itihaash Konna,* and *Meherjaan*

Shongram 71, by British Bangladeshi filmmaker Munsur Ali, urges viewers to grapple with crucial questions of identity, culture, and history from a retrospective postcolonial framework. Like other films discussed in this book, *Shongram 71* situates the independence struggle of Bangladesh beyond its national borders and through intimate relationships between self and Other (in this case, Bengali Muslim and Hindu communities but also *Muktijoddha* and Juddhoshishu). The film is framed through the memories of Karim (Anupam Kher), the son of a freedom fighter who fought in the anticolonial struggle in India. Karim grew up in East Pakistan and fought for the liberation of Bangladesh, and, as the film begins, we see him at the end of his life, in a hospital bed in London reminiscing to a British journalist about a forgotten genocide in modern times. His adopted son, a Juddhoshishu, sits at the foot of the bed as the dying Karim relates the story of the violent birth of Bangladesh and the unresolved questions of loss, responsibility, and reckoning. The Muktijuddho, at the outset, is framed within the long trajectory of anticolonial struggle in a continuum with the 1947 partition of the Indian subcontinent. This helps situate the war as not only a national struggle for independence but one with regional and global roots and consequences.

Karim, played as a young man by Amaan Reza, grew up in the village of Lalghat near the India-Bangladesh border. The relationship between the Muslim Jalaluddin, Karim's father, and Suraj (played by Shubrodho), his friend and comrade in the nationalist struggle, epitomizes the pluralist culture where Hindu and Muslim communities live side by side and share the political dream of an independent Bangladesh. They quote Tagore's poetry and sing Nazrul's songs. Their children play together. As Karim grows, he falls in love with Asha (played by Dilruba Yasmeen Ruhee), who is Hindu. Gradually, a wedge is driven into this harmonious coexistence, and Asha reminds Karim that the West Pakistani army, who Karim believes will not bring them harm because they are of the same nation, are "your brothers [Muslim East Pakistanis]; [but] we are Hindu." When Asha and Karim are stopped by the army officers and they see her sari and teep on her forehead, signifying Bengali and Hindu culture, they are warned, "*Kaffir jaise kapra, sir pe bindi—fir na dekhu*" (Do not dress like the infidel).

"You are a Bengali, not a Pakistani," Major Iftikhar (Arman Parvez Murad) of the West Pakistani army says to Jalaluddin, and Jalaluddin responds by reminding Iftikhar that Bengali and Pakistani should not be seen as mutually exclusive; one is an ethnic identity, the other a national identity. "Governments can come and go but they cannot change my history; I am Bengali and nothing can change that." In another scene, Iftikhar tells Nath, the owner of the local tea shop, "If you had learned to speak Urdu, we could have lived together." Iftikhar asserts Urdu as the authentic language of the Muslims in the subcontinent. Nath responds in indignation, "Does everyone speak Urdu in Pakistan? The Qur'an is written in Arabic not Urdu. Bengali is the language of this land."

As the revolution begins, the community's struggle is brutally suppressed by the Pakistani army, aided by Bengali Muslim razakars. Men and boys are indiscriminately killed, and women and girls are taken to rape camps. Asha's family tries to cross the border to India but is captured on the way. Her mother is killed, and her father is injured. Asha is raped by Iftikhar and manages to escape with the help of a sympathetic Pakistani soldier. She and her father find shelter in a refugee camp across the Indian border. Karim joins the guerilla resistance movement and promises to avenge the deaths of his parents and brother Altaf (Ananta Hira) at the hands of the Pakistanis. His transformation to a freedom fighter is complete when he takes on the struggle of his father, his surrogate uncle Suraj, and his martyred brother. "You have to fight for the right to call it [Bangladesh] your country," he realizes.

With the help of Anu, a Hindu woman who serves Iftikhar in the army camp, Karim and his friends break into the barracks. "This is what a woman has to do to survive," Anu tells the freedom fighters. To keep her mother and younger brother safe, she sexually services the Pakistani officers. "After the war, the same society which could not protect me will reject me. Who will marry me, you?" a defiant Anu asks Karim. "I have someone waiting for me," replies Karim. Hari, his Hindu comrade, steps in: "I will marry you. War is only part of the struggle. Dealing with the consequences and rebuilding our society is next. This country will not forget your sacrifice." In a dramatic scene, when the guerillas capture Iftikhar, they hand a wooden stick to Anu, who lashes out at him, injuring him with all her force, thunderous music playing in the background (he is later killed by Karim). "You are now free," says Hari referring to the sexual coercion Anu was subjected to by the Pakistani army officers. The Bengali fighters are gleeful as they shoot at Pakistani soldiers who surround them in the barracks. Finally, with the help of the Indian army, they win the war. The film uses historic footage from NBC News of Sheikh Mujibur Rahman's iconic declaration of the freedom struggle on March 7, Ziaur Rahman's declaration of independence on March 26, and the Pakistani army's surrender to joint India-Bangladesh forces on December 16.

"The war is over, but are we free? How do you win what is your own right to begin with?" ponders Karim as he boards a bus to India in search of Asha. He finally locates her and Suraj. But Karim's dream is shattered when he sees the *sindhoor* on Asha's forehead, signifying that she is married. Karim's premonition of the ambiguity of freedom is reflected in the scene where he and Asha stand hand in hand behind the iron bars of an open terrace. Asha tells him of her painful crossing over to India, finding herself pregnant with Iftikhar's child, and giving birth to a son who only brought her sadness and hurt. She leaves the child at an orphanage. When Suraj and Asha hear the news that everyone in their village had been killed, Suraj arranges her marriage to a man named Rohit. "No one is to blame," she tells Karim tearfully.

Karim's response to the devastating loss of his family, his beloved, and his innocence is an act of reconciliation, his reckoning with the Other: He chooses to embrace the Juddhoshishu born to Asha, whose father Karim had killed. He accepts responsibility by raising the child of the man who raped the woman he loved. At the end of *Shongram 71*, the child is now a grown man sitting at the foot of his father's hospital bed in London—a scene that hints at the possibility that the freedom fighter migrated out of Bangladesh with his adopted son, perhaps because they were not welcome as citizens in Bangladesh. He finishes sharing his story with British journalist Sarah Myles (Asia Argento), after which he breathes his last breath. When Sarah hands in her report, however, her cynical editor declines to publish the story of this forgotten genocide. He tosses it in the wastebasket, announcing, "No one gives a shit."

Shongram 71 is an important contemporary film to consider for a number of reasons: First, it locates the struggle for Bangladesh's independence within the long trajectory of British and West Pakistani colonization as opposed to continuing the conventional understanding of it as a "civil war." Second, it draws attention to a forgotten struggle for self-determination by presenting the film in the international arena as opposed to a strictly national one. Third, it contributes to the growing critical genre of Bangladeshi national cinema within a world cinema context. Fourth, it fosters critical understanding of war's impact through interpersonal and intimate relationships as well as through a collective uprising. (This point, while clearly important, frequently dominates the conversation to the exclusion of questions about trauma, healing, and postwar responsibility.) Fifth, the story appeals to postwar generations by addressing unresolved questions of identity, gender, culture, and healing. Finally, it pushes our thinking beyond the nationalistic binaries through its emphasis on the ambiguities of survival, legacies, and the consequences of violence on everyday human relationships. The relevance of the film as a memorial form lies in its ability to capitalize on such ambiguities.

Shameem Akhtar's 2000 art film *Itihaash Konna*, which I focus on more closely in Chapter 3, also provides a counternarrative to more traditional masculine and nation-centric representations of the Muktijuddho. Like *Shongram 71*, it, too, emphasizes a reckoning with the Other—not at the state or juridical level but through interpersonal relationships. Notably, Akhtar is one of a few women directors in Bangladeshi art cinema—and a member of the film society movement mentioned earlier—and the film's activist impulse is heightened by casting prominent social activists in the role of actors. Moreover, the fact that the film is presented through an interview with a woman survivor of war explicitly frames it as a tool for mobilizing a campaign to address the atrocities of 1971 and bring perpetrators to justice while emphasizing healing and reconciliation for victims.

In calling for justice, however, Akhtar's film deploys an affective lens, which underpins the notions of intimate histories, empathy, and friendship with the Other—namely, the relationship between a Pakistani citizen with ties to Bangladesh and a Juddhoshishu, war child. Bypassing visual atrocities committed by the Pakistani army and averting retributive violence, this film is more interested in human encounter where the self-Other relationship replaces hostility with care and reconciliation. This ethical encounter occurs through friendship between women of either side of various borders—Bengali and Pakistani, Bengali nationalist and Juddhoshishu, Pakistani and Bangladeshi Juddhoshishu. In doing so, it opens a conversation about a different self-Other relationship between the divided people of South Asia. *Itihaash Konna* consciously attempts to broaden the scope of reconstructing and remembering 1971 beyond the borders of Bangladesh and to reestablish the intertwined history of the region.

The themes of intimacy with the Other, transnationalism, and woman-centered narratives are perhaps nowhere more centrally represented than in Rubaiyat Hossain's debut feature film, *Meherjaan* (which I discuss in depth in Chapter 1). Hossain describes this controversial work as a "women's 'feminine' re-visiting of the Bangladesh national liberation" and as a story of "loving the Other that advocates an aesthetic solution to violence" (*Meherjaan* Press Kit 2011). The film narrates the intertwined stories of four women: Sarah (played by Nasima Selim), a war child searching for the truth about her mother and her past; Neela (Reetu Sattar), who was captured, raped, and tortured by Pakistani soldiers in 1971, and later joins the Muktijuddho with another woman combatant; Meher (older role played by Jaya Bachchan), Neela's cousin, who was only seventeen during the war, when she fell in love with Wasim Khan (Omar Rahim), a renegade Pakistani soldier; and Salma (played by Hossain), another war child born during another conflict—the partition of the Indian subcontinent in 1947. The adolescent Meher (played by Shaina Amin) becomes the lens through which the story is unraveled in flashbacks.

Meherjaan was deliberately promoted as a three-nation film featuring Bangladeshi, Indian, and Pakistani actors, artists, and musicians. The film was shot in Bangladesh, the background music is composed by Indian music director Neil Mukherjee, and it features Lalon Shah's mystic songs from Bangladesh. The actors contribute to what the press kit for the film calls a "symbolic gesture to initiate a process of creative collaboration across the South Asia region" (*Meherjaan* Press Kit 2011). The cross-nationalism speaks to a spirit of healing, symbolized, especially, by the *ghazal* of Urdu poet Faiz Ahmed Faiz, whose famous lines—"When will we see the unsullied green of spring? After how many monsoons will the stains of blood be washed?"— are sung by Pakistani veteran singer Nayyara Noor. Faiz wrote the *ghazal, Dhaka se wapsi par (On Return from Dhaka)*, after his visit to Bangladesh in 1974, where he encountered the painful realities of the Pakistani military killings, including the murder of many of his contemporary progressive intellectuals in the Eastern Wing.

Hossain's reckoning with the Other, like Akhtar's and Ali's, occurs not at the state or juridical level but through interpersonal relationships. In *Meherjaan*, the Juddhoshishu, Sarah, who had been given up for adoption, returns to find her place in the nation. Unlike the state that rejected her and others like her, her aunt, Meher, unquestioningly accepts Sarah as family, inviting her to stay at her home. Sarah's arrival leads Meher to reminisce about her lost love, revisit the trauma of the war, and lay the steps toward mutual healing. Although Sarah, "the passionate nomad," leaves again after finding the answers to her past, she does so only after forming a bond with her aunt, whose own healing is intertwined with Sarah's. "If she had not come, this story would never have been told," says Meher.

Both *Meherjaan* and *Itihaash Konna* reimagine the feminine sphere or domestic space as a place that facilitates the relationships necessary for coming to grips with the past. Most of the scenes between Meher and Sarah are in Meher's present-day home, where they face each other in dialogue. In a scene in which Meher and Sarah discuss an editorial in *Awaaz* penned by Nanajan (Meher's grandfather), in 1946, about the quest for the Bengali-Muslim identity, there is an attempt to bridge differences of time, hurt, and violence. Likewise, the scenes in *Itihaash Konna* depicting an encounter between three women—two friends and a Juddhoshishu—of opposing sides is staged in the private space of the home. Instead of combat footage, in these films, we see the women looking at historical artifacts as props for communication and even mechanisms for healing—for instance, old newspapers, photographs, and, in the case of Meher, a wood sculpture she chisels: "Two human forms

Nasim SELIM as warchild Sarah | Rubaiyat HOSSAIN as Salma Aunt | Reetu SATTAR as "Birangona" Neela

Figure I.3 The leading female roles in *Meherjaan* (dir. Rubaiyat Hossain, 2011).

encircling into each other's body. Their forms mingling, embracing each other. Creating a new form. Loving the Other." The sculpture reflects pieces of all of the women—Sarah, Meher, Neela, and Salma. In this form, though, the bodies are face-to-face. Similarly, after Lalarukh's departure in *Itihaash Konna*, Nanu (grandfather to Juddhoshishu Ananya, and father to activist Monika) takes out a photograph of his deceased daughter—who had committed suicide after her traumatic experience in the rape camp—from the back of a bureau, wipes it clean, and puts it on display. The photograph/sculpture/ newspaper serve as aesthetic devices in the films, hinting at the acceptance of the Other's humanity, a strategy of oppositional film narrative.

Conclusion

Returning to Gayen's three questions about women's roles in war films— What are the social roles women occupy? What is their place in society? What part of the liberation struggle belongs to them?—what these films together urge is a revisioning, a reconceptualization of how women are depicted in wartime cinema. In *Meherjaan* and *Itihaash Konna*, the directors enable a woman-centered vision of healing and reconciliation. In *Shongram 71*, a Hindu woman is the Birangona whose progeny, a child of war, symbolizes the hope to rehabilitate a devastated Muktijoddha (freedom fighter). Nevertheless, this same Birangona of *Shongram 71* cannot return to her village in an independent Bangladesh with Karim. Additionally, Hari, a Muktijoddha, offers marriage to Anu for her honorable rehabilitation to society. A woman's reintegration and location within the nation—outside of a heterosexual union—is thus once again left ambiguous. Even as these films open up a narration in reimagining how women are presented in Muktijuddho cinema, they are yet bound by a masculinist and statist version of the story. Like Fleetwood (2011, 6) surmises with regard to the representation of blackness in visual culture, women in these instances fill in the void, even as they remain the void and also exceed the void's coded attachments, however fleetingly. One can surmise that gender ideology is most sacred in sites relating to the Muktijuddho—the defining event for national identity—and, as such, national cinema as its cultural analogue is bound by its normative memorialization. As a genre, the woman-centered films gesture toward newer and more just attachments to feminine subjectivities.

1

When Love and Violence Meet

Women's Agency and Transformative Politics in Rubaiyat Hossain's Meherjaan

There was nothing heroic about the war of Bangladesh (or any war for that matter).

SAIKIA, *Women, War, and the Making of Bangladesh*, 95.

The release of Rubaiyat Hossain's film, *Meherjaan* (2011), a story about loving the Other, set amid the Bangladesh Liberation War of 1971, met with strong responses from Bangladeshi audiences across generations and political persuasions. At the core of some of these responses lies a hypermasculinist rejection of unsettling a politics of truth regarding the war, which has come to occupy a "sacrosanct" space within the Bangladeshi national imaginary (Alamgir and D'Costa 2011). In this chapter, I explore the anxieties underlying the gendered responses to *Meherjaan*, particularly regarding themes of absent or omnipresent trauma, the nonnormative relationship of nation to gender and sexuality, and the notion of loving the Other. I explore these themes at two levels: the political message the film transmits, unwittingly or not, and its aesthetic choices and affects. Finally, I comment on the potential of this woman-centered and feminist film to further a dialogue of healing and reconciliation in the Indian subcontinent. Such a dialogue is much needed, as the legacy of the violent partitions (1947, 1971) continues to stir personal and political rifts across the region.

There has been a robust tradition in Bangladesh to write and make films, theater, and television dramas about the topic of the Liberation War, which has put forth conventional norms of representations but, as I mentioned in the Introduction, in recent years, key texts and films have appeared that disrupt the nationalist archive. These newer efforts have departed from that tradition and brought into view a critical discussion of war, genocide, and gender justice on a transnational scale. Seen together, *Me-*

Figure 1.1 Film poster for *Meherjaan* (dir. Rubaiyat Hossain, 2011).

herjaan, too, contributes to this new genre of cultural production that seeks to illuminate internal and external tensions surrounding the representation of war, gender, memory, and justice for a wider regional and global audience.

Meherjaan generated controversy among audiences in Bangladesh and the larger diaspora, including at a screening and discussion on the film I organized at Harvard University in 2011. I argue that embedded in the film's narrative is a potential for a cross-border reckoning about the gendered consequences of war and healing in the subcontinent—a reckoning that also produces anxieties and strong responses. To do this, I draw on Saikia's *Women, War, and the Making of Bangladesh* (2011), a historical analysis of women's experiences of 1971, as I see both that study and *Meherjaan* as social texts that intend to unsettle fixed notions of "truth" and confront the deeper remnants of colonization—that is, the internalized oppression that lies within postcolonial subjects. In doing so, both texts seek to remake the self and humanize the Other. The transformative politics and aesthetics of *Meherjaan*, I argue, compel a rethinking of the entrenched relationship between nation, gender, sexuality, and identity that is born of injury and trauma. They urge a shift in perspective—from a focus on the lived and imagined liberatory potential of identities resulting from trauma to one that embraces a principle of shared humanity, vulnerability, and universal love. Both *Meherjaan* and Saikia's gendered tellings of 1971 are attempts to restore an ethical script to history and to evoke an authentic decolonization of subjectivity and personal identity (2011, 9).

Film Synopsis

As I began to explore in the Introduction, *Meherjaan*, Hossain's debut feature film, narrates the intertwined stories of four women. The first is Sarah (Nasima Selim), an adopted Juddhoshishu who comes to Bangladesh to search for the truth about her mother and her past. Next are Neela (Reetu Sattar), who was captured, raped, and tortured by the Pakistani army, in 1971, and who subsequently gave birth to Sarah; and Neela's cousin Meher (played as an older woman by Jaya Bachchan), who was only seventeen during the war (played as an adolescent by Shaina Amin), when she fell in love with Wasim Khan (Omar Rahim), a renegade Pakistani soldier. Sarah's search leads her to the older Meher, her mother Neela's biological cousin, which stirs Meher's memories of 1971. The adolescent Meher, then, becomes the lens through which the story is unraveled in flashbacks. Finally, there is Salma (performed by Hossain), another war child born during a different conflict: this one, the partition of the Indian subcontinent in 1947. Salma is seduced by a romantic notion of war and pines for the heroic soldier to ride off with into the sunset. Salma's clairvoyance, an uncanny ability to absorb the vicissitudes of war and proffer contentious insights, is perhaps connected to her own birth during the tumultuous times of 1947. While the film weaves in and out of the past, much of it is set in the idyllic home and village of Khwaja Sahib (Victor Banerjee)—Nanajan—the benevolent patriarch, grandfather of Meher and Neela, and father of Salma.

Meher's family takes refuge in her maternal grandfather's home, in a village relatively untouched by violence even as the war rages elsewhere in the country. Nanajan, portrayed as a deeply learned, pious, and compassionate benefactor, gives shelter to the freedom fighters but does not allow the Peace Committee[1] to set up base at his village, regardless of both subtle and overt threats from razakars. He has a deep historical and pluralist understanding of the Bengali grassroots struggle for autonomy (he cites the philosophies of Hazrat Shah Jalal and Stree Chaitanya as having influenced the Bengali Muslim culture) and is not swayed by the ruse of a unified Pakistan for Muslims of both wings. "True religious consciousness," he says to Shumon (Azad Abul Kalam Pavel), a Bengali Communist Party member, "does not make one blind." And, to the Peace Committee representative, he points out, "In the Census of 1872, it was discovered that half of the population of this low-lying delta were Muslims. The 1940 Lahore Proposal didn't mention Bengal at all. Muslims of Lahore and Bengal are not the same.[2] There are differences."

Meher finds the surrounding village liberating as she roams without a care in the world. She befriends Arup (Rifat Chowdhury) and Rahee (Arup Rahee), a Sufi couple bearing a message of love and unity through their song and poetry. One day while Meher is in the countryside, an injured Baloch soldier[3] who has defected from his unit, Wasim Khan, saves her from capture by Pakistani troops. Meher, in turn, finds him shelter at the home of Arup and Rahee, who embody queer masculinity and sexuality in the film. While the three nurse Wasim back to health, Meher and Wasim share their misinformed views of each other's cultures and communities and grow to love one another despite the immense weight of historical difference. When Meher's family discovers the romance, however, they are outraged and disappointed.

While Meher's love for the enemy soldier is blossoming, Neela, who had survived rape and torture, finds her desire for revenge against Pakistani soldiers intensifying. In contrast to these agentic women, their male cousin, Sami (Rajeev Ahmed), is portrayed as having more bluster than mettle. On one hand, he wants to restore honor to Neela and, in doing so, to the nation; yet, on the other, when faced with the reality of war, he does not want to fight in it. Instead, he finds the pursuit of his love interest (Meher) more compelling. Rejected by Meher and duly emasculated with a slap to his face, Sami directs his jealous rage at Wasim, the "(noble) enemy" within reach. Meanwhile, Neela submits to the marriage proposal of Shumon, the Communist, although a rather cryptic scene leaves us wondering about the nature of this submission. In a conversation with Shumon, Neela alludes to nonwartime violence she has experienced as well as her general distrust of men. Nanajan, however, an otherwise progressive and gentle soul, rejects the union of Shumon and Neela based on an archaic religious law whereby marriage between individuals who have suckled the same woman is prohibited. (We learn that when Neela's mother died, Shumon's mother was her nursemaid.) Disappointed and desperate, Neela leaves with a female soldier named Joba (Tansina Shawan) to join the fight for liberation: "This time with weapons," she says to Joba.

In a parallel plot, Salma—Nanajan's daughter, a character both wise and comical—finds her hero in freedom fighter Shimul, but not before giving Meher her blessing to love Wasim. As the story concludes, the idyllic village and home are destroyed and Nanajan is killed, ostensibly by the Pakistani army in one of the few scenes of overt violence. Years later, the troubled Sarah, who has come searching for her origins, finds comfort in Meher's affection. Notably, in the film, it is the women who are most intimately affected by war—and the ones who begin the healing.

Like Hossain's film, Saikia's provocative book, *Women, War, and the Making of Bangladesh*, challenges a number of cherished and inherited "truths" regarding the Bangladesh Liberation War[4]—truths that have taken the form of literary and filmic texts, personal essays and memoirs, some scholarly engagements, and archives of district-level accounts of war crimes, all of which have overwhelmingly memorialized the war as a triumphant narrative of masculinist liberation. Women's wartime experiences and struggles in these narratives have not only been invisibilized but also reduced to sexual victimization, locked in "the private sphere and . . . dealt with as private matters by the victims' families [or] often solely by the victim who hides in shame" (2011, 54). Saikia's book, on the other hand, is groundbreaking for a number of reasons. It is one of a small number of scholarly publications for a global audience that sheds light on a lesser known—or, as alluded to in the discussion of Munsur Ali's *Shongram 71* in the Introduction, mostly forgotten—conflict in the history of modern South Asia, it prioritizes women's narratives as the primary vehicle for reconstructing this forgotten history, and it debunks a number of national myths that have shaped the consciousness of the post-1971 nation of Bangladesh. Saikia, like Hossain, counters the reductive renditions that obscure women's narratives. She urges readers to delve deeper to "develop an ethical memory" to "initiate multiple tellings of 1971." In doing so, she hopes to "cultivate a site for the divided people of South Asia, in India, Pakistan and Bangladesh, to contemplate a different self and Other relationship" (5).

Saikia's attempt to broaden the scope of reconstructing and remembering 1971 beyond the borders of Bangladesh is parallel to *Meherjaan*'s impulse to reestablish the intertwined history of the region. Unraveling this complex history, however, dislodges a number of perceived truths. For Saikia, these include the misguided idea that suggests Pakistan was the sole colonial power oppressing Bangladeshis before 1971 (31), the notion that there were clear boundaries and distinctions between enemies and victims (namely, Pakistanis vs. Bengalis), and the claim of a Bengali genocide—which she

defines as a "cold and rational plan and not irrational, random acts of killing" (47). Contrary to this definition, her findings determine that "no single
group had a monopoly on committing violence, nor did one single group
control the production of death in East Pakistan" (49). Consequently, since
the internal violence has not been confronted in Bangladesh, Saikia is suspicious of a truth-and-reconciliation process or a war crimes tribunal. She
asks, "Who will try the criminals? And who has the authority to do so?" She
notes that, in the current climate of distrust between the governments of Bangladesh and Pakistan, these processes could not be properly administered
and, most important, would not solve the problems of women, who are yet
to be recognized as political actors. After all, as Saikia poignantly asks, "What
kind of memory inhabits the site of pain that has never been resolved or visited?" (7).

Saikia's text is a useful companion piece to *Meherjaan*, which, as mentioned in the Introduction, was promoted as a three-nation film. It was shot
in Bangladesh and features Bangladeshi, Indian, and Pakistani actors and
artists. The multinational actors contribute to a "symbolic gesture to initiate a
process of creative collaboration across the South Asia region."[5] Like Saikia,
Hossain, too, emphasizes a "reckoning" with the Other—not necessarily
through legislative or judicial efforts but through interpersonal relationships. While Saikia foregrounds the religiocultural principle of *insaniyat*
(humanity) for the reckoning between victim and perpetrator, Hossain's
film deploys a lens of universal love, shared vulnerability, and *insaniyat*
toward an undifferentiated Other. Saikia speaks directly to the brutality of
war and gendered violence, all the while deconstructing categorical renderings of "victim" and "perpetrator." Hossain, however, seemingly bypasses
this nuanced rendering and encourages viewers to question their own prej-
udices about the enemy Other and to reflect on a condition of vulnerability
shared by all. Released in the same year, both texts have been deemed controversial in the subcontinent, with *Meherjaan* receiving the lion's share of
criticisms. The blogosphere was ablaze with sexually charged accusations
maligning Hossain and her crew's morals and motives. Many members of
her crew received threats. Even though Hossain has been described as a
"leftist" with a "critical vision," at the time of the movie's planned release, the
situation was further complicated when other influential Awami League
political elites (e.g., Tarana Halim, who is also an artist and cultural activist)
joined the protest. The army was deployed at the theaters where the film
played in its short duration, adding to the threatening environment. Amid
such furor, the distributor, who is himself a freedom fighter, pulled the film
from the theaters only a week after its release, despite sold-out showings.

I contend that *Meherjaan*'s undoing was the result of its emphasis on
shared vulnerabilities and humanity.[6] The film for the most part bypasses

depictions of overt violence and trauma and does not repeat the trope of evil enemies and innocent victims; instead, it encourages love and reconciliation between aggrieved parties. Both texts raise a series of questions: Are enemies equally worthy of compassion and love as members of the same nation? Does a moral retelling of the liberation struggle require distinctions between enemy and victim? Can shared vulnerability as a condition of humanity supersede a desire for retribution? Is there feminist potential in the intersection of love, violence, and transformative politics—such as advanced in *Meherjaan*—for the recovery of women's experiences, agency, and subjectivity? It is indisputable that there is subjugation surrounding women's experiences of 1971 in the annals of history. Yet, the mere evocation of a woman's rendition of the period has not lent moral credibility to *Meherjaan*. Zafar Sobhan (2011) observes that, despite the film's attempt to break out of the "grand narrative" and to choose matters of the heart as the vehicle to do so, to centralize a romance between a Bengali woman and a Pakistani soldier with the intention of offering a female narrative of the war "ultimately does a disservice to the very female narrative that the director professes it is her goal to give voice to. The question can be asked: who does Meher speak for other than the director?" Sobhan sees the film deflecting attention from more important stories of the war, something that other critics have also suggested. While there is, indeed, a global and regional marginalization of 1971, it appears, from Sobhan's critique, an attempt to trouble the narrative of heroism and valor is simply not the way to go about establishing a historical narrative.

What is interesting in Sobhan's criticism above and another more recent email response I received from a film critic, about the merit of a woman's narrative to counter a grand narrative, is that both take issue with the alliance with an enemy soldier, which they believe "taints" the authenticity of the nation—and the inspiration for the Liberation War. Such an alliance, according to the masculinist responses to the film, betrays the essence of the nationalist struggle for separation from Pakistan, an essence which appears to be embedded on women's bodies. Bengali women must uphold the purity of the nation, the nationalist sentiment, and its heroic struggle. Any wavering from that is considered a distraction, at least, and a betrayal, at worst. Here is an indignant and indicative correspondence I received from a film critic who is palpably outraged by the film's alleged distortion of the "truth" and diminishing of the heroism of the male Muktijoddhas:

> In a film dealing with particular historical events a director must use his/her imagination without altering and distorting the actual events. Yes, history is sometimes constructed. But when it is done that hardly remains "history" rather it becomes a falsification. Such

attempts are criticized. In order to be imaginative a filmmaker cannot change events of the past which was the whole truth, not any "constructed" version by any party. Can anyone deny the carnage conducted in Dhaka on March 25, 1971? What would you say if a filmmaker shows that not the Pakistani army, but Bengalis killed the intellectuals in Dhaka University that night along with many other innocent civilians? Would that be considered a good attempt by anyone who is acquainted with the events of March 1971? So, we cannot reject authenticity. In fact, we must stick to it. A "constructed" history is not history at all, but when we talk about history we must give precedence to actual reality and authenticity.

And here, Rubaiyat Hossain failed miserably. She can surely show the emotional involvement between a Pakistani soldier and a Bengali girl. But for doing so why did she find it necessary to present the freedom fighters as nincompoops? You saw the film still I would like to mention that three freedom fighters were shown in that film. One of them joined the war and soon returned, that means he was a deserter. And he even said "I don't want to die." When by risking their lives the freedom fighters were fighting to free their motherland from occupying forces, did any freedom fighter say such a thing? Another one said, "The war makes me feel very tired." And then, during the war, he got married, and not only that but a scene showed that he entered a decorated room with his newlywed wife to enjoy the first night of their married life. This scene, I would say, is obnoxious!! Because it is a sheer distortion of the temperament of our freedom fighters. No one during the war was thinking of getting married. And Rubaiyat Hossain cannot depict a freedom fighter this way that he could get married in such a gorgeous manner during the war neglecting his more important duty of fighting the enemy. And the third freedom fighter asked the village influential for his permission to conduct [guerilla] operation in his village. The influential man did not give him the permission and the freedom fighters did not conduct operations in his village. Did freedom fighters require the permission of a landlord to fight the Pakistanis? And did any Bengali landlord supporting the Liberation War try to refrain the freedom fighters from fighting the Pakistanis?

. . . In order to provide a counter narrative can Rubaiyat Hossain show things that did not take place in 1971? We need to keep this in mind that her film was set in Bangladesh in 1971 and so she must portray the actual reality, not a constructed one. As to the erasure of marginal subject position, this director was surely guilty of erasing their actual contribution and attitude. And concerning the women's narrative of 1971, we notice that in *Meherjaan* the heinous rape of Bengali women by the Pakistani army has hardly been portrayed. A character appears who was raped by the Pakistanis, but the brutality of the Pakistanis has hardly been conveyed through the narrative of the film.

All this, and especially the scene of an idyllic village where a Pakistani man and a Bengali woman can enjoy their moments during a genocidal war cannot convey the sense of terrible anxiety and horror that people experienced in Bangladesh in 1971. Having seen this film, the question comes to the mind if the director knows about the history of 1971 at all. And interrogating a dominant narrative is one thing, and misrepresenting the actual events is another. This film, thus, accomplishes nothing. And I just don't see how this film meaningfully conveys a number of "anxieties" around gender and nationalism. If she would have made an entirely imaginary film, perhaps such criticisms would not be levelled at the film but she chose to make the film in the backdrop of 1971 so she cannot ignore the necessity of acknowledging the contribution of many people. She cannot make the bold appear as feeble, she cannot make a time marked by a great deal of bloodshed look like a peaceful time where lovers can roam the countryside without any fear. It is very important to maintain "authenticity" when one deals with real events. (Personal email, January 17, 2021)

This lengthy and angry response to the film—and the filmmaker—as desecrating Bangladesh's history and honor, I argue below, surfaces a series of anxieties around gender, sexuality, and nationalism. In particular, this strongly worded reflection of the film brings to light the ongoing tussle over "who speaks about 1971" and a masculinist claim to authenticity. Notably, the critic sees in men the only freedom fighters in the film, and rape of women by Pakistanis as an obligatory plot line to any film about 1971. The indignation over the filmmaker's gender—a young female director, educated in the West, who was also relatively new to the industry—perhaps contributed to the writer's intense discomfort with the film, scrutiny of its director, and authoritative claim to legitimacy.

The release of *Meherjaan* coincided with two noteworthy and related developments. First, the Awami League government in Bangladesh initiated the much-awaited war crimes tribunal to prosecute the Bangladeshi razakars. Second, *Dead Reckoning* (2011), the controversial book by Sharmila Bose that denies the genocide, was published. Instead of coalescing a critical engagement with history, in this climate, Hossain's film engendered highly emotional responses that accused it of promoting union with Pakistan (*Pak-*

isongom) and detracting from the quest for political justice in Bangladesh. Even the cultural elite in Bangladesh have described the making of this film as "a bit premature" (Zaker quoted in Ethirajan 2011b).

There are obvious ways the film departs from conventional depictions of the Liberation War. First, the war is both sensually omnipresent and visually absent. Aesthetically, it is dissonant to the subject of war and violence. The violence, in fact, is either averted (Meher's rescue by Wasim, Nanajan's refusal to harbor any political group in the village) or transmitted in the background through melancholic music and distended sounds (during Meher and Salma's "retreats" to the dollhouse) and long scenes belying abandonment, emptiness, and desertion (the repeated shots of the hanging bench). Second, unlike these long melancholic shots, the plot, which is front and center, weaves in and out of the stories of the four women who are constantly in motion. All of the women are agentic—that is, they project a notion of "embodied resistance" (Hobson 2008, 232), and they narrate their own stories, which is an act that women, especially Birangona, have not been able to do in Bangladesh. The agency of women depicted by bodies in motion and overt sensuousness is not subtle, although none of the female characters can be said to be representative of the "emblematic survivor" (Rothe 2011, 36). Rather, what we observe is "a disambiguation of trauma culture characters towards a more complex representation perhaps through the use of parody, satire, hyperbole, trivialization of survivors" (36). Third, the righteous nationalist uprising in East Pakistan is not the only conflict that is featured. Rather, we learn about multiple power struggles between the Communists, secular nationalists, pro-Pakistani collaborators (e.g., the Peace Committee), and the rural indigenous populations who are largely left out of the jockeying for power. Moreover, we learn that family and community struggles can be at odds with the nationalist struggle. Fourth, we also learn about the intertwined histories of the region and the multiple legacies of allegiances that spring forth from that shared and embattled past. We learn how religion, spirituality, and mysticism found multiple expressions in people's lives. One of the opening scenes of the film shows the adult Meher praying while her surroundings are dotted by insignia of Islam, Hinduism, Buddhism, and Christianity—the multiple religions of the subcontinent. Finally, victims and perpetrators in the war are not that easily categorized. The film portrays the enemy Other as vulnerable and worthy of empathy, while the self is ambivalent about retribution, instead searching for a more transcendental engagement with the Other. The narrator is at once childlike—as in the voice of seventeen-year-old Meher addressing "Dear Diary"— yet mature, reasoned, and moral ("I have saved someone's life. I have loved someone. I did what my heart desired"). Conventional notions of gender and sexuality as dichotomous and hierarchical are disrupted. The central

Figure 1.2 Adult Meher in prayer surrounded by multireligious insignia
(*Meherjaan* [dir. Rubaiyat Hossain, 2011]).

plot is both heteronormative (allegory of the woman and the soldier in the framed painting) and fantastical (a love that never comes to fruition, so its legitimacy is subverted), complicated by subplots of same-sex love and eroticism (caressing scenes of lovers and landscapes, self-adornment by Nanajan and Meher) and a yearning for unity with the divine self (through the Sufi-inspired poetry of Arup and Rahee). The "topography of affect" (Srinivas 2005, 324) creates an aesthetic that is beautiful and poetic, but there is violence and trauma on the flip side, with the slaying of Nanajan and the erratic behavior of Neela. Hossain's *Meherjaan* as a border-crossing film attempts to work through a number of nationalist anxieties deeply connected to traumatic histories of conflict and violence, and, in doing so, it imagines how an ethics of reciprocity and care could be enabled in the breach.

Anxiety 1: Trauma as Absent-Present

Perhaps the single most damning criticism directed at *Meherjaan* has been that the film obscures the trauma of 1971 and trivializes the suffering of women despite the director's insistence that it is a feminist and even a nationalist film. Commentators, like the one I quoted at length earlier in the chapter, who are otherwise open to critical perspectives of this period took issue with what they saw as conceptual flaws of the film, including the Bollywood-influenced color and dress schemes and the use of ultrafeminine imagery as the backdrop to a fantastical romance in the midst of a raging war. To the audience, the visual landscape of the film was utterly dissonant with its subject matter. As Naeem Mohaiemen describes, "Scenarios are built as a dissociated dollhouse, within which the ugly context is a force-fit and the attempt at counter narrative loses its way. The brutality of genocide and the geography of ravage vanish, while starry-eyed lovers stroll, undisturbed, through lilting mustard fields" (2011, 83). Sobhan (2011) appreciates the cinematography even though he finds it inappropriate for similar reasons: "Although the film is beautifully shot and scored, I didn't find its evocation of time and place convincing. For the most part, it did not succeed in taking me back to 1971 or persuading me that there was a war raging in the background." Hossain responded to this line of criticism by saying, "Because I have not shown any war within the canvas of my cinema, they are interpreting it like I deny that there was genocide, which is really not the case. There are so many indications in the film that a war is going on." Explaining her aesthetic choices, she added, "It's a film-maker's choice on how they want to represent a certain topic. I can make a movie about a murder and not show a drop of blood" (quoted in Ethirajan 2011b). These aesthetic choices, according to critic Mookherjee (2011), contribute to the credibility problem of the film because audiences read them as political choices instead. Captured in the words of Ferdousi Priyobhashini, a survivor of 1971, "There is a silent message in the movie that we can forget about [the war]. This historical sentiment cannot be erased" (quoted in Ethirajan 2011b).

Contrary to these criticisms, I argue that trauma subtly permeates the entire aesthetics and sensibility of the film. Eschewing the overt acts that habituated audiences would easily recognize, Hossain instead communicates trauma through a structure of feeling, creating that topography of affect through distended sound, intense imagery, nonlinear narrative, and music. In the first minutes of the film, seventeen-year-old Meher recalls the scenes of death and destruction she witnessed en route to her grandfather's village. The scene is intensely beautiful—young Meher lying on an intricately carved bed with fluffy pink cushions beside an open window through which the bucolic landscape is slightly visible. The beauty of the setting is dissonant with the memories Meher recounts. Hossain skillfully uses conventional codes of femininity to disturb a dialectics of the relationship between supposed male activity and female passivity (Netto 2005). Yet, it is a memory of which Meher cannot speak: "I don't tell anyone, not even Mother. I must erase these memories," she writes in her diary. Right at the outset, just like the aesthetic dissonance, Hossain establishes a dissonance between public and private voice— a recurring theme, particularly with regard to women's trauma.

Trauma is further communicated through a set of discordant and fragmented occurrences. Salma Khala, Meher's clairvoyant aunt, draws her into
her makeshift dollhouse—a huge almirah—to show her a painting given to
her by her father, Nanajan. It depicts a young woman providing succor to her
knight. As the story goes, the soldier falls asleep listening to the woman singing, and when he awakens, she is gone. He looks for her for the rest of his life
but is unable to find her. This romantic story of love and separation foreshadows Meher's own unfulfilled love story. It is inside the almirah, a frame
within a frame, where Salma spins the story of love in a time of war; in the
next instance, switching to reality, the confused Meher asks, "Do you know
that the country is at war? Are you prepared for it?" When Neela, Meher's
cousin, arrives at the village, Nanajan senses her before he actually sees her.
He is awakened from his peaceful slumber in the garden with the white
doves flitting about and wants to visit the Sufi shrine immediately after greet-
ing her. Neela is obviously distraught; everything about her demeanor—her
frequent fainting, walking about listlessly, and even speaking out loudly about
being captured, raped, and tortured by the Pakistani army—sets her apart as
a character in distress. The women in the family speak in hushed tones about
Neela's rape and worry that nobody will want to marry her. Salma tells Meher
that Neela is *khanelaga* (touched by a Pakistani). Neela's male cousin, Sami—
well fed and coddled by his mother—wants to join the war to avenge Neela's
rape. Disrupting the gendered nationalist narrative of male valor and female
shame, Neela intervenes to break the silence: "I will tell everyone that I was
abducted and raped. I will not stay silent." Yet, this depiction appears to be
too subtle in the eyes of some viewers. In an email exchange about the film,
a critic writes:

> We must not distort historical facts when we attempt to make a crit-
> ical exploration. As I said, in presenting newer information about
> the rape of women in Bangladesh can we say the Pakistani soldiers
> did not rape Bengali girls in 1971? Or can we say the freedom fight-
> ers were nothing but a bunch of weaklings? . . . What did it show actu-
> ally? How did it come under the rubric of a women's film, or a war
> film, or a socially-conscious film, or a historical film? It just com-
> bined some nonsensical shots that were totally out-of-sync with the
> very situation the film attempts to describe. It did not address the
> war, nor the history, nor the emancipation of women. (Personal email,
> January 17, 2021)

Much of the criticism of *Meherjaan* centered on the character Neela and
her sexual expression. In the film, Neela's insistence on speaking the truth
about her experience on her own terms is met with discomfort by both her

Figure 1.3 Shumon comforting Neela (*Meherjaan* [dir. Rubaiyat Hossain, 2011]).

family and the Communist Party leader, Shumon, another of the film's heavy-set, less-than-heroic Bengali male characters. When Neela, a former Student Communist Union member, openly talks to him about her rape, Shumon evades the conversation by responding, "Let's talk about something else." Later, when Shumon asks Neela not to be prejudiced against all men because of "what happened to [her]," she charges back, "How would you know what happened to me?" referencing that women were not given the space to talk about their experiences during or even after the war. Furthermore, she confesses, "It wasn't the first time either," referring to the continuum of oppression of women. Subsequently, when Shumon puts his arm around Neela in an attempt to soothe her, she turns to him questioningly, doubtfully. Shumon enveloping Neela here can be read as an act of both comforting her and silencing her.

In her work on subjectivity and violence with regard to the partition of the Indian subcontinent, Veena Das (2007) argues that the discursive formations of the traumatic emergence of nation-states assign a particular type of subjectivity to women as victims of rape and abduction (59). Women's own assertions of their subjectivity, however, cannot be fully determined by these assignations. Das suggests that, "through complex transactions between body and language," women can both provide witness to the harm done to the whole social fabric and express their own injuries. These expressions do not fit available frameworks of power/resistance or absolute repression of women. Rather, they have to be understood as delicate and layered acts of self-creation (78). In this exchange between Neela and Shumon, we gain insight into a particular subjectivity of Neela, born of trauma, that her community can neither recognize nor contain.

A scene in the film that brings into sharp relief the ever-present sensibility of trauma and the uncontained subjectivity of women born out of trauma is when Neela, unafraid of speaking the truth, calls Shumon a coward. They are walking among some trees. Neela is framed rather provocatively in a sleeveless blouse and nylon sari that exposes her arms and midriff. Leaning against a tree, she asks Shumon whether he is intimidated by her, which he clearly is. He looks away nervously and says, "No." When she calls him a coward, however, the usually mild-mannered Shumon changes in an instant. With his wounded male ego, he grabs Neela by the arm and asks, "What did you just call me?" She grabs him right back, wrestles with him, and says, accusingly, "You touched my body! You enjoy touching women, don't you?" The scene fades, and, in the next one, we observe Shumon walking a few steps in front of a subdued and defeated Neela, her head cast downward. The sun is setting, and dusk casts a shadow on the ground as they slowly walk home.

Trauma is also intricately woven into the persona of Sarah, the Juddhoshishu who returns to Bangladesh in search of her mother and answers about her past. In addition to the anguish of those questions, Sarah is also heartbroken by the loss of her lover, which she thinks is part of an ongoing trajectory of abandonment that defines her life: "Why does everyone leave me? Is it my fault?" Upon her arrival, she approaches the adult Meher, who unlocks an almirah in the corner of her room, takes out a locked wooden box, lifts its lid, and pries out objects that prompt her to flash back to a past that she had long kept confined. Inside this metaphorical Pandora's box are her father's glasses, her grandfather's *tasbeeh* (prayer beads used by Muslims), and her cousin's sari, along with her own voice, in the shape of the diary. As the items are released, the healing begins as a way to resolve the trauma. "Giving words to sorrow is so healing," Meher tells Sarah. "Things are not always as they appear. Let me tell you a story."

When Meher presents Sarah with Neela's well-worn nylon sari, Sarah wraps it around herself and curls up in a fetal position—a return to the original trauma of her conception and birth as an unwanted child, the product of a brutal atrocity, which the family, community, society, and government took great measures to eject from history. This scene speaks to the paradox of women's place in postliberation Bangladesh: While Sheikh Mujib had theoretically elevated women participants of war by bestowing the honorific Birangona on them—although in reality it reified gendered narrative of valor and shame—he also declared their progenies tainted, unwanted, bad blood that needed to be flushed out to purify the nation. Social workers undertook an active state-sponsored program of abortion and foreign adoption at the end of the war. In the film, Sarah's return to Bangladesh and Meher's unquestioning acceptance of her denotes the story of the original trauma and shame that was never allowed to find expression, let alone heal. Interestingly, Sarah is also coded as queer in the film: She refers to her female friend who has left her, she is dressed in pants and a T-shirt, and she has short-cropped hair. Coded as an Other, Sarah is also an agent of healing and love.

It is in this scene that the founding trauma—Neela's rape and giving birth to Sarah—gets transferred onto Sarah. This is also the scene where Meher unlocks her box of memories and her story becomes the central narrative, which arguably transfers attention away from both Sarah and Neela. Critics have called this a conceptual flaw, but I see it as an instance of reaffirming the film's instrumental use of love as the lens through which to represent trauma. Transference also creates a cascading effect of disparate stories of the four women during the war—all centrally speaking to the war—as the narrative weaves in and out of their lives. Arguably, the film only shows the stories of Birangona in partial, nonlinear, and marginal ways—a narrative choice that speaks to the representation of trauma in a discordant topography of affect. This narrative choice also alludes to the notion that trauma cannot be fully recuperated but can be told and retold through pieces of memory, where certain parts are glossed over while others are overemphasized. It refers to the film's aesthetic mechanism for reflecting on secondary trauma—the witnessing of trauma—and an ethical way of consuming that trauma some forty years past. It further alludes to Das's (2007) claim that violated women's subjectivities cannot be fully determined by their experience of violence. Sarah and Meher—not directly violated but certainly wounded by the violence of war—in particular, engage in a process of separation from trauma and remembrance in the shape of mourning. They are located within this indeterminate space of forgetting, remembering, and healing.

Aesthetically, in refusing to objectify trauma, the film opens up a dialogue between the past and present. Speaking to the genre of Holocaust films, Guerin and Hallas (2007) argue no representation can even begin to communicate the truth about traumatic experience, yet representation, however inadequate, is necessary—for documentation, for education, and for imagination. Artistic representation such as *Meherjaan*, however, can be criticized for not meeting the "burden of evidence" and held up to certain subjective standards of "responsible" and "ethical" representation. Guerin and Hallas find these criteria of accuracy and authenticity to be an undue burden for the function of art. They point to the apparent paradox here: that art is both embraced for its perceived ability to represent historical trauma and burdened as evidentiary. What gets lost in these expectations is the performative function of art; it is replaced by the constative and the need for "factual" representation. Claims of truth, in fact, may or may not be the most important consideration in art (LaCapra 2001). Leshu Torchin (2007) calls the processes of producing and consuming historical trauma "bearing witness"—recuperating a forgotten history in the service of genocide recognition and public consciousness. The film is meant to have transformative power, which can not only represent the atrocity but also invoke an ethical transformation in the spectator. In such circumstances, Tina Wasserman (2007) posits, it is important to discover a critical language to reencounter the traumatic past within the context of the present—that the aesthetic of representation reflects the full incomprehensibility of historical trauma. The glaring absence or the absent-presence of trauma in *Meherjaan* underscores such inadequacy of trauma representation.

Anxiety 2: Loving the Other: A Metaphor for the Loss of and Longing for National Unity

The most intense love stories are those that are difficult to consummate. In Sufi philosophy love relationship between the divine and the devotee always remains fueled by the consciousness of the impossibility of ultimate union. Meherjaan love story is driven by such impossible material conditions of union, while indefatigable emotional desire to unite throbs throughout the narrative.

RUBAIYAT HOSSAIN, *Meherjaan* Press Kit.

The enemy, as women revealed, was within, not outside the community of insan (human beings).

SAIKIA, *Women, War, and the Making of Bangladesh*, 92.

The Bengali-self finds itself haunted by its own shadow.

SAIKIA, *Women, War, and the Making of Bangladesh*, 79.

Writing a people's history of 1971, I suggest, is a way of developing a shared responsiveness for allowing transformation within the self while simultaneously acknowledging interconnectedness with others.

SAIKIA, *Women, War, and the Making of Bangladesh*, 8.

Meherjaan is dedicated to women who fought in the Liberation War of 1971 with or without weapons; it is a tribute to their unrecognized, undocumented, and unappreciated roles. Instead of foregrounding the trauma as paramount, the film focuses on humanity, empathy, and reconciliation in a plot that is ostensibly about loving the Other. Hossain uses the nation as metaphor in developing two impossible unions: the central romance between Meher and Wasim Khan, and a peripheral yet equally important union between adult Meher and her niece, the war child Sarah.

Wasim, a young and handsome Baloch soldier, is deemed a traitor to Pakistan for refusing to fire on Bengali Muslims at a mosque. He is captured by the freedom fighters but manages to escape likely execution, by either the hands of his own regiment or the Bengalis. An injured Wasim hides in the woods of the village where Meher and her family have also taken refuge, and he saves Meher from falling into the hands of the Pakistani army. She, in turn, with the help of the Sufi bauls Arup and Rahee, nurses him back to health. Over the course of this rehabilitation, they fall in love, and Wasim increasingly takes on Sufi-Bengali attire and mannerisms.[7]

Meher struggles to contain her feelings for Wasim as the war rages in the background and within her own family. This struggle takes the shape of a moral conflict over religion and nation. She first asks Nanajan whether helping the wounded is a commandment in Islam, and his response is, "I believe in that, hence I am in this state"—alluding to his own nonviolent and compassionate position even as he is approached to cooperate with members of the Peace Committee, Communist Party, and freedom fighters in his village. His response is a staunch "no" to each group, while still maintaining a responsibility to the peasantry of his village, who he believes are both religious and revolutionary. The doors to his house are always open to the poor and those needing shelter from any injustice, regardless of their political or religious affiliation.

Meher then approaches her cousin Neela, who is obviously traumatized by her imprisonment and rape. Her response to Meher's dilemma about what to do with a wounded Pakistani soldier is to "slaughter him." Meher is at an intractable crossroads here: that of her religious and moral obligation to help the person in need (a fellow Muslim, and one who has not killed or harmed a Bengali) versus a patriotic obligation to avenge her cousin's rape and support her people's nationalist cause. It is Salma, Meher's clairvoyant aunt, who finally gives her the permission to help the wounded soldier. If Nanajan is the voice of morality and Neela that of the traumatized nation, Salma is the eccentric, mentally undeveloped yet surprisingly perceptive in her desire for love and union. It is this voice to which Meher chooses to listen.

Meher's load is lightened by the fact that Wasim is not a brute who indiscriminately murders, pillages, and rapes Bengalis. Rather, he is a noble Other with a conscience—an enemy who is open to transformation thus deserving of empathy. At the same time, he is utterly vulnerable, wounded, and likely to be executed by either of the warring parties. When Meher asks Wasim why he saved her, his response is, "I too have a mother and sisters in Quetta." When she further probes why the Pakistani army is torturing and killing Bengalis, he reflects, "A nation trains its army to face the enemy. But sadly, today we are aiming weapons at our own people." A noteworthy example of loving the Other is the film's representation of the characters coded as queer. Similar to the love between Wasim and Meher, and Sarah and Meher, the Sufi couple also defy basic love laws that govern their social existence. According to Brinda Bose, transgressions of love laws "are the result of conscious decisions by the emotionally over-charged characters. The very circumstances of their choice(s) affirm the political judgment that surely it could not simply be bodily need; the sublimely erotic experience is also the pursuit of a utopia in which ideas and ideals, greater than what a momentary sexual pleasure offers, coalesce" (1998, 60). Bose affirms such queer desires that disrupt convention as a form of personal political power. While the word on the street is that the renegade soldier is "seven feet tall, well-built with strong muscles," the Wasim that Meher knows is kind ("My heart would not listen," he says, describing his reluctance to open fire on Muslims at a mosque), gentle (we see him stroking a baby goat, picking touch-me-not flowers), and righteous (his adamant belief in the purity of their love). His understanding and admiration of the love between Arup and Rahee is expressed in the scene where the three men, each an Other, sit in the courtyard of the Sufi couple's home. Rahee is wearing a magenta lungi and is bare chested. He is primping in front of a handheld mirror and has a flower tucked in his long tresses. Arup is sitting across from him, and between them is an open fire, which Wasim—also sitting bare chested and in a dhoti—uses to warm his hands. When Arup coughs, Rahee gets up to fetch a glass of water. Arup says to Wasim, gesturing to Rahee: "He is my soul mate. . . . Do you understand what I say?" Wasim nods knowingly.

The forbidden romance between Meher and Wasim serves as a metaphor for the impossible union and the ultimate separation between East and West Pakistan. From inside her dollhouse Salma tells Meher, "You can love him but cannot marry him." Meher's internal struggle rages: She cannot deny her feelings toward Wasim, yet she feels deep guilt. "What do I know? I am a terrible person. Being a Bengali girl, I have sheltered a Pakistani soldier. I am a traitor," she confesses to Wasim. The conflict between religion and nation resurfaces as Wasim takes her hand and reminds her, "In our religion saving a life is a noble deed." Meher snatches her hand away. In a later scene, Wasim ruminates, "Our lands are different. Our languages are different. But our hopes are one." Meher responds, "You are our enemy now. Perhaps our love is impossible." In this scene, Wasim is center screen and Meher's profile is visible just behind his shoulder, as though it is one body with two heads—the ambivalent Janus face of a nation, one looking forward, the other facing backward (Bhabha 1990). Wasim walks forward, and Meher becomes completely invisible. "I have no retreat left," he says, referring to his position as the traitor to West Pakistan and the enemy to its Eastern Wing. Meher reemerges on the screen and says to Wasim, "You have shelter in me forever." The two embrace passionately. It is important to note here that as a Baloch, Wasim's status in Pakistan is also marginal and somewhat parallel to that of Bengalis in Pakistan.[8]

Bose points out that desire, particularly of the personal kind, has always been underrated in comparison to revolutions and seen as insignificant in relation to the "epic sweep of mass movements" (1998, 60). Similarly, the trope of sentimental love between protagonists of opposing nations may appear apolitical and trumped by narratives that highlight the heroic and triumphant separation of the Eastern Wing from its oppressor. Bose, however, urges a rethinking of the erotic utopia—as depicted in the film through soft lighting and a bucolic backdrop awash in pink and pretty imagery—as political. Meher's "fatal attraction" to Wasim is perceived as lacking the political commitment of participation in the uprising of East Pakistan. The choice of sentimental love is read as suspect and as a betrayal to the nation/ community. The foregrounding of gender and agency is perceived as "silly" when the real conflict should be the militant masculinized nationalist agenda. Kavita Daiya (2011, 594) cautions that the trope of "inter-ethnic couple-dom" in the context of Bollywood films can serve to sanction the project of normalizing, particularly, forms of social reproduction, namely the creation of compliant heteronormative citizen subjects. At the same time, there still are minor perspectives that can defy the social reproduction of heteronormativity in these stories about romantic and familial intimacies.

As we saw in the critic's response earlier in the chapter, the (im)possible and tormented union of the two wings of a nation is a theme that has not been well received by audiences in Bangladesh, who are more sympathetic to a narrative highlighting the heroic separation of the Eastern Wing from its oppressor. Such responses belie the impossibility of entertaining a narrative of 1971 that diverges from the masculinized grand narrative of heroic male soldiers, abject female victims, and the brutal Pakistani army. It is the conventional emplotment of 1971, reproduced and maintained by historical and cultural discourse (Afsan Chowdhury 2011). "I tried to break out of the stereotype of the Bengali hero versus Pakistani brute in the backdrop of the 1971 war, and that is what my countrymen are so upset with," said Hossain in an interview with Al Jazeera. In the same interview, Jehangir Kabir Nanak, a minister of the Awami League government, countered: "What she thinks is stereotype is actually the truth. The Pakistanis killed us like flies and raped our women like beasts. They even massacred our intellectuals just before they surrendered" (quoted in Bhaumik 2011).

Afsan Chowdhury, one of the most celebrated and respected authors in 1971, claims that a "myth-driven history of 1971" controls the current imagination of the Liberation War. Some key notions that such a past rests on include a fixation on numbers killed and raped in the genocide to legitimize

Figure 1.4 Meher and Wasim, an impossible union
(*Meherjaan* [dir. Rubaiyat Hossain, 2011]).

the Bengali suffering, a notion that "Bengalis were naturally good people and Pakistanis were naturally bad ones," and that a "'spirit of 1971' prevailed that year though that is not described. It wasn't there before and now must be preserved though no one says what that is" (Afsan Chowdhury 2011). In a debate organized by the Arts Council in Bangladesh featuring prominent intellectuals and artists, Mustaeen Zahir criticized the active production of hatred and racism toward Pakistan in the name of the Liberation War. Another participant, Piyas Karim, agreed that, as a nation, Bangladesh needs to be accountable to this sentiment of hatred (he called it "fascism"), which has been in the making for decades. Both Zahir and Karim offered as evidence of a national insecurity problem the tendency to malign any person of a divergent view as razakar (*Meherjaan* Debate 7, 2011).

In the same debate, Farhad Mazhar suggests that the root of the anxious responses to this film is that a character such as Wasim is simply unimaginable and unacceptable to the Bengali psyche:

While we have owned our Liberation War, we have not at the same time taken ownership of our Bengali racism. . . . In our subconscious, this racism is active. And that is why, a man like Wasim—and I admit that the film is very bad. A man like Wasim, a Baloch—who deserted his own regiment, who did not open fire upon Bengalis at a mosque, who is a fugitive, who is not even literally a Pakistani, nor a Bengali, he is literally a person who is just going to be killed. Still, he could not win the hearts of the Bengalis. What I mean is even in our imagination, we found him unacceptable. (Mazhar quoted in *Meherjaan* Debate 7; translation mine)

Mazhar points out that, historically, Pakistan saw an ethnic Bengali and a religious Muslim identity as being irreconcilable, and Bengalis had to prove their Bengali-Muslim identity with blood. As a result, this history of conflict over an authentic (Muslim) identity makes Bengali and Islam appear irreconcilable. Mazhar continues, "We [Bengalis] cannot allow a union between Wasim and a Bengali woman. He symbolizes not only Pakistan but also 'the religion.'"

This question of acceptance is addressed in the scene when Wasim is "on trial" in Khwaja Sahib's house. Viewers see Wasim standing on the right side of the room next to an enraged Sami (the coddled freedom fighter), who is ready to shred the enemy to pieces, and Meher's disbelieving father, who slaps his daughter for her wayward behavior. Across the room to the left stands a weeping and defiant Meher with her aunt. Meher's mother is shown as almost unconscious with shock. The audience observes the room through the eyes of Nanajan, who at one point leaves and then crosses back over the threshold to deliver his judgment. It is a long shot, the camera view stretching to an open window beyond the clashing parties on either side.

Meher is most vocal in this scene. She sarcastically cuts her cousin Sami down to size by referencing his reluctance to join the fight and desire to marry Meher instead: "If you wish to fight the Pak army do it on the battlefield. Don't try to show your bravery here." Wasim, the noble Pakistani soldier, is positioned next to Sami, the less than valiant Bengali fighter. Both Meher and Wasim speak to absolve the other of guilt: "Meherjaan is innocent. She saved my life. She has done no wrong. Please don't blame her for her act of compassion." And from Meher: "He hasn't killed a single Bengali, Nanajan. He has nowhere to go. . . . He is not at fault." Wasim shows that he is ready to face the consequences of his countrymen's actions—"If only my blood will soothe your anger then kill me. I stand before you"—and Nanajan is able to see beyond the hatred as he delivers his final verdict: "As an individual he is not guilty." It is a nonviolent resolution, a recognition of the humanity and vulnerability of the Other, reached within the space of Nanajan's home. This scene is a strong contrast to an earlier one where Nanajan is treated as a "guest" in his own home by an imperialistic Pakistani general who mocks him for his loyalty to the Bengali resistance.

As stated earlier, some critics of the film have pointed to a seeming "conceptual flaw" in the plot when Meher diverts the narrative to foreground her own story and subsequently sidelines the story of Neela. As another iteration of the film's central theme of loving the Other, I argue that Sarah's story can only be sensible if coevally developed with Meher's and Wasim's (im) possible union. A noble enemy like Wasim is still unimaginable in the Bangladeshi national psyche, and an active production of anti-Pakistani masculinist discourse sustains that impossibility. The source of the hatred hinges on the original trauma of the rape of Bengali women and forced impregnation as a war strategy. The desire to "flush out" the enemy through state-led policies of abortion and foreign adoption institutionalized the hatred of the Other. That leads to the second (im)possible union in the film: the union of Meher and Sarah. In that sense, Meher's unquestioning acceptance of Sarah is a feminine revisioning of history that includes the acceptance of the Juddhoshishu and a rejection of masculinist war narratives.

The encounters between Meher and Sarah are mostly staged in Meher's present-day home, facing each other in dialogue and often using props— historical artifacts, objects, books, and newspapers—to aid communication. In a scene in which they discuss a 1946 editorial in *Awaaz*, penned by Nanajan, about the quest for the Bengali-Muslim identity, there is an attempt to bridge differences of time, hurt, and violence. This is exemplified in the following exchange between the two women:

Sarah: When I came here I didn't know what to expect and now I am going away with so much.
Meher: So much of what, Sarah?
Sarah: So much positivity.
Meher: Will you come again?
Sarah: Do you want me to?
Meher: Your coming has opened a window that I had long shut. I was always so guilty. I felt, am I making a mistake by loving someone who was supposed to be my enemy?
Sarah: No. Your story gives me hope.
Meher: Giving words to sorrow is so healing.

Faiz Ahmed Faiz, the Pakistani poet who wrote his famous *ghazal*, *Dhaka se wapsi par* (*On Return from Dhaka*) after his visit to Bangladesh, imagines this healing as an impossible question. His trip to Dhaka, in 1974, opened his eyes to the painful realities of what the Pakistani army did in the war. In the film, Meher flashes to her tearful goodbye to Wasim, accompanied by Nayyara Noor's voice singing a poem by Faiz:

After those many encounters
That easy intimacy
We are strangers now

After how many meetings
Will we be that close again?
We are strangers now
When will we again see
The beauty of innocent greenery
After how many monsoons will the
Blood be washed from the branches?
So relentless was the end of love
So heartless

The end of love—and end of an era—is also marked by the murder of Nanajan in his own garden just as the Pakistani army reenters the village. It is left ambiguous as to who actually pulls the trigger because in preceding scenes there were freedom fighters, Communist Party members, and Peace Committee representatives mobilizing to take control of the village. The notion of the "enemy within" and the ambiguity of truth is thus cast into sharp relief.

Almost four decades later, having encountered the progeny of war, Meher finally faces her pain and her past and gives it expression in the shape of a wood sculpture she chisels: "Two human forms encircling into each other's body. Their forms mingling embracing each other. Creating a new form. Loving the Other." It is reminiscent of the earlier scene where Meher and Wasim's bodies merge into one with the two faces, looking backward and forward. In the new form, however, the bodies are face-to-face. The second (im)possible union in the film is still possible, only fleetingly. Sarah, "the passionate nomad," having found answers to her past, leaves again—but not before securing a familial bond. The sculpture reflects pieces of all of the women—Sarah, Meher, Neela, Salma—and echoes the soldier and the woman embracing in the picture that Salma carries. The sculpture serves as an aesthetic device hinting at the acceptance of the humanity of the Other, while also positing the body as a site of intervention. The director makes use of an "embodied resistance" through a subversive rendering of the body politic (Hobson 2008, 232), a strategy of oppositional narrative in the film.

The sculpture is also a metaphor for the "unacceptable and unimaginable" union between the Bengali self and its Other. Created by Meher, it symbolizes women's ability to transform self and society where men have failed. The sculpture represents an unhealed trauma that has not been worked through. And in Meher's decision to not remain faithful to the known and inherited discourse of trauma in 1971, she creates an opening in the film for reflection, criticism, and healing. Ananya Jahanara Kabir has argued that as a genre, film functions as "testimonial narratives for survivors" (2005, 178). In her work on partition narratives, she suggests that film provides a means

Figure 1.5 Sculpture symbolizing union, trauma, and healing (*Meherjaan* [dir. Rubaiyat Hossain, 2011]).

for narrative integration of traumatic memory and opens up possibilities for mourning and reconciliation. The emplotment of trauma in *Meherjaan* outside of its iconic grid allows one step toward the possibility of mourning and reconciliation.

Anxiety 3: Gender, Sexuality, Nation

It is high time we acknowledged the great genetic stew of a family circle that our history hides, and that our DNA relentlessly reveals. But let us not project modern notions of romance upon unions born of trauma, of dependence and constraint. Let us not use easy claims of love as a further deflection from confronting the infinitely more painful emotional hierarchies with which our peculiar institutions have left us battling still.

WILLIAMS, "What's Love Got to Do with It?" 10.

The heroines of *Meherjaan* are unabashedly agentic and sensuous. Sumita Chakravarty (2003) points out that sexuality in narrative cinema can evoke attitudes that are critical to history and society. Love and longing "take on meaning only as part of a larger political project of self-understanding, simultaneously social and subjective. Erotic can function as a composite metaphor for the invocation of value systems, beliefs and practices through which a society calls itself into being at specific historical and cultural moments" (82). The scenes of the lush green rural landscape, the immense ocean and rippling riverbanks, the soft lighting and settings awash in pink hues, the love songs of the baul and heartrending lyrics of Faiz's famous poem—all of these exude a deep sensuousness. Whether between Meher and Wasim, or Arup and Rahee, or the self and the divine, love is as bountiful as the verdant fields. Nanajan, himself a part of the idyllic setting in his crisp white pajama *panjabi* and topee ensemble, asks, "Which of Lord's bounties will you and you deny?" The plentiful love and adulation bind humans to each other and to God. Nanajan and Meher adorn themselves in *atar* (perfumed oils), *shurma* (kohl), and flowers, ostensibly before prayers. The desire for union between self and the divine and between self and Other—and the impossibility of each—"throbs throughout the narrative," Hossain said (*Meherjaan* Screening 2011). Rahee tells Wasim, "Love is the absolute, love is dharma." He expresses this yearning to unite with the divine, as he sings:

> *When will I unite with thee*
> *Quench the thirst of my heart*
> *I would live in sheer bliss then*
> *In sheer bliss, My Lord.*
> *Tell me now where is my divine love*

The quest for unattainable and divine love is transformative: It transforms Wasim from "enemy Other" to a more Bengali self. He gradually transforms his clothing from the soldier's uniform to a dhoti and pajama *panjabi*; he changes his diet, accepting from Meher a bowl of rice and green chilis. Nevertheless, he fails to evoke an ounce of compassion in the Bengali psyche, as, it seems, Neela fails to garner sympathy as a representative of Birangona. Neela, who exudes sensuality in her husky voice, *shurma*-rimmed eyes, flowing tresses, and urban attire, is also deemed unacceptable and unimaginable—particularly as a rape victim. Morshedul Islam, a noted alternative filmmaker in Bangladesh, exemplifies this problematic treatment of Birangonas' sexual agency. Islam is contemptuous over the irreverent depiction of Birangona women and the liberation struggle in the film:

My next observation is about the most important character in the film—the raped woman. As an audience member, I did not feel an ounce of sympathy or respect for that character—as a Birangona. The way she carried on, her dressing, everything. Perhaps, the next generation will defend this portrayal by saying that they want to depict a Birangona as a strong woman. And, Neela was depicted as someone who was a member of the student league of the Communist Party. She also says that it is not the first time that she experienced rape. What is the meaning of this? Why include such a storyline? What this did was soften the issue of rape by Pakistani army. As a result, that character did not move us. The director misrepresented the Birangona and trivialized their experience. This will neither educate the next generation about their experience, nor will it stir any sympathy in their minds. (Islam quoted in *Meherjaan* Debate 1; translation mine)

Islam calls for a stricter adherence to a conventional narrative of 1971—a surprising stance coming from a filmmaker who is presumably aware of the function of art:

Those of us who have experienced the Liberation War do not find any resemblance to it in the film. The village in which the film is set, the way the three female characters behaved, the character of Nana-jan—it is not possible to understand what was implied by these depictions! They certainly did not represent the spirit of 1971. It was not like that. The freedom fighters in the film were extremely weak characters. One of them is shown as not wanting to fight! And, his mother is weeping and telling him not to go! This did not happen during the war. Sons willingly joined the fight, and mothers encouraged them to do so. Sometimes these men wrote letters to their family members before joining the resistance. The film further shows the freedom fighter returning in the middle of the war and expressing fatigue and disinterest in fighting, but at the same time expressing desire for getting married! (Islam quoted in *Meherjaan* Debate 1; translation mine)

Islam accuses Hossain of diverging from a patriotic rendition of 1971; he expresses grave discomfort with the depiction of Bengali men as weak and Birangona women, particularly Neela, as wayward. These comments illuminate that in Muktijuddho cinema a certain *shadhinotar chetona* (which is replete with a particular gender ideology and a concept I elaborate on in Chapter 2) is equally sacred. Representation of martyrs and Birangona are delimited and hierarchical. When freedom fighters are shown as less than heroic, when mothers are less interested in sacrifice for their nations than protecting their sons, when women openly talk about sexual violation, these story lines radically depart from the ways in which the war has been memorialized (Mookherjee 2011). Islam's response to the treatment of the freedom fighter's "interest" in marriage ironically alludes to Hossain's critique of the patriarchal postwar policy of the state. Sami's marriage proposal to Meher is a keen reminder of Sheikh Mujibur Rahman's urging of freedom fighters to honor and respect Birangona women and marry them. Even though Meher is not a survivor of sexual violence in the film, the marriage proposal nevertheless is a gesture of protection toward women at a time of conflict. Some

Muktijoddhas are known to have demanded dowry or some form of compensation for marrying Birangona women. In some cases such marriages did not work out.

Not only is the *shadhinotar chetona* sacrosanct; it seems to embody a certain nonagentic depiction of Birangonas. It is striking that the progressive filmmaker Islam cannot muster any sympathy for Neela because she dares to speak aloud not only about rape by Pakistani soldiers but also violence against women in nonwartime. For Islam, the two cannot be connected because such a structural view of women's oppression softens the atrocities committed by Pakistanis. It is important for him that *Meherjaan* sufficiently distinguish the trauma of "enemy" rape by Pakistanis versus rape of Bengali women by Bengali men. While rape was certainly used as a weapon of war in 1971, recent scholarly literature has demonstrated that Bengali and Bihari women were raped by Bengali, Indian, and Pakistani men during and after the war (Saikia 2011). Deviations from the conventional narrative of brutal Pakistani violence, however, are not acceptable. As Mazhar (*Meherjaan* Debate 7) points out, the humanity of Wasim as a Pakistani soldier is simply unimaginable in the Bengali psyche. This is particularly so, I think, because the film shows a diminished masculinity of the Bengali men and the absence of a categorical enemy Other who kills, rapes, and pillages. For instance, the identity of the person who killed Khwaja Sahib is blurry, and, although Neela was raped by Pakistani soldiers, there is also an insinuation that her own countrymen raped her previously. Moreover, the audience is upset by Neela's "inappropriate" dress and demeanor and finds it insulting to women who fought in the war. In an article jointly penned by Ferdousi Priyobhashini, one of the few survivors of rape by Pakistani soldiers to speak publicly of her experience, and academics from Dhaka University, the authors strongly criticized the film as a betrayal to the history of the Liberation War and an insult to all freedom fighters and Birangonas. They were particularly offended by the depiction of the three main female characters as "sex symbols" and specifically Neela as "sexy" and "wanton" in male company (Ferdaus et al. 2011); and by Salma's repeated requests that her father arrange a '*mut'a* [temporary] marriage'[9] for her. They argue that the story of Meher's falling in love with the enemy Other is mired in a patriarchal obsession with women's reliance on men and marriage. Condemned as "Paki folk fantasy" and deemed detrimental to the war crimes tribunal at a sensitive moment, these writers suggest that the film is Pakistani propaganda.

What are the consequences when there is insufficient differentiation between victim and perpetrator? When their identities, their traumas, and their agencies are blurred? Can shared vulnerability evoke recognition and empathy for an enemy? Wasim's moral dilemma has no place in the Bengali psyche, the Bengali freedom fighters are insufficiently heroic, and the women are not virtuous enough to be genuine victims.

In her work on partition-related literature and film, Ananya Jahanara Kabir (2005) suggests that partition as cultural and collective memory and trauma shapes group identity. The memorializations are deeply ethnicized and gendered, and they erupt when different groups within a nation claim or reject the memory of war in different and competing ways. It also puts the responsibility on art to mourn and memorialize historic losses. Kabir recounts the experience of watching a television show about partition in college in India where the postindependence audience erupted in laughter in the most unexpected of moments. Likewise, I was bewildered by laughter from the audience—mostly young, diasporic, many non-Bengalis—at similarly painful scenes at the screening of *Meherjaan* at Harvard University. For instance, there was a comedy-type reaction following the scene where Neela raises a sickle and tells Meher that she would slaughter Pakistani soldiers if she encountered them. Later, in conversations with some members of the audience, they shared that they did not find it as offensive as they thought they might, that the bad acting and clunky plot (the "dear diary" narrative, the homosexuality) made them laugh out loud. Following the screening, an audience member wrote derisively in the blog Sachalayatan about the four feminist academic panelists who "climbed on to the stage after the screen" and his suppressed desire to scream "*Bandemataram!*"[10] at Hossain for trivializing such an intense historic event into her fantasy film.[11] Some older members of the audience, however, remained silent during the question-and-answer period. During conversations with them later, some expressed that the topic was important and courageous, but the film was poorly executed, that it held no resemblance to 1971, and that it served as entertainment/propaganda, not as proper history. Some older men insinuated that I must be pro-Pakistani to have organized such an event and that I needed to familiarize myself with more authentic representations. (Several novels were suggested as good sources of history.)

Kabir concludes that the laughter from the younger generation at the screening of the partition serial in Delhi denoted a "failure of narrative" to mobilize an aware and responsible collective (2005, 189). That is, while the traumatic past of partition is regularly memorialized in private spaces—oral histories, films, and television—it is unmatched through academic studies. School and college textbooks gloss over 1971, women are hardly mentioned in them, and successive regimes in Bangladesh have tried to manipulate the information according to their own political agendas. As a result, while the trauma of 1971 has indelibly shaped the fabric of post-1971 life in Bangladesh, the memorializations are highly contested. One needs to ask, Who gets to celebrate 1971 as victory? Who determines it was heroic? Whose experiences remain untold? The question of truth is important: it can be seen in the ways that ordinary people police the boundaries of what is true and what can be said out loud, as a means of defending their personal national boundaries. It is the embodiment of nationalist power itself. While breaking away from a faithful representation of trauma, Hossain's film opens the debate about authentic and irreverent narratives and what we as a fractured community choose to gain from such conversations.

Patricia Williams (1998) posits in her well-known essay, "What's Love Got to Do with It?" that although relationships between two parties of unequal social and political standing may occur—such as that between President Thomas Jefferson and the slave Sally Hemmings—we need to rethink the use of a sentimental framework of love to represent them or else risk obscuring those very real power structures. While applauding Hossain for boldly initiating a conversation about reconciliation, feminist scholar Jyoti Puri (2016) suggests that the film overlooks a complex history of hurt and violence with an aesthetic of sentimentality. In the process, it obscures relationships of power and inequality based on gender. She asks, "What is the difference between 'loving the other' and falling in love with a more powerful enemy?" (*Meherjaan* Screening 2011). Responding to Puri's criticism, Hossain explains,

> I researched the nationalist representations of the raped women of 1971, and during that time I conducted a few interviews with survivors. One of them gave me a very complex story of falling in love with a soldier while she was being raped by the others. When she described this story to me, she described it with a lot of tenderness. After I had done my research and went through all these narratives of violence, I really found a lot of hope in her story and the story of these two human beings who are able to come close to each other on the basis of compassion, in the midst of a conflict situation. So that's where the inspiration for the story comes from. But of course in the film's story, the girl who is raped is different from the girl who falls in love with the soldier. (*Meherjaan* Screening 2011)

It is critical to remember that even though heterosexual romance is the primary lens through which we witness a time of terrible devastation, none of these unions ultimately comes to fruition: certainly not Meher and Wasim, a relationship simultaneously erotic and impossible, but also Salma and Shimul, whose marriage is only *mut'a*, an extraordinary wartime union. Salma repeatedly points to the extraordinariness of the time—"*Desh e ekta juddhho choltese, er jonno ki tomar kono prostuti ase?*" (Are you aware there is a war going on in the country? Are you prepared?). We learn later from adult Meher that Salma and Shimul leave the country after Nanajan's death. Even if heterosexuality is ostensibly the focus, the treatment of war as masculinist domination and the subplots of same-sex eroticism displace its legitimacy through the loving relationship between Arup and Rahee, the erotic cinematography in relation to the bodies of women—particularly the dollhouse shots of Salma and Meher—and, ultimately, the arrival of Sarah, the war child who is also coded as queer, an Other in more ways than one. It is upon her arrival that the healing from the masculinist nationalist struggle begins, and it is significant that the two characters who initiate this dialogue are female. These elements provide a counternarrative to the charge that *Meherjaan* is trapped within the patriarchal grid, instead presenting the heterosexual union as a too-simple solution to a devastating history of hurt.

Priscilla Netto (2005) argues that using conventional codes of femininity disturbs conventional dialectics in the relationship between supposed male activity and female passivity and that the body can be used as the site of intervention in doing so. *Meherjaan* is framed within a feminine aesthetic—intense colors, pink prettiness, erotic landscapes, and female bodies in motion. It suggests a feminine passivity even in the characters' obsession with love and marriage. Nevertheless, at the same time, it subverts the conventional understanding of the feminine, just as it subverts the conventional understanding of heterosexual love and marriage. By revealing the fragility of the masculinist grand narratives of war and sexuality, by rendering heterosexual union impossible, the film undermines those conventional codes that it seemingly embraces.

Empathy, Responsibility, and Reconciliation: Is *Meherjaan* a Feminist Film?

What would it take not only to apprehend the precarious character of lives lost in war, but to have that apprehension coincide with an ethical and political opposition to the losses war entails? Among the questions that follow from this situation are: How is affect produced by this structure of the frame? And what is the relation of affect to ethical and political judgment and practice?

BUTLER, *Frames of War*, 13.

Despite Hossain's unequivocal presentation of her debut film as "woman-centered" and nationalist, some of its most vocal critics—the cultural and political elites, including feminists—disagree on both counts. Feminist scholars often contend with the relationship of woman to nation. One such scholar, Kathleen McHugh (2009), writes about Virginia Woolf's *Three Guineas* that "women's worldly space was not independent of country, of the national, but based on spatial paradox: they were at once inside, marginal, in the private sphere of the nation-state (within patriarchal ideas, institutions, and histories in which women have no place) and, at the same time, not contained by, in excess of that state by reason of these internal and internalized exclusions and difference" (112). McHugh's claim shines light on how women are both insider and outsider to nationalist and colonialist struggles, and a layered perspective is necessary to mount a deeper understanding of this complex and contradictory location women occupy. Bina D'Costa (2011), too, notes the complex relationship of woman to nation; she claims that Pakistani civil society seems to be more open to discussing the wrongs committed in 1971 than its Bangladeshi counterpart is (143). D'Costa posits that Bangladeshi justice-seeking movements must address "internal turmoil" as well as hold Pakistan accountable to the 1971 atrocities. The dual process of internal and external reckoning, no doubt, is tantamount to opening a Pandora's box with reconciliation rather than revenge in mind.

McHugh wants to move beyond the ghettoizing tendencies in film studies to specify "women filmmakers" or "women in film," which she believes limits women's film production as specialized or exceptional. Rather, she locates "women's place in cinema within transnational influences and relationships" to generate a broader understanding of "structures of opportunity," ideological underpinnings, production, reception, and circulation of films that are feminist (2009, 126). This allows for a deeper understanding of the worldly space women occupy and the internal exclusions and differences that are particularly critical to feminist filmmaking. Similarly, Ella Shohat (2003) locates "transnational film feminisms" as a distinctive historical modality advancing a political project that critiques both nationalism and colonialism in relation to feminism. Here the transnational is defined as "spaces and practices acted upon by border-crossing agents, be they dominant or marginal" (Shohat citing Francoise Lionnet and Shu-mei Shih, 119)—a definition that takes into consideration the filmmaker's own training and cinematic approach as well as the location of her work beyond the national in an age of rising global mass culture. It offers the scope to historicize women's struggles within the broader legacy of colonial processes and realities of globalization and sheds light on cross-border connections in feminist filmic representations and interpretations.

That Hossain's treatment of feminism and nationalism is intellectually and politically transnational fits well into Shohat's definition. Hossain studied in Bangladesh, the United Kingdom, and the United States, and she was influenced by feminist scholarship and activism as well as by commercial film enterprises such as Bollywood. She confronts the silencing effect of nationalism on women and has been inspired by Noeleen Heyzer's writing about the Korean comfort women,[12] with whom she draws parallels in putting the Birangona within a larger global context of women's wartime oppression. Like Heyzer, Hossain suggests that we consider an "aesthetic solution" to a history of violence and look beyond feminist studies for a "more powerful power," a "power which is 'life sustaining, liberating, and transforming.' I believe love and compassion is that power" (*Meherjaan* Press Kit 2011). Seen in a transnational framework where women's wartime experiences are placed within a global movement for justice, *Meherjaan* is instrumental in mobilizing awareness and action and developing collective critique and resistance. The film is transformative, as it has launched a dialogue about women's 1971 experiences within and beyond a nationalist and national framework and beyond the narrowly constructed notion of "women's films."

What *Meherjaan* brings to the fore is the impasse inherent to the formulaic relationship between gender, nation, sexuality, and identity. From the place of entrenched nationalist stories and gendered identities—forged through trauma, war, and wounding—the impasse appears almost inevitable in that it is born of the stock identities of victim, aggressor, Birangona, freedom fighter, Bengali, Pakistani. These identities are inherently defensive, exclusive, rigid, oppositional, and combative in their formation and formulation; they are wounded attachments that are built through survivalist impulses of Us versus Them. The subversive characters of the enemy Other—the agentic Birangona, men with men, women with women—make transcendence possible because they disrupt easy formulas by their very existence. They are the crack through which light gets in, the deconstructive moments where we see that the inherent instability of the post-1971 nationalist identity is built on a foundation of wounds, partiality, and brokenness. In shedding light on the precariousness of life and of shared vulnerability, *Meherjaan* opens up an ethical and political response to war. This is based on the notion of a radical equality and a claim to love, honor, and protect the precarious life of the Other (Butler 2009, 177). It entails honoring the impulse to resist aggression as resistance itself and honoring the ability to love beyond oneself—to love someone who is not the self and unlike the self, to see the loving presence of another, and to see through to a condition of humanity transcendent of material conditions and entrenched identities. Merging with the love of the divine also alludes to unity and to becoming whole again, thereby transcending wounds through the merger with the universal principle of love and humanity. Painful as it is to confront these themes, and resistant as we might be to disrupt entrenched positions, the highly emotional responses to *Meherjaan* ultimately speak to its success.

Moreover, the film sets in motion a conversation about the necessity of an ethical reckoning of the 1971 genocide and, particularly, the many faces of that genocide. Such a reckoning stands the chance to recuperate a forgotten history—particularly for women and minorities such as Hindus and Biharis[13]—and, in the process, to activate diverse publics. The film also calls for a resistance to the hypermasculinist responses it has received. For instance, we need to reflect on artistic representations and responsibilities to 1971: Should art be burdened with "truth" and, if so, whose truth? Are we ready to accept that representations of 1971 might, even should, be nonformulaic in their questioning of what Afsan Chowdhury (2011) calls the production of a mythical spirit of 1971? Is it possible to unpack that spirit, contest some of these mythical projections, and evoke emotion and resistance that, ultimately, pull to transcend the narrative of a glorious war? In that vein, we can strive for an ethical reckoning that challenges the binary understandings of victim/perpetrator, Bengali/Pakistani, and elicits a deeper appreciation of differentiated agency, suffering, and humanity.

It is important to situate *Meherjaan* within the new genre of cultural production centered on gendered experiences of the nation and the larger transnational movement of healing and reconciliation. A feminine revisiting of 1971 moves toward a gendered healing and a reconciliation with the debased feminine, where femininity is the location of love, caring, and nurturing and the household is the place where we learn an ethics of care. The film offers a redirection of the violence of one's formation, a reconciliation of femininity with masculinity, the tempering of aggressive masculinity with care, and the resurgence of cooperation and community through the work of women and the revaluing of femininity as the place of love. This love encompasses feminized men loving men, women loving women, and self loving the divine in a quest for unity and wholeness. The nationalist movement also seeks wholeness—the integrity of Bangladeshi identity—but it does so by creating a narrative of greatness and liberation. Such wholeness, sought through woundedness, is unlikely to succeed. Wholeness sought through love is, indeed, the reconciliation with the divine; that is, our higher, ethical selves that transcend qualities of humanity and community.[14] This shift in our imagination—from trauma and wounding to love and unity—permeates the feminine aesthetic and politic of *Meherjaan*.

2

Ethical Reckoning

Gender, Vulnerability, and Agency in
Nasiruddin Yousuff's Guerilla

As we have seen, film and literature are critical mediums through which collective memory, interpersonal reckoning, and national solidarity have been shaped and maintained in Bangladesh. The relationship between film, literature, and human rights and the contested terrain of representation, articulation, and artistic approximation of unspeakable violence is well documented. This is particularly true in the genres of Holocaust cinema (Goldberg 2007) and Palestinian cinema (Dabashi 2006). These genres of national cinema, or human rights cinema—a genre that I explore in depth in Chapters 4 and 5—are crucial for attending to and generating far reaching and enduring social and historical consciousness, even political action. In Bangladesh, Muktijuddho films serve that purpose: They contribute to the creation of a collective consciousness about national liberation and its emergence following mass atrocities, genocide, and gendered violence.

In this chapter, I build on the idea of Bangladeshi national cinema *as* human rights cinema. I explore its role in documenting and engendering understanding about women, vulnerability, and agency within a Muktijuddho gender ideology. Drawing from feminist sociologist Patricia Hill Collins's (2004) conceptualization of a Black gender ideology, I propose that in cinematic traditions, an idealized Muktijuddho gender ideology influences and entrenches gendered social norms and reinforces perceptions of masculinity and femininity in war. These perceptions serve to justify patterns of legibility, recognition, and rejection for discursive practices of national inclusion and exclusion.

Figure 2.1 Film poster for *Guerilla* (dir. Nasiruddin Yousuff, 2011).

As I did in the Introduction, I again look to Gayen's study (2013) of women's representations in Muktijuddho cinema and consider her three questions, and one of my own, to guide me:

1. What social roles do women occupy in Liberation War films?
2. What do these cinematic representations imply about women's place in society?
3. What modes of participation in the liberation struggle are available to women?
4. What are the terms through which subjects can become visible as victims/survivors of violence and agents of nation?

I focus here on an important and critically acclaimed war film, *Guerilla*.

Contextualizing the Woman Muktijoddha

Director Nasiruddin Yousuff, himself a freedom fighter, created *Guerilla* (2011), the first commercially released Muktijuddho film that centers around a female combatant. The film is based on acclaimed writer Syed Shamsul Haque's novel *Nishiddho Lobon* (*Forbidden Salt*, 1990). *Guerilla* traces the story of Bilqis Banu, a middle-class Bengali Muslim[1] woman who becomes increasingly involved in the freedom struggle. It is through her awakening that we see the story unfold. Breaking with the cinematic tradition of gendered representations of the war, where the combat role is reserved as masculine and the vulnerable victim is feminine, *Guerilla* invokes a double meaning of combat and struggle: one played out on the front lines of war, the other fought within social and cultural norms of patriarchy. The heroine is a Muktijoddha for both national liberation and woman's emancipation. Throughout the film, we see a play on the title *Guerilla*, where presumably an innocent and docile Bengali woman is capable of acting as an insurgent in the face of personal, communal, and national threat. Her rebellious and passionate nature is the flip side to her soft femininity. The motif of agency in death and sacrifice is ultimately embraced, while the question of women's place and integration in the independent nation remains unclear.

In December 2017, in celebration of the forty-sixth anniversary of Bangladesh's Victory Day, 157 outlets across the country featured historic films about the Muktijuddho. Joya Ahsan, the lead actor of *Guerilla*, attended one of the open admission screenings of the film, noting the showing's significance in reviving a popular tradition of community film and theater culture as well as promoting *shadhinotar chetona* among younger audiences. In an interview with *Prothom Alo*, a national daily newspaper, Ahsan invited readers to join her in this national initiative, calling it an artistic blueprint to Muktijuddho, and she spoke about her own investment in *Guerilla* as the daughter of a Muktijoddha. "When I was working on this film, I thought of myself as a fearless guerilla fighter just like my father. It was a feeling like no other" (Masud 2017; translation mine).

The film's rendering of Muktijuddho goes beyond the national and, simultaneously, locates the Bengali struggle for self-determination within global anticolonial movements. There is a moment in the film where we come to visualize the freedom struggle through a revolutionary lens—spanning class, gender, religion, urban, rural, global, and geographic divides—to articulate a shared vision of truth through love, peace, and revolution. In this moment, the adolescent daughter of the real-life martyr Altaf Mahmud,[2] who is portrayed by Ahmed Rubel in the film, sings *Joy Shotter Joy* ("Victory to Truth"). The Bengali freedom struggle is depicted through a montage, personified through an image of its charismatic leader, Sheikh Mujib, as the culminating figure within an array of other revolutionary leaders: Fidel Castro, Che Guevara, Martin Luther King Jr., and Mahatma Gandhi. The audiovisual cues hearken back to a certain historical mapping of Muktijuddho onto a series of global anticolonial and liberatory struggles. This is a nod to the cultural activists, and filmmakers like Zahir Raihan and Alamgir Kabir, whose revolutionary vision and work in the 1960s and 1970s were the foundation to Muktijuddho cinematic genre. As noted by Naadir Junaid (2020), Kabir was involved in revolutionary politics in Europe, traveled to Algeria and Cuba, and became a member of the National Liberation Front (FLN), the nationalist political party that fought to achieve Algeria's independence from French colonial rule. Further, Kabir was in conversation with activists in the Palestinian liberation movement and the Campaign against Racial Discrimination in the UK. Kabir was sent to prison in France for his involvement in guerilla resistance movements and later in East Pakistan for organizing the East Bengal Liberation Front. Fahmida Akhter (2020) locates the work of Raihan and Kabir within the landscape of Third Cinema, emerging in Latin American political filmic discourse, which was inspired by revolutionary thought and action of the global decolonizing struggles. Speaking to the revolutionary impetus of Zahir Raihan's *Stop Genocide* (1971), Akhter quotes Alamgir's endorsement of the film as representing "the relentless struggle for better life being waged all around the world by working men and women" as well as documenting the genocidal violence in 1971 (Akhter 2020, 235). Despite the revolutionary vision, Akhter argues that the film however portrays women symbolically through an essentialist association of female body to nation. This global 1960s revolutionary spirit, and the feminization of women in war cinema, emanates in the scene where Altaf is shown sitting in a breezy verandah clad in white, nodding to and encouraging his daughter's passionate singing. His wife, wearing a cotton sari, comes in with a cup of tea and joins them, completing the picture of the Bengali middle-class cultural activist home.

Yousuff's *Guerilla* is a quintessentially nationalist film as well as a political film inspired in the spirit of the Muktijuddho genre and its founding artists the way they also intended to narrate a particular story of the birth of Bangladesh. This narration aligns with ruling government of Awami League—the political party leading the ushering in of independence and its secular nationalistic allegiances to Bengali identity. The government not only partially funded the film's production but also waived the tax on the sale of tickets. The film went on to win the National Film Awards in a record-breaking ten categories. (This stands in stark contrast to *Meherjaan*, which was released within months of *Guerilla*. Whereas *Meherjaan* elicited an angry furor over its "misrepresentation" of history, *Guerilla* amassed unprecedented accolades.) *Guerilla*'s massive popularity and high-level recognition speak to several motifs that have come to be mythologized in the memorialization of the war, specifically when the Awami League Party came into power in 2008 on the platform of justice for martyrs and healing for the nation. The opening scene shows Sheikh Mujib (also affectionately called *Bangabondhu*, "friend of Bengal") as the unequivocal leader and proclaimer of independence. (The Awami League's archrival, the Bangladesh Nationalist Party, has claimed that its deceased leader, President Ziaur Rahman,[3] was actually the first to proclaim it.) This perspective solidifies the film's allegiance to the revolutionary and leftist vision of the Bengali cultural intelligentsia.

Guerilla Synopsis

The film opens to the impending violence of March 25, 1971, the night known as Operation Searchlight, when the Pakistani army unleashed a military strike on unarmed civilians of its Eastern Wing, massacring thousands.

Figure 2.2 War images (*Guerilla* [dir. Nasiruddin Yousuff, 2011]).

Bilqis and her husband, Hasan, are in their home when the sound of Sheikh Mujib's voice playing on the radio—declaring the independence of Bangladesh on the cusp of the war—was ringing in the background while widespread agitation ensued on the streets. Hasan tries to placate an anxious Bilqis with humor, suggesting that if he does not return home from work—which foreshadows his imminent disappearance—she can take pride in his *korbaan* (sacrifice) in resisting Pakistani occupation. When he does not return home that night, Bilqis embarks on a search for her missing husband and joins the freedom struggle alongside Bengalis from all walks of life.

In Hasan's absence, Bilqis carries on with her day job at a bank, all the while acting as an insurgent: collecting donations for the war, transporting spools of revolutionary poems and songs composed by Altaf Mahmud to the underground networks of *Shadhin Bangla Betar Kendro*,[4] arranging medical care and transportation for comrades, and even planting explosives at high-level Pakistani military events. In one such scene, Bilqis arrives wearing a red sari, dramatically transformed into an elegant, high-class woman who speaks English and sips wine (under duress, then spits it out). She accompanies Mrs. Khan, who, in contrast, is dressed in black. She is an upper-class widow and mother who consorts with Pakistanis to aid the Bengali freedom struggle. At this party, Mrs. Khan makes the ultimate sacrifice by acquiescing to the request of the Pakistani army officers and staying back with them at the party, even though she is aware that Bilqis and her cadre had planted an explosive in the bathroom. Mrs. Khan's farewell gesture to Bilqis is a raised fist, signifying both goodbye and the revolutionary symbol of solidarity and resistance.

Bilqis's character fights on two fronts: She is both an insurgent in the war and a woman resisting patriarchal social norms. As a composite figure,

Figure 2.3 Mrs. Khan and Bilqis at the party with West Pakistani army officers (*Guerilla* [dir. Nasiruddin Yousuff, 2011]).

she navigates her roles as wife, mother, insurgent, combatant, and ultimately martyr. She always stands apart as different, as Other. At a security checkpoint, for example, the Pakistani guard inspects her identity card and notes that she does not look Bengali. In another scene, Bilqis asks Hasan why he married her since she did not measure up to his Dhaka University women friends who were "smart" and "modern" and totally unlike her (*gaaiya* or backward and "unsmart"). Hasan's reply reflects the patriarchal standard whereby a woman has to be demure and sexy as well as feisty and compliant: He states that Bilqis may come across as a village belle but inside she is a "savage" (*aasto jongli*)—a trait that arouses him. He reaches for her with a passionate embrace, and Bilqis responds coyly, "I can bite" (*kamrabo kintu*). In another instance that codes Bilqis as Other, her mother-in-law admonishes her as "manly" in her activities as well as high and mighty in her demeanor, and she likens Bilqis to "Maharani Queen Victoria." Here, the film exposes another patriarchal double standard that even women uphold: Despite Bilqis's unwavering service to her mother-in-law, the older woman on her deathbed calls her "the monster who devoured her son" and left her life empty of meaning.

The turning point in the film occurs when the narrative and the war front shift from urban to rural Bangladesh. With the death of Bilqis's mother-in-law and the capture of her comrades, namely Altaf Mahmud, she has no more refuge in the city. Mahmud's wife, another female combatant, hurries over to Bilqis's home and asks her to flee and go undercover. Donning

Figure 2.4a Bilqis on the train to Joleswari (*Guerilla* [dir. Nasiruddin Yousuff, 2011]).

Figure 2.4b Bilqis leaves the city wearing a burka (*Guerilla* [dir. Nasiruddin Yousuff, 2011]).

a burka[5] for protection and as a form of disguise (clothing in the film has alternative meanings, as insurgent practice or religious allegiance), Bilqis boards a train to return to her ancestral home of Joleswari. On the train, she witnesses Pakistani militias harassing Hindu passengers, identified by their absence of burkas and topees.[6] She chastises the men on the train for being silent as a Hindu woman is dragged away.[7] An indignant Bilqis takes off her own burka to reveal her long black hair and simple printed cotton sari, a trademark of Bengali women activists to this day. She leans out of the train for some fresh air and looks out to the horizon. It is from this point that we witness a gradual shift in Bilqis's appearance and disposition: From the defiant activist traversing the city, she gradually transforms into a listless, disheveled, and unbalanced (thirsty, depleted, and hallucinating) figure, resembling what Nayanika Mookherjee (2015) has described as the trope of the ghostly absent-present Birangona.

The film ends with Bilqis taking her own life after learning of the death of her freedom fighter brother, Khokon, finding his body and attempting to give it a proper burial (*Antigone* style, hearkening the message of respect to the dead, gender roles, and justice),[8] and getting captured by the Pakistani army. In a dramatic scene, as Bilqis comes to resemble more and more the figure of the madwoman or the iconic representation of the ghostly Birangona, she prevents her own rape by detonating a hand grenade she finds in the room, killing both herself and General Shamshad Khan, the Pakistani threatening her. Interestingly, the assailant here is played by the same actor (Shatabdi Wadud) who played the role of General Sarfraz Khan, killed by freedom fighters earlier in the film; this signifies that the villainous Pakistani officers are portrayed as interchangeable. Bilqis's death—the exit of the woman combatant/Birangona by suicide—is a familiar trope in Muktijuddho films, where death is seen as preferable to rape. The credits roll to Kazi Nazrul Islam's "Bidrohi"[9] ("The Rebel"), with music by Altaf Mahmud and vocals by Chandan Chowdhury, and the following script runs across the screen: "On 16 December finally Bangladesh was liberated. Syeda Bilqis Banu is one of those three million martyrs who gave their life for the independence of Bangladesh in 1971." This poses a significant ambiguity, as Bilqis is both recognized as a martyr who sacrificed her life for the freedom struggle and is perceived as having surrendered because she preferred self-annihilation to rape.

Disrupting Patriarchal Discourses

Despite having a woman Muktijoddha as its heroine, Yousuff frames female agency within patriarchal norms. His intention is to glorify the history of the Muktijuddho and to solidify its heroic image, yet he does so through a narrative of female resistance that is both disruptive and acquiescent. Nevertheless, the question of women's belonging to the nation is of feminist concern, and, by not quite dislodging the woman from the nation, Yousuff strives to expand the gender role landscape. Literary scholar Sally McWilliams (2009) provides a useful analysis of narrative strategies employed in fiction and film to examine a specific feminist representation of the politics of reading women's positionality and agency within trauma narratives. Arguably, what Yousuff achieves is a woman-centered narrative that presents a woman's awakening within a metanarrative of patriarchy. His narrative strategies create new envisionings as they challenge hegemonic narratives of masculine agency, identity, and nationalism. *Guerilla* marks a departure from previous nationalist cinema by deviating from sexual violence as the usual entry point for women in war films. In doing so, it shows that this singular act of violence does not define women's participation in the war; rather, we see Bilqis's character develop more multidimensionality—as a wife, daughter-in-law, sister, comrade, insurgent, and the most valued: martyr. Further, the film begets a consciousness of gender violence within patriarchal social norms that is not necessarily tightly linked to wartime violence only; rather, it serves to point to its structural dimension. Bilqis resists Pakistani occupation and defies the societal, familial, and cultural constraints that limit women's agency.

The film decenters masculinist power by integrating the marginalized Other as integral to the construction of historical and cultural knowledge. Thus, *Guerilla* provides a space for new possibilities and acts as an interventionist film, one in which patriarchal, nationalistic discourses are disrupted, not subverted. At the same time, however, the film is unable to escape patriarchal gender norms that transcend wartime—the female combatant, like the Birangona, cannot coexist with the nation because such a role, real or perceived, has not been imagined. Even in this genre-bending film, the female combatants occupy traditional gendered roles: as mothers (Mrs. Khan, who calls out for her son at the moment of death, and the comrade who transports spools of recordings in her baby's stroller) and/or as wives and sisters (Bilqis in turn searching for her husband and attempting to give her brother a proper burial).

This brings me back to the question, "What are the conditions in which a woman could be perceived as combatant, survivor, and full citizen?" Here, the work of feminist sociologist Patricia Hill Collins on Black sexual politics is pertinent. Speaking to the historic oppression of Black people from slavery to the present, Collins posits that in feminist literature and film, sexuality represents a central site of the oppression of women, with rape as its dominant narrative trope (Collins 2004); and in antiracist discourses, where sexuality is still central, the lynching of Black people has embodied the trope. The visual spectacle of lynching to maintain control over the Black population had a public dimension, whereas the rape of Black women remained a private suffering. For Black men, who are already rendered helpless by the prospect of lynching, their inability to protect Black women from rape is further emasculating to their diminished sense of self. Rather than conceptualizing lynching and rape as either race- or gender-specific mechanisms of social control, Collins approaches institutionalized rape and lynching as different expressions of the same social control: that which oppresses and dehumanizes Black people.

In a similar vein, the dominant Muktijuddho narrative was conceptualized through gendered tropes of the heroic male freedom fighter (Muktijoddha) and the victimized woman (Birangona), where the public sacrifice of the former has been valorized and the private suffering of the latter has been covered and co-opted to fit various political objectives. Here, I do want to acknowledge Mookherjee's (2015) important work arguing that the rape of women has not been erased or silenced so much as censored and instrumentally utilized in human rights, state, and cultural memorialization purposes. Clearly, relegating feminine suffering to shame and secrecy has not given voice to the multifaceted struggles of women during war, let alone ongoing postwar struggles in rehabilitation and reintegration. Even when *Guerilla* defies the dominant narrative by focusing on a female combatant, the character cannot remain in the independent nation as a hero or a citizen. For that to occur, Collins's gender ideology would have to be integrated into the film so that the violence against *Mukhtijoddhas*—both men and women— was articulated as different expressions of social control and systematic repression of the Bengali populace. Here, too, failure to protect women (and nation) is a sign of failure to enact hegemonic masculinity, which was denied to Bengali men as racialized inferiors. Pakistani generals in the film comment on the smaller size and darker skin of Bengali freedom fighters and refer to them as "pygmy Muktijoddhas." Rethinking dominant conceptualizations of wartime gender roles—women's as sacrificial, men's as heroic—to see both as sites of social and political repression would open up ways to rethink the Muktijuddho gender ideology, which renders women's struggle insufficiently admissible and visible.

Further, borrowing from transnational feminist insights, I draw on the work of sociologist Jyoti Puri (2016), who offers the methodology of the juxtaposition of dissimilar contexts to illuminate how power works. By juxtaposing anti-Black and anti-Bengali racism/oppression, we can see how one context helps illuminate the other. Puri has illustrated that, unlike a simple comparison, juxtaposition can also serve as an epistemological device. She suggests that it "does not rest on establishing a common yardstick between the two cases. It also does not necessitate papering over differences in order to establish comparability of cases. Instead, juxtaposition entails exploring how each case is supplemented by being placed in thoughtful relation to the other" (4). Puri contrasts police targeting of *Hijra*[10] communities in India to anti-Black police responses in the United States: "Juxtaposition offers the possibility of thinking across these two distinct moments [in this case, Black and Bengali Muslim] and two dissimilar settings [in this case, trajectories] to deepen understandings of how institutional racism [institutional oppression] continues to imperil and devalue the lives of some while being rationalized as necessary" (6). This methodological tool helps in understanding the workings of power in dissimilar contexts while putting the oppression of racialized or variously Othered populations in a transnational frame.

The work of feminist philosopher Erinn Cunniff Gilson (2016) is useful in tracing the theoretical interventions around gender, vulnerability, and agency in *Guerilla*. Gilson takes up the complicated positioning of vulnerability in sexual violence discourse to demonstrate how it is associated both with femininity and with weakness and dependency. As a feminized concept, its association with femininity is made more problematic by assigning it inferior status. Bilqis's death by suicide has meaning only in terms of the dominant script of Muktijuddho gender ideology, where women represent vulnerability. Bilqis exercises limited agency, but it comes at the cost of her own life. Interestingly, while the on-screen debauchery of the Pakistani general Shamshad is in full view, the simultaneous assault on Shiraj, a Muktijoddha whom Bilqis claims as her younger brother to try to hide his Hindu identity, happens off-screen. Here, the vulnerability of both Bilqis and Shiraj is feminized as a gendered and racialized Other to the hegemonic Pakistani Muslim male military figure: Bilqis because she is a woman, and Shiraj because the soldiers strip his clothing to discover he is uncircumcised and thus presumed Hindu. Bilqis hears his tortured screams as she fends off her assailant. If vulnerability, as Murphy (2011) argues, is tantamount to violability, Bilqis is vulnerable by nature and must take responsibility for protecting herself—and her agency in *Guerilla* comes from taking this responsibility and choosing self-annihilation over rape. A woman who has been violated cannot be a martyr or celebrated as a Muktijoddha, nor can the violation of a male Muktijoddha be publicly depicted. Shiraj's violation is legible through diegetic sounds of his anguished screams. Such roles as the woman martyr or the violated male Muktijoddha are beyond conceptualization in the national imagination. As Gilson notes,

> Inferior strength and sexualization comprise the specificity of feminine vulnerability and constitute it as a dualist, reductively negative form of vulnerability: one is vulnerable because one's body is the kind of object on which others, active male subjects, seek to act and because one cannot prevent them from doing so. Given hegemonic perceptions of gender and sexuality, to be a woman is to inhabit the kind of body that is perceived as inciting lust and thus as inviting sexual attention, whether desired or not. Conceived in this reductive way, women's vulnerability is not just susceptibility to any kind of harm but rather is thought of in terms of a particularly sexual vulnerability. (2016, 75–76)

Due to the physical presumption of vulnerability, "woman" in the context of violent conflict is read as "victim," so it becomes difficult to reimagine how gender can interact with war in a more nuanced and multifaceted way. While *Guerilla* stretches the boundaries of woman as victim, the heroine's bravery and glory is ultimately tied to her decision to kill herself rather than be raped. Bilqis opens herself up to violence and violation simply by being female bodied; her vulnerability is embedded within her physicality and thus impossible to shed.

Gilson reminds us: "The conventional concept of victimization comprises a set of norms that operate as criteria delimiting who will be socially recognized as a victim and who will not be. These norms require victims to fit a particular profile to count, that is, to be convincing . ˙. [to be] a 'true' victim . . . one must be vulnerable in culturally appropriate ways" (2016, 80). Recall that *Meherjaan*, from Chapter 1, offers an example of a victim who did not "behave" as a victim in the socially accepted way. The Birangona Neela demonstrates female sexual expressivity, for which she is decried widely as wanton, sexualized, and unworthy of sympathy. Whereas other Birangona are valorized for their sacrifice—at least in theory, as signified by their title—Neela is not recognizable as a victim. Director Hossain has described her film as a "women's 'feminine' re-visiting of the Bangladesh national liberation" (*Meherjaan* Press Kit 2011). The furor over Neela's depiction centered around criticism that it buries the trauma of the war and makes light of women's suffering, despite the director's insistence that the film is both feminist and nationalist. Released only a few months prior to *Guerilla*, the film was pulled from theaters because of massive protests, including threats to its director and crew.

In *The Spectral Wound: Sexual Violence, Public Memories, and the Bangladesh War of 1971*, Mookherjee (2015) shows how the Birangona's narrative buries the complexities of her life story even while allowing her trauma of rape to be told, not forgotten or silenced. It is not the knowledge of rape that brings social sanction but the speaking of it in public. The critical question is how to reconcile the private suffering of women with the public national suffering and women's embodiment of it. An ethical recognition of gendered vulnerability in the Muktijuddho narratives entails, as Gilson suggests, recognizing the in-betweenness and intertwined spaces of what appears to be diametrically opposed ways of being: terms such as *strength* and *weakness, activity* and *passivity, agency* and *the absence of capacity to act*. Drawing on the work of Brene Brown (2012), Gilson contends that "vulnerability itself is the condition that enables one to deal with and heal from exploitation. It is therapeutically necessary insofar as to heal is not to secure oneself so as to be invulnerable and inviolable but rather to come to be able to experience one's vulnerability with some semblance of safety" (2016, 92). The question is, Can Muktijuddho films accommodate such in-betweenness and complexities of women's experiences and struggles?

Woman in/and the Nation: Looking Ahead

Mookherjee argues that, in Bangladesh, the issue of wartime rape is neither invisible nor a secret. When Sheikh Mujib used the term "Birangona," he created space for women survivors to be publicly viewed as citizens who had been wronged and to whom the nation owed an ethical debt. Nevertheless, their postwar lives exemplify the fact that they continue to be a "spectral wound" on the nation's body. As Mookherjee argues, even those who reconciled with their families must live with *khota* (scorn) as part of their mode of being (Mookherjee 2015). Saikia (2011) offers insight into the violence that Bengali and Bihari women experienced during the war. Her research, which took her to both Bangladesh and Pakistan, juxtaposes memories of both victim and perpetrator. She states:

> What is of real concern to women is to consider and question how their lack of recognition as human is made possible. The power of nation and masculinity in 1971 became impervious to the responsibility of protecting, but became the force of terror. There is thus a profound connection between the person acting or being acted upon, and the realm of structures created by human power and need, which turns against humanity time and again. Women's testimonies question how power endowed to institutions triumphed over human beings who created it. (Saikia 2011, 112)

Both Mookherjee and Saikia refer to the complex processes that actively (in)visibilize Birangona women from and in nationalist memorializations of history and war: They appear—but predominantly as a spectral wound or testimony to the trope of plunder. As an appendage to the project of nation building, national cinema, too, has deployed similar gendered tropes. However, films such as *Guerilla* and other relatively new productions I have undertaken in this book attempt to probe these difficult questions and problematic representations; they explore the possibility of healing and reconciliation within the realm of intimate and interpersonal relations. Taken together, they urge a reconceptualization of how women are depicted in wartime cinema: in *Meherjaan*, a vision of healing and reconciliation is firmly woman centered; in *Guerilla*, Muktijuddho cinema narrates its first story of a woman combatant, albeit one who is only redeemed through self-annihilation; in *Shongram 71*, a Hindu Birangona with a child of war presents hope for the future—when Karim, a devastated Muktijoddha, adopts the child—yet remains an impediment to reintegration/reconciliation into society, as the Birangona herself cannot return to the new nation of Bangladesh. *Shongram 71*, in particular, complicates the representation of the Birangona by making her responsible for a double rejection, first by refusing Karim's invitation to return to their native village and then by leaving her Juddhoshishu at an orphanage. Such a heteropatriarchal family unit—a Hindu Birangona, her Juddhoshishu, and a Muktijoddha (Karim)—defies conceptualization, both in the newly independent Bangladesh and in the films that would later depict it. While *Shongram 71* and *Guerilla* have had limited success in envisioning a disruption to the Muktijuddho ideology, *Meherjaan* has faced such vehement criticism and protest that it cannot be screened in public theaters in Bangladesh. It is clear that the depiction of anything other than normative gender ideology in national cinema about the Muktijuddho is a deep cultural taboo. One can surmise that gender ideology is most sacred in sites relating to the Muktijuddho—the defining event for national identity—and as such, national cinema as its cultural analogue is bound by its normative memorialization.

In their influential work, Black feminist scholars Treva Lindsey (2013) and Jennifer Nash (2008) have engaged with the sexual subjugation of Black women during slavery in the United States and its powerful legacies. Lindsey argues that a "politics of respectability" (57) influences how African American women and communities delineate what constitutes objectification and hypersexuality and that contemporary films in the United States provide unique sites to dissect such renderings of women's subjugation and sexuality. Nash asks whether the legacy of silencing or "sexual conservatism" (52) foreclose transgressive possibilities of reclaiming a more nuanced female sexual expressivity. She reminds us that Black feminism has functioned as a "critical social theory" in its engagement with visual culture. She defines what Patricia Hill Collins terms "controlling images" as "dominant representations that produce and entrench racial-sexual mythologies" (57). The social purpose for controlling images is "to provide a justification for the state's continued disciplining of the black female body" (57). "Controlling images" is a useful term to describe how images of the Birangonas convey ideological power and secure conceptions of their sexual subjugation. Like the state's regulation of the Black female body, the regulation of the Birangonas has also rendered their bodies a public site, "a space onto which social debates and collective anxieties about morality, religion, policy and the state are inscribed" (97). This representation becomes normative rather than analytical and at the expense of women's sexual heterogeneity, multiplicity, and diversity. Against such normative production, Nash urges feminist scholars to ask how objectification is mobilized in specific historical contexts and what could be alternative readings—a representational space for women to view themselves and each other as sexual subjects.

Like Nash and Lindsey, I would argue that filmic representations of women's sexual subjugation in 1971 have been normatively depicted in commercial cinema highlighting their victimization, erasure by death or suicide, shame, or mental instability. In contrast, films such as *Meherjaan* and *Itihaash Konna* prioritize women's narratives as the primary vehicle for reconstructing this normalized circulation of history. Feminist scholar Kavita Daiya (2008) has illustrated how within partition narratives the female body comes to symbolize the project of nationalism to the extent that it serves as a metaphor for women's perceived otherness. In Bangladeshi films, the methodical reproduction of the "authentic Birangona" reifies the otherness through similar iconic imagery (Mookherjee 2015).

Finally, I return to my own question: What are the terms through which subjects can become visible as victims/survivors of violence and agents of nation? At the very least, the films under discussion in this chapter attempt in small ways to redirect our conversation from paternalist nationalism to a fragmented but layered understanding of, and aspirations toward, healing and the intricate and intimate relations within nations, communities, and individuals in the subcontinent torn asunder by colonial violence. These and the films taken up in subsequent chapters are attempts at "feminine re-visioning," to borrow a term from Rubaiyat Hossain, of, or an ethical reckoning with, masculinist narrations of war, nationalism, and agency.

3

Ethical Encounters

Friendship and Healing in Shameem Akhtar's
Itihaash Konna

This chapter explores the idea of friendship—that is, a deep knowledge of another—between women and across nations as a basis for social and political transformation. Over centuries, philosophers have built a large body of literature about various aspects of friendship. Philosopher David Annis emphasizes that there is an "epistemic aspect" to friendship, a "sharing of information about one's experiences, beliefs, values, and so on; friendship requires getting to know the person" (1987, 349). Friendship, then, is a relationship that aspires to be intimate, personal, caring, and empathetic; it is a practice of self-disclosure and vulnerability that aspires to attachment and connection. While friendships can be underpinned by different pulls— convenience, shared location, mutual interest—philosophers have, for generations, celebrated friendships based on shared ethical orientations. In *Nicomachean Ethics*, for example, Aristotle (384–322 B.C.E.) praised friendships based on shared virtue. In these relationships, friends are drawn to each other precisely because they share each other's ethical orientation, and, as Dean Cocking and Jeanette Kennett note, in choosing a friend who shares our "virtues," "friendship is based on self-love . . . [because] our choice of the friend is based on an appreciation of the similarity of the other to oneself" (1998, 506). For Aristotle, these friendships are noble, valuable, and worthy of time and care.

Other philosophers suggest that friendship is a particular ethical relationship because of its mutuality. Eric Hoffman, for example, notes that "friends . . . have thrown their fortunes together to some extent, and within

Figure 3.1 Sara Zaker
as Lalarukh in *Itihaash
Konna* (dir. Shameem
Akhtar, 2000).

the sphere of mutuality they have established might discharge their debt by
the simple recognition that the other friend would do the same if the situation were reversed" (1997, 111). Friendship, then, binds us to another and
makes us responsible to each other ethically. Another perspective is that this
makes friendship a unique relationship of vulnerability. As philosopher
Sandra Lynch writes, "We are vulnerable to pain and disappointment in
friendship, since friends have in common with enemies the capacity to hurt
us" (2005, x). It is the capacity of friends to hurt each other, the "vulnerability and fragility" of the relationship, that makes friendship both potentially
transformative and potentially risky (5).

This chapter builds on the philosophical literature concerning friendship's challenges and pleasures to theorize and celebrate a different kind of
friendship: that which requires us to unravel our assumptions and biases and
to clear the colonial, sexist, ableist, and racial debris from our perceptual apparatus to truly see one another. Friendship, here, is imagined as a relationship that allows for the possibility of intimacy and affiliation across borders
and boundaries, including gender, race, class, ethnicity, and nation. In this
chapter, I consider and examine a dissident female friendship: one portrayed in the Bangladeshi film *Itihaash Konna* (*Daughters of History*, 2000).

"Dissident friendship" is a term coined by postcolonial theorist Leela
Gandhi in her book *Affective Communities*. It describes friendships that cross
boundaries and reveal that power does not monopolize our intimate lives
(2006, 10). Gandhi's concept of dissident friendship builds on Aristotle's
well-known insistence on philia (friendship) as a model for a political citizenship based on similarity and familial relations in the household. Gandhi
also invokes the work of Jacques Derrida (1930–2004) on friendship and reads
the Aristotelian philia as a basis for modernity's "logic of political simili-
tude" that excludes "the Other" (1994, 28–29). The alternative she embraces

derives from her reading of Epicurean *philoxenia*, or "guest friendship," which explicitly welcomes the stranger and is thus open to "the Other" (29).

While this chapter focuses on friendships between women, it is important to note that some scholars have seen male-male friendships as particularly dissident. French philosopher and social theorist Michel Foucault (1926–1984), for instance, argues that where women have long had access to each other's bodies, "man's body has been forbidden to other men in a much more drastic way. . . . It's only in certain periods and since the nineteenth century that life between men not only was tolerated but rigorously necessary: very simply, during war" (Richlin 1997, 139). Foucault then celebrates the affective bonds and deep friendships that can emerge through male-male intimacy and suggests that these bonds can help forge new forms of political life. He thus advocates what he terms "friendship as a way of life" and celebrates the creative kinds of coalitions and affiliations that can emerge through the intimacy of friendship.

Classical thought has characterized friendship as ethical, public, and— importantly—exclusively masculine; this has been the starting point in Europe and North America for philosophical discourses about friendship. Given this categorical exclusion, are all women's friendships by definition "dissident"? Scholars such as Sushmita Chatterjee (2016) have also drawn attention to "guest friendship"—friendship with "the Other"—raising important questions about the nature of affiliation: Can cross-cultural friendships sidestep or even undo the effects of patriarchy and imperialism, or do they reinscribe them? Does friendship's basis in affect offer a challenge to liberal individualism and neoliberal notions and practices of power?

Friendship, as defined by feminist scholars Richa Nagar and Sangtin Writers (2006), is a collective journey among women across differences involving personal transformation and political struggle and striving toward solidarity, reciprocity, and accountability. Women of color and transnational feminists have focused on differences between, among, and within women, including cross-cultural differences. Feminist theorist Maria Lugones (1995) has described such friendships as "bonding among women across differences" (141). For Lugones, such friendships are particularly powerful because they allow "the radical theoretical and practical reconstruction of the relations among women" (141). Understood as such, dissident friendship recognizes the logic of plural realities and remains open to the possibility of self-reflexivity and transformation in perception. That is, instead of the impulse to make the Other into an image of one's own, in friendship "one comes to see oneself as constructed in . . . [the Other's] reality in ways different from the ways one is constructed in the reality one started from. Thus, pluralist friendship enhances self knowledge" (143). This "enhancement" involves a mutually meaningful and empathetic relationship with the Other. It is a demanding position because one dislodges one's own centrality and strives to work across inequalities rather than simply acknowledging them; but it is a rewarding, transformative, and politically revolutionary position. In dissident friendship, then, lies the possibility of our resistance to the divisive and fragmenting lies of structural power; the potential for global compassion, generosity, empathy, and love; and the foundation of a world that works on behalf of life. While alliance, community, and solidarity are amply discussed in literature dealing with social change, friendship is often believed to be outside the realm of social and political transformation. I consider instead the possibility that friendship—especially dissident friendship—allows for the expression of crucially important emotions, such as love and vulnerability, which more formal political alliances often dismiss.

To further a discussion on solidarity among women, I consider the film *Itihaash Konna* within a context of women-of-color theories of friendship politics and transnational film feminism. To do this, I deploy a transnational feminist analysis (Stone-Mediatore 2003)—that is, paying attention to the ways in which far-reaching relations of domination shape and influence the lived realities of communities and individuals across borders. *Itihaash Konna*, I argue, is an important film that helps illuminate the complicated histories and politics of nation-states, war, and gender as they impinge on interpersonal relationships across time and space. Gandhi (2006) takes up the politics of marginal friendship, drawing attention to hitherto ignored individuals and groups who renounced the privileges of imperialism and allied with victims of their own expansionist cultures. Devoting attention to these presumed "nonplayers," Gandhi's work seeks to illuminate some "minor" forms of anti-imperialism that emerged in Europe, specifically in Britain at the end of the nineteenth century; these are the friendships that she termed "dissident." Akhtar's film, I argue, helps us draw attention to similarly presumed-minor relationships between women that defy the logic of colonial and nationalist hierarchies. Relationships between women can be seen in a context that is much more complex than a mere separation of the colonized and the colonizer, particularly for women who are part of either side of nationalist projects.

While Gandhi's purpose is, in part, historical redress, I am inspired by her impulse to unpack the politics of dissident friendship to think through relationships between women across differences, or more specifically between a lesser colonizer and the colonized. By "lesser colonizer," I mean those who were in some ways on the fringes of imperial society—women, LGBTQs, and people of color. For example, Jan Jindy Pettman (2006) elucidates the intersection of privilege and oppression of white European women in settler-colonial societies. They were at once marginalized because of their gender yet privileged by their racial identity. Even in colonial societies, hierarchical class structures put certain native groups closer to centers of power. Uma Narayan (1995) has demonstrated the similarities between the ideology of sexism and colonial racism, where physical and moral attributes were used to define women of the colonizer society and the colonized (men and women) as the weaker sex/race. Yet, despite being of the "weaker sex," colonizer women played vital roles in maintaining the colonial project and taking on the "white man's burden" that put them in paternalist positions in relation to the colonized. Like their male counterparts, they replicated the colonial structure of at once oppressing the natives while at the same time couching that subjugation in the ethic of care. This system, which robbed the colonized of full humanity and rights, was justified by an ethic of responsibility and obligation of the oppressor to provide moral and cultural guidance to the "less enlightened." Even within these hierarchical conditions, relationships emerged to varying degrees that hinted at affinity and friendship. Whether forged accidentally or purposefully, friendship is a vehicle for furthering political and social goals within intimate spaces.

In another essay, Narayan takes up the idea of dialogue between members of heterogeneous groups in encounters that can take the form of friendship or politics. She states:

> Working across differences is a morally and politically important enterprise in either context. Both in political contexts and in the context of friendship, such differences in elements of background and identity can be enriching resources, epistemologically, politically and personally. Learning to understand and respect these differences can make more complex our understanding of ourselves and our societies, can broaden the range of our politics and enrich the variety of connections we have as persons. (1988, 32)

I join Gandhi's insistence of paying attention to dissident friendships with Narayan's urging that relationships between individuals of heterogeneous backgrounds with discrepant power positions in society can elicit a deeper understanding of human connection.

Dissident Friendships across Borders and Power Structures

I find Shameem Akhtar's *Itihaash Konna* to be a significant contemporary text to engage the ideal of lasting social and political change through the practice of female friendship between women of differential gender positionality, however fleeting and difficult that may be. The film is set amid the ruins of the devastating Liberation War that established Bangladesh as a nation independent from its "colonial occupier," West Pakistan. I argue that the film offers an example of a dissident friendship between Lalarukh (played by Sara Zaker), a Pakistani researcher working on documenting war crimes that the Pakistani military committed on Bengalis in 1971, and Monika (played by Rahnuma Ahmed), her Bengali activist friend whose family survived the violence. Through the course of the film, both women experience transformations of consciousness through their intertwined struggles. As a Pakistani, Lalarukh bears the burden of the genocide that her own government and military forces unleashed on the Bengali population. Yet, she finds herself conflicted: On the one hand, she was born in East Pakistan and is empathetic toward the Bengalis affected by the war, particularly her childhood friend Monika; yet, on the other, she must make sense of the silence and sanctioned ignorance of her own family, including her Bengali mother, during the war. Monika's and Lalarukh's contrapuntal trajectories of the war and its consequences—as part of the oppressor and the oppressed nations—form the premise of a dissident alliance.

The dynamic between West and East Pakistan following the partition of the Indian subcontinent summarily inherited the legacy of British colonial rule in the region. Akhtar's film engages this legacy and offers an opportunity to probe the violent inheritance, especially because the relationship between the two women is indelibly framed as a colonial one. Even though Lalarukh had family ties to East Pakistan and Monika had ties to West, the war severed those ties. That left Lalarukh squarely as an agent of the oppressor nation and Monika as an activist seeking to document and mobilize a response to the 1971 genocide, mass sexual violence, and forced pregnancies. The dynamic between the women allows readers to consider the underside of liberation—the incomplete independence of a postcolonial nation and the kinds of social alliances possible within it, which are nevertheless deeply imbricated in older colonial histories. The power of an idealized nationalism that is elusive in providing freedom and security to and security to women, that fails to foster trust between women, inherently tests women's intimate bonding. Further, national independence did not necessarily liberate Bengali women from patriarchal oppression in either wartime or peace.

While these alliances may be minor narratives, I believe they are significant for three reasons: First, they offer another instance of understanding the colonial encounter beyond its categorical West/non-West binary; second, they illuminate ways in which the colonial power structure replicates itself even in marginal sites and relationships and allows us to think of friendship—at times clandestine, conflictual, even unacknowledged—as a mode for social and potentially political transformation for diffuse groups and individuals; and third, it takes as the premise of such transformation the desire to recognize a mutual humanity based on compassion and empathy. I use terms such as "humanity," "compassion," and "empathy" with some caution here and do not mean to evoke romanticized or cultural relativist notions of unity within diversity. Again, I refer to Narayan, who unequivocally states that empathic sensitivity in unions across differences does not simply hinge on "good will" (1988). Similarly, feminist theorist Jane Mansbridge (1995) defines empathy as a gesture toward human connection, as opposed to emotions such as pity, condescension, or self-righteousness. It is what Adrienne Rich calls furthering "the conscious work of turning Otherness into a keen lens of empathy, that we can bring into being a politics based on concrete heartfelt understanding of what it means to be Other" (1995, 400). Alliance across differences for the purpose of this project, then, is a connection that (1) exists across differences, (2) has to be strived for, and (3) is based on shared humanity. I explore whether such alliances are inevitably crushed within dominant patriarchal colonial relations or whether they can cause a change in self-and-Other perception and potentially contribute to social and political transformation and, in the process, become transgressive.

In this chapter, I have largely used the terms "alliance," "community," "solidarity," and "friendship" interchangeably. While alliance, community, and solidarity are generously discussed in literature dealing with social change, friendship is often believed to be outside the realm of social and political transformation. I intend to trouble that assumption to convince readers that friendship reenvisioned can be the basis of (potentially transformative) solidarity precisely because it is premised on a kind of human connection that may be lacking in other types of unions. What makes friendship an interesting medium to discuss is that it allows for the expression of emotion, which in more formal political unions is more often than not dismissed. Instead of rejecting emotions, Narayan (1988) proposes that emotions can infuse our experiences and knowledge of reality in a way that exposes the subtle workings of power more insightfully and intensely; hence, we should not presume their role in explaining human connection to be outside of politics. An exploration of friendship allows us to understand power and oppression that are more immediate, complex, and subtle. In addition, following Gandhi's cue, friendship in this project refers to a collaboration between the "most unlikely of associates" (2006, 10). It may take the form of minor or seemingly insignificant gestures of affinity to the Other at the risk of endangering the self's security in her own community. I am particularly interested in exploring when and whether "dissident crosscultural friendship"—sometimes between these unlikely associates of oppressor and oppressed communities—trumps, or is trumped by, other kinds of loyalties women might have to family, community, or nation in the pursuit of social justice (Elora Chowdhury 2016).

Feminist theorist Maria Lugones has also talked about friendship as "bonding among women across differences." Such bonding does not presuppose unconditionality but does recognize the situationality of each person while being cognizant of their plural realities. According to Lugones, friendship can be based on "practical love" and knowledge of and commitment to the other person. She says:

> Because I think a commitment to perceptual changes is central to the possibility of bonding across differences and the commitment is part of friendship, I think that friendship is a good concept to start the radical theoretical and practical reconstruction of the relations among women. (Lugones 1995, 141)

Understood as such, friendship recognizes the logic of plural realities and remains open to the possibility of self-reflexivity and transformation in perception. That is, instead of the impulse to make the Other into an image of one's own, in friendship one sees one's own image as closer to that of the Other. This enhancement is not merely a co-optation of the Other in the service of self-actualization but involves a mutually meaningful and empathetic relationship with the Other. It is an epistemically demanding position because one dislodges one's own centrality and strives to work across inequalities rather than simply acknowledging that they exist.

I approach this analysis of *Itihaash Konna* through a combination of filmic and transnational feminist analyses. I share Shari Stone-Mediatore's definition of transnational feminism, which is an analytical and political project that goes beyond unpacking gender ideologies to confronting far-reaching relations of domination spanning, but that which is not limited to political, economic, and cultural spheres. These relations of domination "cross over national boundaries and produce historically specific cooperative as well as hierarchical relations among women of different nations, races and classes" (Stone-Mediatore 2003, 129). This mode of analysis is also exemplified in Ella Shohat's (2003) work, discussed in further detail below, where she points out the multiple oppressive structures of colonialism and nationalism, spanning across geographic borders of the nation and shaping women's experiences. A transnational feminist approach elucidates that women are part of various groups across communities and nations and thereby part of different, yet sometimes converging, struggles. Additionally, this approach suggests that women's myriad struggles—such as colonization, patriarchy, and poverty—whether individual or collective, are often inseparable from structural oppressions shaping their lives and their communities. A transnational feminist lens provides a way to understand the paradoxical dynamic of conflict and cooperation that shape women's relations with one another.

This analysis of *Itihaash Konna* explores the idea of friendship between women across cultures as a mode for enacting social responsibility and care for the Other. Through an investigation of the conflictual yet cooperative alliance between Lalarukh and Monika—women representing either side of a historical conflict—I reflect on the idea of dissident friendship and argue that relationships between individuals of heterogeneous backgrounds with discrepant power positions can elicit a deeper understanding of human connection. I discuss how, despite being on oppositional sides of the Bengali nationalist struggle and having suffered tremendous violence and losses that render their friendship vulnerable to betrayal, both women have singular goals of establishing the existence of war crimes by documenting victims' experiences and mobilizing awareness and support to elicit an apology from the Pakistani state. In the process, however, both must confront their own silences and complicities and engage in critical self-reflection if not transformation.

The landmark feminist collection *This Bridge Called My Back* explores the personal and collective challenges women must face in the process of forging political and social alliances and solidarity. In its foreword, Cherríe Moraga expresses the book's unique intention of creating a space for dialogue among women as opposed to between men and women. She argues that understanding the specific conditions of oppression of women, be it for marginalized communities in the United States or elsewhere, is key to building a more effective "Third World feminism," which she describes as follows:

> In the last three years I have learned that Third World feminism does not provide the kind of easy political framework that women of color are running to in droves. We are not so much a "natural" affinity group, as women who have come together out of political necessity. The idea of Third World feminism has proved to be much easier between the covers of a book than between real live women. There are many issues that divide us; and, recognizing that fact can make that dream at times seem quite remote. (Moraga 1983)

Together with Stone-Mediatore, Moraga's vision is an effective medium to both illuminate and analyze the "internal differences" within groups, even women's groups, which feminist debates have shown are never coherent. When thinking about and organizing around women's oppression, the cooperative yet conflictual lens that transnational feminism provides is a medium that humanizes the suffering of others different from "us" even as it recognizes friendship, community, and solidarity, not as natural alliances but as being sought through active engagement and reflection. Such alliances can take on dissident forms across cultures and are steps to the realization of that remote dream Moraga talks about for feminism—human connection that nourishes self-growth as well as fosters community.

Woman, Nation, Conflict in *Itihaash Konna*

As we have discussed in previous chapters, the tradition of casting stories about the Muktijuddho into conventional norms of representation has lately been disturbed by key texts and films that have given voice to an erasure in Bangladesh around women's varied experiences of the Bangladesh Liberation War. These critical films and works of both fiction and nonfiction have launched a crucial and critical discussion of war, genocide, and gender justice on a transnational scale. Like this greater body of work, Shameem Akhtar's films, and, in particular, *Itihaash Konna* (1999), illuminate for a regional and global audience internal and external tensions surrounding the representation of war, gender, memory, and justice.

I suggest that this new genre attempts to restore an ethical dimension to intimate/interpersonal encounters of healing and to the decolonization of subjectivity and personal identity (Saikia 2011, 9). The films in this genre challenge a number of cherished and inherited "truths" regarding the Liberation War (Elora Chowdhury 2012). They are, to different degrees, groundbreaking; their scope is more global, as they shed light on a conflict in the history of modern South Asia that is, outside of Bangladesh, largely forgotten. Some of these texts are also provocative because, as stated previously, they debunk a number of national myths that have shaped the consciousness of Bangladesh, primarily the triumphant narrative of male valor and female victimization. In contrast, these texts prioritize women's narratives as the primary vehicle for reconstructing this forgotten history.

Unlike the predominant masculinist narratives, the female characters of *Itihaash Konna* are agentic and project what Janell Hobson calls "embodied resistance" (2008, 232) even as none of them represent the "emblematic survivor" (Rothe 2011, 36) of 1971. Emblematic survivors are recognizable in Bangladesh war films as iconic representatives of victimized women—the rape victim, who is disheveled in appearance, is mentally unstable, and exits the narrative by suicide or by death, frequently by suicide. Countering reductive renditions, Akhtar's film urges an ethical memorialization and initiates multiple tellings of 1971. As we have seen in the work of Hossain and Saikia, Akhtar, too, emphasizes an interpersonal "reckoning" with the Other. One of the few films about the Liberation War directed by a woman and foregrounding the standpoint of women, *Itihaash Konna* deals with genocide, rape, and war children through the lens of a moral reckoning ("separation versus liberation" of East Pakistan in 1971) and responsibility on either side.

This reckoning is explored through the challenges to and potentials of dissident friendship: Lalarukh's and Monika's long and beleaguered relationship, which has been severed by the bloody birth of Bangladesh and reflected in the intertwined histories of their two nations. Monika was born in Rawalpindi, West Pakistan, and Lalarukh in Dhaka, East Pakistan. They studied together in Dhaka until Lalarukh's family left for West Pakistan in March 1971, just days prior to Operation Searchlight, the brutal strike by West Pakistan against Bengali civilians. This massive assault was especially felt at Dhaka University, the largest public university in Bangladesh, as it targeted academics and students, particularly from the Hindu minority. The film depicts many scenes where Lalarukh visits various sites on the campus that commemorate the massacre.

Many years after the independence of Bangladesh, the two friends reacquaint as adults and activists in a seminar on genocide in London. Thereafter, Lalarukh comes to Dhaka to conduct research and is hosted by Monika, who is archiving an oral history project about the women survivors of the war. Lalarukh's return to Dhaka, twenty-eight years after her family left at the cusp of the war, is bittersweet. She expresses her noble objective to Monika: "I intend to work for an apology [at the state level]." Monika is skeptical of Lalarukh's intentions to learn about war-affected families in her brief one-week visit. She is also hesitant to rekindle their personal friendship, given Lalarukh's long absence and silence about the war. One scene depicts the two as seated on Monika's bed. Monika looks fatigued, bearing the weight of the war's devastation. Lalarukh probes, "I want to know everything. I have a personal stake in this." The viewer is reminded of an earlier scene when Lalarukh insists that she has a right to return to this land, as her mother was Bengali. A stubborn Monika responds, "Two people can have totally different experiences of a war. These distinct experiences can change a relationship forever." Monika presses her friend about the Pakistani silence regarding atrocities committed during the war. Lalarukh tries to defend her position by touting the then government propaganda about Bengalis dancing to the tune of India and acting as separatists. Her family was in the dark, says Lalarukh in defense, given the news blackout about what was happening in East Pakistan. Monika reminds her of the international movement on behalf of Bangladesh liberation—the concert in Madison Square Garden and the statements by Tariq Ali, a Pakistani intellectual who criticized the military repression. She admonishes Lalarukh about her silence and complicity.

Lalarukh is further confounded by the unspeakable coldness from her friend's family members. The once-lively house she visited in her childhood seems to be shrouded in misery and gloom. Monika's father, Nanu (an affectionate term for maternal grandfather, played by Abul Khair), refuses to meet Lalarukh face-to-face, even though he ensures proper hospitality for the guest. The silence is finally broken as the family sits down together for a feast on the day of Lalarukh's departure for Pakistan. Once again, Monika and Lalarukh, seated across from each other at the table, debate the merits of an acknowledgment of war crimes and an apology from Pakistan. Nanu, seated at the head of the table, directly confronts Lalarukh, asking whether she would forgive the rape of her own sixteen-year-old daughter. "If she is raped, would you be able to forgive [the rapist]?" Lalarukh lowers her glance and admits, "No." She adds, "But, I would want a trial and punishment for the perpetrator." Nanu responds, "What about the victim? How would justice be served for them?" The confrontation leads Nanu to reveal that Ananya (Nasrin Siraj), daughter of his younger daughter Konika, is a Juddhoshishu, a child of rape, and that Konika committed suicide months after Ananya's birth. Prior to this scene Ananya has been unaware of her status as a war child—perhaps her family's attempt to protect her from the pain and trauma of that identity. It is at this encounter that the character Konok Khala (Bonna Lohani), who raised Ananya, quietly exits the frame—a departure that might be read as a kind of "exit narrative." A member of the Hindu community, Konok's entire family was massacred in 1971, and she was held captive in the same rape camp as Konika. Her exit from the gathering and the frame of the Birangona at this critical scene has been critiqued by feminist scholars in regard to the disappearances of Birangonas. Without doubt, it reemphasizes the question of acceptance and justice for the victims of sexual violence, a question that remains largely unattended and unresolved in the postwar social and political discourses.

Itihaash Konna attempts to reckon with the Other by suturing torn interpersonal relationships: namely, an irreconcilable conflict was institutionalized at the moment of original trauma, when war babies were declared tainted and ejected from the nation (the womb) by state-sponsored postwar policies of abortion or foreign adoption. It is Lalarukh's arrival that opens up the conversation about Ananya, the Juddhoshishu, and Konika, her mother who committed suicide following her birth. Unlike the state, however, the family unquestioningly accepts Ananya as their own. Lalarukh's mission is to write about the genocide and mobilize a movement for a national apology. Monika finds common ground in that objective, as it would imply recognition of war crimes—even though her father, the elder survivor of war, is not sure that this would be meaningful for victims. This scene and encounter are critical conjunctures where past, present, and future questions around healing and reconciliation are set in motion. It can be read as an "ethical reckoning," where the war child (Ananya) takes center stage alongside feminist activists (Monika and Lalarukh). When the now-adult Ananya (whose name means "exceptional" in Bengali) first meets Lalarukh, Lalarukh introduces herself as a *bideshi* (foreigner), to which Ananya replies, "Not a foreigner, a Pakistani"—hinting at the intimacy of her identity that is like no other. Ananya becomes Lalarukh's guide and research assistant during her stay, taking her on a tour of the various war memorials and museums in the city. Lalarukh is left overwhelmed by the intensity and enormity of the atrocities and consequent losses. Ananya comforts her, and, in turn, Lalarukh urges Ananya to address her as *tumi*—the less formal version of the pronoun "you," which is reserved for friends. Ananya ponders over the request and says, "It will take time."

Ananya's brief association with Lalarukh leads to a different kind of reckoning between the younger woman and her older aunt, Monika. It is as though the latter comes to see the former in a new light, transformed into her own person. This transformation is apparent in a conversation between aunt and niece: "You've grown up; I've never heard you speak like this," says Monika when Ananya raises the question of the somber household and lack of festivities there. Ananya says, not without a hint of reproach, "You did not want to realize it." She asks her aunt about her childhood friendship with Lalarukh, when everything was different and more exuberant—the house, Nanu, Monika. The film raises the question of a possible (or impossible) union between Monika and Ananya and between Ananya and Lalarukh. These (im)possible unions break down the seemingly irreconcilable conflict that was institutionalized at the moment Juddhoshishus were deemed disposable. It is noteworthy that, similar to Sarah's arrival in *Meherjaan*, Lalarukh's arrival here leads to the opening of the Pandora's box of memories, breaking the silence in the house, and taking steps toward healing. Ananya's full story can only make sense if coevally developed with Lalarukh's and Monika's (im)possible union. Rather than assigning Ananya to the periphery, the film simultaneously develops the conflicted relationships between the three women as representative of the historical conflict(s) between woman and nation. The rejection—even hatred—of the Juddhoshishu hinges on the original trauma of the rape of Bengali women and forced impregnation as a war strategy. The desire to "flush out" the enemy through state-led policies of abortion and foreign adoption institutionalized the hatred of the Other. In that sense, Ananya's union with Lalarukh (and Monika) is a feminine reenvisioning of history that includes the acceptance of the war child and a rejection of masculinist war narratives. Again, I refer to feminist scholar Kavita Daiya (2008), who has shown how the project of nationalism in partition narratives has been thrust on the female body to the extent that it serves as a metaphor for women's perceived otherness. In Bangladeshi films, the methodical reproduction of the "authentic Birangona" reifies the otherness through similar iconic imagery (Mookherjee 2015). The state-imposed regulation of Birangonas rendered women's bodies as a public site onto which "social debates and collective anxieties about morality, religion, policy and the state are inscribed" (Nash 2008, 57).

Lalarukh's return to Bangladesh stirs up repressed emotions, opens old wounds, and instigates an intimate as well as political reckoning across time, space, and history. Ananya comes to know the truth about her birth and the identity of Konok Khala, her surrogate mother. Nanu confronts Lalarukh about her quest for "justice" and asks whether the victims of 1971 will be appeased by it. Following this encounter, he takes out a dusty old picture of his dead daughter, Konika, and puts it on the bureau. He is finally able to place her in the open and face that painful history. Ananya comes to terms with the story of her birth and the realization that it is inextricably interwoven with the individual and collective journeys of Monika and Lalarukh. Lalarukh leaves with a heavy heart, asking Monika and her family to "take care of Ananya." Following her departure, Lalarukh writes a letter to Monika from Pakistan admitting her and her family's complicity by not speaking up against the atrocities of 1971. The question of women survivors may remain incomplete, yet the healing begins with them. Ananya continues to work on the oral history project with Lalarukh and Monika, becoming the bridge between the women separated by the burden of historical conflict. Monika begins to look at Ananya in a new light, and both women, aunt and niece, come to realize their shared struggle. The soundtrack by Shimul Yusuf plays, "Tears of yesteryears as life goes on."

Akhtar's film provides an opportunity to read the complex machinations of gender, nation, and patriarchy, particularly as they operate between women of opposing national contexts, while exploring both the limits and the possibilities of solidarity in spite of these forces. More specifically, it enables a discussion of circumstances where women's loyalty to family, nation, and the community's specific structures is disrupted by the possibility of an alliance built on a "common" gender-based oppression. It is an instance to test the ideas of contrapuntal histories of the oppressor-oppressed and the possibilities of cross-cultural dissident friendship within that context.

Transnational Feminism, Film, and Ethical Encounters

Feminist filmmakers and scholars have long noted the anomalous relationship of woman to nation. Scholar Kathleen McHugh (2009, 112) states:

> Notably, women's worldly space was not independent of country, of the national, but based on spatial paradox: they were at once inside, marginal, in the private sphere of the nation-state (within patriar-

chal ideas, institutions, and histories in which women have no place) and, at the same time, not contained by, in excess of that state by reason of these internal and internalized exclusions and difference.

This points to the complex and contradictory space women occupy—both within and outside of nationalist and colonialist struggles—and requires a multilayered perspective to gain a deeper understanding of this space. Part of this perspective entails placing women in cinema "within transnational influences and relationships" to understand those characteristics that define a film as feminist and are particularly critical to feminist filmmaking— among them, "structures of opportunity," ideology, production, reception, and circulation (McHugh 2009, 126). Ella Shohat (2003), too, speaks of "transnational film feminisms" as a decisive political project that critiques both nationalism and colonialism vis-à-vis feminism. The transnational analytic lens and agents—filmmakers and financiers—offer the scope to historicize women's struggles within the broader legacy of colonial process- es and realities of nationalist struggles; they shed light on cross-border con- nections in feminist filmic representations and interpretations. Seen within a transnational framework where women's wartime experiences can be placed within a global movement for justice, Akhtar's sensitive treatment of war's consequences on women is instrumental in mobilizing awareness and action while developing collective critiques and resistance. *Itihaash Konna* can be seen as transformative in launching a dialogue about women's 1971 experiences within and beyond a nationalist and national framework and beyond a narrowly constructed notion of liberation.

The film is also instrumental in opening a conversation about the neces- sity of an ethical reckoning of the 1971 genocide. Such a reckoning stands the chance to recuperate—even if only partially—forgotten histories, par- ticularly for women. It is important to situate *Itihaash Konna* within the new genre of cultural production centered on gendered experiences of the nation and the larger transnational movement of healing and reconciliation, where femininity is the site of caring and nurturing. Instead of retribu- tion—the focus of much political discourse in postindependent Bangla- desh—the film looks at internal tensions, interpersonal healing, and gen- dered justice. This shift hints at an emerging new direction in feminist scholarship about women's experiences of 1971.

I return here to the question of dissident friendship, community, and solidarity between women and explore further the circumstances in which these are or are not trumped by loyalties women have to their families, com- munities, or nations. Of course, the ideas of friendship and community in feminist discourses are contested. In the collection of essays *Feminism and Community* (Weiss and Friedman 1995), the contributors distinguish between "traditional" and feminist communities. They argue that, in traditional settings, significant relationships of female support and acts of resistance can coexist with hierarchical and exploitative ones; in feminist communities, however, internal struggles can inhibit women from achieving the desired political transformation—for both themselves and others. These two settings, then, are neither mutually exclusive nor completely antithetical to one another. Rather, the authors suggest that "both can be the sites of genuine friendship, social support, and collaborative political activism among women" (Weiss and Friedman 1995, xii).

The arenas Akhtar highlights in *Itihaash Konna* are conflictual, reflected by the Bengali nationalist and the naive yet hopeful Pakistani researcher. The dual settings are populated by the two women, both of whom are motivated by political activism and a certain reconciliation. Within these settings also exist collaborative relationships among women who come from opposite ends of the spectrum, forming unexpected alliances. At the same time, it is useful to keep in mind Weiss and Friedman's cautionary note to keep from engaging in uncritical celebration of women's agency and resistance within traditional communities, but instead to listen carefully to women in all contexts to learn the specific insights they have to offer in the larger struggle for social transformation (1995, 162). While Lalarukh and Monika may not have achieved much, in the sense of official or lasting peace between the two nations, through their sometimes dissident, always conflicted alliance, viewers come to learn how the identities—or positionalities—of each are constituted through their specific national and gender locations. These positionalities dictate the limits of their agency and the risks each can take on behalf of women's freedom. In the final reckoning, even Monika admits to the value of Lalarukh's work, which aims to raise awareness in Pakistan and globally so that the state moves toward an acknowledgment of and, ultimately, an apology for war crimes.

Feminist political theorist Iris Marion Young (1995) has argued for a broader understanding of individuality and community that does not pit one in a negative relation against the other. *Itihaash Konna* allows us to expand this debate and to recognize that, when striving for solidarity, women's relationships can be heterogeneous, complex, and conflicting. Solidarity is a demanding ideal, and the attainment of it can be ambiguous and fleeting. These ephemeral moments nevertheless allude to "disruptive possibilities" (Friedman 1995, 200) and can lead to important transformations in female consciousness in the broader and ongoing struggle to create more enabling conditions of mutual care.

4

Muktijuddho Film as Disruptive Archive, Filmmaker as Witness

Yes, I have heard of the term Birangona. But who does it refer to? *Birangona* is someone who has been taken away and berthed with Pakistanis.

ELDERLY MALE COMMUNITY MEMBER

Birangona has to be married to Bir or she herself must be courageous. If she were brave, could she have been raped? She was raped because she was not a *Birangona*.

ROMA CHOUDHURY

If women get raped, it is they who become pregnant. They are living proof [not the men] of the rape; the scar is on their body. Men bear no proof.

ROMA CHOUDHURY

I have put her on a pedestal, haven't I?

HUSBAND OF RONJITA MONDOL

Accounts of the Bangladesh Liberation War of 1971 and its aftermath are shaped by competing investments in memory and political projects of nation building (D'Costa 2010, 54), and we have seen this dynamic play out in the films we have studied thus far. The newer genre of cultural production attempts in various ways to rewrite the model of traditional history that casts the war as a glorious struggle, with male heroes and female victims. This model, as we have seen, features religious, ethnic, geographic, and cultural schisms between what was East and West Pakistan; resulting in a nine-month war that delivered massive losses and violence, the enduring memory of which is constitutive of a national trauma and identity. While women's roles have not been entirely ignored in historiography, they have been typified within an honor-shame-stigma complex and alternatively subjected to "authorial co-options" (Fitzsimons-Quail 2015, 27). Against these reductive narratives, which Van Schendel (2015, 5) calls part of a more nuanced and analytical second-generation historiography, Saikia (2011) examines narratives of women who experienced violence by

Figure 4.1a Film poster for *Rising Silence* (dir. Leesa Gazi, 2019).

জলের শরীরে বেঁধা বিষকাঁটা: বাউরি ইতিহাস, মাতৃভূমি, 'বীরাঙ্গনা'

BishKanta

বিষকাঁটা

The Poison Thorn

Direction & Cinematography by Farzana Boby
Duration 41 min.

Figure 4.1b Film poster for *The Poison Thorn* (dir. Farzana Boby, 2015).

Pakistani, Bengali, Bihari, and Indian men spanning the pro- and antiliberation forces. In so doing, she sheds light on the multiple wars within 1971 and writes diverse women's agential roles during and after the war back into the national history.

While the official Bangladeshi narrative focuses on a singular story of Bengali victimhood and Pakistani oppression, Saikia suggests that the claim to trauma and violence is not an exclusively Bengali experience. She cites as evidence the pogroms perpetrated by Bangladeshis/Bengalis in East Pakistan/Bangladesh against the minority Bihari population—a group of non-Bengali Urdu-speaking migrants from Bihar whose allegiance was to West Pakistan. She reveals how ordinary people committed atrocities to the extent that victims and perpetrators are not clearly distinguishable (2011, 18). In the absence of official documents, scholars have turned to oral histories, film, and literary texts, which in turn also perpetuate a kind of erasure/suppression of women. Saikia establishes connections in this literary genre between the Bengali women, land, and nation, whereby the rape of Bengali women comes to stand for the rape of Bangladesh. The Birangona narratives are manipulated by various actors and shrouded in "shame and fear of the accusation of complicity and collusion." Saikia's research shows that "the lack of a serious demand to probe the circumstances and agents of gender violence has enabled the internalized oppression within Bangladesh to continue, where rumors, gossip, and slander abound" (53). Additionally, Saikia posits, Birangonas, although projected as heroes, are also viewed by some as "being complicit in the crime of her rape" (112). This sort of co-optation and "epistemic silence," she says, is instrumental to the production of official histories in the service of nation building. The Muktijuddho cinema genre, particularly woman-centered films, both reifies and intermittently subverts and alludes to an against-the-grain, alternative reading of Bengali Birangona subjectivity. Subsequently, such filmic narratives gesture toward a (re)imagining of agency, freedom, justice, and feminist knowledge making.

Documenting Trauma

In writing about the narration of crisis in cinema, Hesford and Kozol (2001, 4) ask an important question: Why should such a genre even evoke criticism, lest it run the risk of lessening the horrors that it purports to "accurately and compellingly depict?" They ask, "How, to put it most bluntly, do you critique a documentary about genocide and state-sanctioned rape that appears to offer a true depiction of this horror?" Like Hesford and Kozol, I, too, am invested in the "pedagogical value" of making visible the narrative and filmic construction of memorializing projects to illuminate the "meaning-making gaze of the literary critic, film critic, and other cultural workers" (9). Following Hesford and Kozol's lead, I argue that "cultural representations of the 'real' compete with interests in the interstices of power, authority and resistance" (2). Even justice-driven projects—such as the films I examine below—must be consumed both critically without diminishing their importance and, simultaneously, for their historical value for marginalized groups to resist dominant narratives of their own experiences of victimization. However, as Hesford and Kozol urge, "authenticity cannot secure an absolutely privileged position for either dominance or resistance" (3)—that is, an examination of how cultural forms and material conditions interconnect in producing notions of voice and justice is critical in struggles for legitimacy and recognition.

In this chapter, I explore the ways in which two such nondominant documentaries—Leesa Gazi's *Rising Silence* (2018) and Farzana Boby's *Bish Kanta* (*The Poison Thorn*, 2015)—contribute to, affirm, and disrupt a Muktijuddho gender ideology as well as contest the power in which they are embedded in the process. These films contribute to the growing genre of cultural texts and productions that offer gendered histories and complicate the "glorious war" narrative by focusing primarily on marginalized stories of women to recuperate more nuanced tellings of the birth of a nation. It is noteworthy that the two films vary in length and overall technical quality. *Bish Kanta*, at forty minutes, was filmed with a Handycam Camcorder as part of the filmmaker's own realist pedagogy, while *Rising Silence*, at seventy-five minutes, is HD format, filmed with a small technical crew as part of a London-based theater collective; *Rising Silence* received far greater endorsements, support, and circulation. I engage primarily with *Rising Silence* and secondarily with *Bish Kanta*.

In this analysis, I turn to critical feminist literature on cultural productions that defy a masculinist nationalist reading to recover submerged histories of women—arguably, the goal of both films. Drawing on transnational feminist theorizing around nationalism and war, memorialization projects, and visual culture as a critical mode of human rights knowledge production, I decode an alternative reading of how these two films illuminate submerged histories and contribute to what Viviana MacManus (2020) calls a "disruptive archive" of nationalist history yet still perpetuate a certain ongoing fixing of the honor-shame-stigma complex. I am interested in how nationalist politics and a transnational feminist aesthetic simultaneously underpin the goal of such feminist recovery projects and whom and what they serve in the broader question of gender violence and gender justice. Further, I discuss the filmmakers' assumptions regarding women's experiences and whether these films reinscribe an assigned role for women in nation building or allow a recognition of alternate modalities of being (Weheliye 2014, 15). Some critical questions guide this analysis: To what extent do these films defy and disrupt an extant masculinist statist rhetoric? In what ways do they reify symbolic roles of women within a nationalist struggle, and to what extent are these roles subverted, fleshed out, reimagined? What are the epistemological and political implications of narrating submerged histories of women survivors of sexual violence?

Necropolitics and Gendered Dehumanization

Philosopher and political theorist Achille Mbembé discusses the concepts of biopolitics, which strips the conditions of certain populations to a state of "bare life," and necropolitics, a state where the threat of death becomes the technique of governance (2003, 12). Bare life thus is premised on an overarching threat of death, where power lies in determining who can live in what conditions and who ought to die. This right to determine life-and-death conditions is what Mbembé defines as sovereignty and the politics prevailing in war. Naomi Hossain (2018) explores how in global imperial geopolitical relations the Bay of Bengal historically came to be framed within a bare life discourse, whereby the nation of Bangladesh was written in through cyclone, war, and famine. Geopolitics cast a certain biopower over the Bangladeshi population at the nation's very inception even though Bangladesh has over the decades proven to develop better social and economic protections. Drawing on Georgio Agamben's (2005) idea of "bare life," Hossain asks the question, "What did it mean for a whole country to be designated 'bare life'?" (2018, 3). While to outsiders it may appear that the cyclone of Bhola in 1970 and the famine of 1974 were instances of natural and human devastations, the West Pakistani authorities' failure to prevent or mitigate the destruction for years prior and, of course, outright military aggression in 1971 triggered the tragedy that first catapulted Bangladesh into a global and developmentalist imaginary. This image making, as characterized in a Thames Television film on the Bhola cyclone as well as visuals for musician George Harrison's 1971 single "Bangla Desh," was certainly aided through the decades of economic and political neglect, exclusions from sovereign power, and exploitation rendering the Eastern Wing of Pakistan vulnerable and cast as in need of triage. Indeed, in the 1970s, Bangladesh appeared as a reflection of the bare life categorization, made deficient as it was through biopower and war- and disaster-ridden, exacerbated by its exclusion from global political support.

Dominant feminist theories of nationalism have not adequately accounted for a necropolitical framework; nor has the seminal work of Michel Foucault on biopolitics ensured a gendered interpretation of those power dynamics. Tazreena Sajjad casts a genocidal motivation for sexual violence when speaking about the Bangladesh war conditions. She defines genocidal rape as an assault on the body and on the larger polity in an attempt to control and harm a socioeconomic or biological process (2009, 225). Feminist scholars such as MacManus (2020) and Melissa Wright (2011) further expand on this critical gap with regard to racialized and sexualized biopolitical frames by teasing out the vulnerabilities of a gendered dehumanization process, undergirding the biopolitics and necropolitics of the state, particularly as shown through audiovisual and cultural texts. Wright and MacManus expose how some dominant understandings lack a gendered as well as a racial lens, and Weheliye suggests a "recalibration" of these power discourses to shed light on hierarchies of "racialized, gendered, sexualized, economized, and nationalized social existence," which better conceptualize the dominion of modern politics (2014, 1). Weheliye asserts that the framework of the bare life discourse fails to recognize "alternative modes of life alongside the violence, subjection, exploitation, and racialization that define the modern human" (1–2). I believe this expansion is critical to understanding the ways in which both *Rising Silence* and *Bish Kanta* render visible the conditions of life and subjecthood of Birangona women. Both films illuminate the racialized and gendered dehumanization processes that constructed the personhoods of Bengali men and women vis-à-vis West Pakistani personhood.

Recovering submerged histories of women, of gendered oppression, violence, and resistance, with particular attention to narrative—as evinced in the two films here—is important within the field of transnational feminism. I use a feminist cultural studies approach to analyze a historical juncture, and ideologies that characterized an event, paying attention to how cultural producers represent the tensions and gaps in narrations. Feminist critic Jean Franco, who studies massive state-engineered atrocities in Latin America, writes that cultural texts like "faded photographs, fragmented testimonies, exhumed bodies, harvests of bones" leave long-lasting memories that can be excavated for collective healing and memorialization (2013, 11). This harvest can appear, as we have seen, in various forms: literature, oral histories, embodied expressions, and visual cultural texts that exhume buried memories of gendered, state-sponsored violence. Oral historians argue that this exhumation not only recovers otherwise marginalized voices but also constructs political subjectivities, consciousness, and collective identity—particularly of those in the margins. Knowledge produced through such mediated storytelling contributes to what MacManus terms a "disruptive archive, a dissident feminist archive that counters repressive state, military, and even masculinist activist narratives" (2020, 18). Moreover, this alternative feminist epistemology often signals how trauma informs modes of narration and how loss that is borne out of trauma is integral to knowledge and is never fully recoverable. This traumatic narration is illuminated in *Rising Silence* in a scene where Gazi sits side by side in a paddy field with Shurjyo Begum, a Birangona woman from Sirajganj, as she narrates her experiences of rape and torture from 1971. Shurjyo Begum says, "When I lie down I see the army coming . . . monsters," and her voice trails off. She looks out in the horizon and says, "I can still see them coming." A haunting moment in the film, this particular segment evokes for the viewer the fragmented memories of a survivor of violence, the embodied knowledge borne out of it, and a kind of release and solidarity that is hinted at by the sharing of that knowledge with the filmmaker and the viewer. It is a gesture toward politicizing the "combed over" (Mookherjee 2015, 23) narratives of women in the quest toward creating more just knowledge and collective reckoning of the past.

Through constructing disruptive archives, women can transform dehumanizing, violent memories of repression into politicized projects that seek what Wendy Brown terms a more "comprehensive justice" for crimes of the state. These projects then have the dual goal of knowledge production and social justice (2004, 453). The two films we consider here reveal the specificities of subjectivity and knowledge that rise out of trauma, created in a context of compromised living. They are evident when Halima Khatun, Birangona and survivor of war, tells Boby, "I left home because of my mother. She did not support me or care for me. Once I tried to hang myself, another time I took poison. My war has not stopped. I continue fighting." Her experience of trauma that continues to compromise her life echoes Shurjyo Begum's, "I can still see them coming": "I still see them when I fall asleep. So I wake up screaming. I have been screaming for the last 40 years."

Compromised life is evident in the particular violence unleashed by the Pakistani military, the carceral politics of the state, and the methodical killing of Bengali men; in the assignation of inferior racialized characteristics to Bengali men, who were deemed smaller, darker, and less masculine than the more "racially evolved" West Pakistanis; in the use of rape as a tool of war to both humiliate the East Pakistani society and impregnate and thereby create a more docile population to control; and in the postwar titles bestowed to men (*Bir* Muktijoddha) and women (Birangona) by the new Bangladeshi state. The differential recognition of wartime heroism is also evident in the memorialization of Muktijoddhas as martyrs and the erection of statues and structures to honor them during the immediate postwar era; meanwhile, it was only in 2015 that Birangonas were granted state-sanctioned stipends and recognition as freedom fighters (Gazi).

This layered dehumanization process is laid out in Wright's gender violence work regarding femicide in the city of Juarez, Mexico, and is a useful lens through which to explicate the gendered dehumanization process during war. Wright identifies a violent gendering of space that justifies the violence and death suffered by both men and women, with different rationales for each. Wright argues that government officials render women who "walk the streets" as disreputable and unworthy, so that their murders are legitimized as a form of cleansing (2011, 711), and the men who are killed in drug violence are also rendered valueless and, therefore, expendable. The role of gender undergirds the violence—these deaths provide the "raw material for politics" against the so-called drug war (713). MacManus (2020, 65) describes violence used against women political resisters in the "Dirty War" in Mexico and Argentina, where they were subjected to sexual violence within a framework of carceral politics of the state. In this context, both male and female dissidents were relegated to a condition of necropolitics—their lives stripped of "use" to the nation. Both Wright and MacManus suggest that masculinist narratives of the state and even leftist political groups misrecognize this gendered war mechanism; they argue for a more humane and healing legacy that acknowledges the victims' experiences, which are not readily seen as worthy in official or mainstream narratives. MacManus's purpose is precisely to engage with cultural and audiovisual texts evoking, acknowledging, and honoring this legacy—the "haunting" legacy, as she calls it (quoted in Gordon 1997)—and to unsettle and rescript that exclusionary narrative of who counts as human (2020, 104). I extend MacManus's and Wright's framing to the context of the Bangladesh Liberation War, where West Pakistan state deployed differential and gendered violence—either side of the same coin of systemic colonial violence described in Chapter 2—on the bodies of Bengali men and women. This, too, is arguably a kind of carceral politics, a racialized and sexualized annihilation of Bengali personhood. Fox (2019) argues that rescripting, through memorialization projects, can influence trajectories of public policy, civic engagement, and collective identity formation and citizenship. It is a way to "flip the discourse" of victimization to show how violence is core, not occasional or exceptional, to state operation (Wright 2011, 724).

This racialized and gendered analysis of necropolitics and sovereignty is useful to show the ways in which cultural producers have harnessed and excavated women's narratives in an effort to memorialize 1971 and seek healing and recognition for its victimized women. Muktijuddho films are a vehicle through which to imagine and reimagine the foundational violence and its rippling aftermath. Both Gazi's *Rising Silence* and Boby's *Bish Kanta* illustrate the gendered necropolitics of the state and the ways of being that have been induced by war and state-organized violence and their continuing violent aftermath. Both documentaries revolve around the stories of Birangona women, who narrate their experiences while at the same time reflecting on state and social rehabilitation processes. Family and community voices provide the sociocultural context in which the featured women struggle for survival and recognition. While the Pakistani state targeted the Bengali population as a whole in 1971, as we have seen, they deployed different tactics in the assault against males and females, who were targeted differentially and rendered expendable and exploitable. The predominant Bengali narrative of the war, portraying the mass murder of men and the sexual oppression of women, thus unfolded the continuing conditions of necropolitics: men, even in social recognition, were elevated as *Bir* Muktijoddhas, while the women, even with their honorific title Birangona, were shamed and ostracized. Even though the title is meant to uphold women survivors to an eminent position of honor in society, Shehreen Islam (2012, 213–238) argues that it presupposed a docile subjectivity for women who then had to "earn" their place in the rehabilitation programs within the parameters of the role. The paternalistic state attitude and attendant policies of abortion and foreign adoption, to expunge the nation of tainted Pakistani babies, extended its ownership and control of women's bodies—a further assertion of gendered and racialized biopower.

In *Rising Silence*, we see not only this differential subjecthood but also the paradoxical consequence of telling women's trauma narratives through experiences of sexual violence. The documentary reemphasizes the social and cultural scrutiny of survivors within a framework of gendered morality. There is an overreliance on women's bodies as victims and a linear tracing of trauma/victimization, survival, and agency. We see this especially in the depiction of Rijia Begum, the last featured story in *Rising Silence*. Wandering the streets and slums of Dhaka, Rijia Begum narrates her horrific experience of rape by Bengali collaborators and the Pakistani army in 1971. She is shown lighting candles at a Sufi shrine while renowned mystic poet Jalal

Khan's song plays in the background in freedom fighter Birangona Rijia Begum's voice, "*Keho Korey Becha Kena Keho Kandey*":

> *Can I find you in exchange for the tears in my two eyes?*
> *Do not cry, oh, master of my mind, by the side of the road.*
> *If you wish to find him in this life, go to His bazaar.*

Rijia Begum speaks defiantly of the many hurts and insults hurled at her on the streets:

> They ask why I don't die? Why I don't go away? I say, if I leave or die do you think you'll have an extra portion of rice to eat? When Allah orders, they'll take me away. They'll not take me away because you say so! Do you feel wretched when you see me, you bastards? Who do you take me for? I ask people around here, Where do you think each of us comes from? Search your roots first, then come and talk to me.

The scene depicting Rijia Begum speaking to the crowds is spliced with vibrant shots of Dhaka city, a busy metropolis in contrast to the flat, bucolic scenes in the previous stories. There is a striking image of a tall man wearing a red-and-green bandana, striding confidently through the streets carrying a bunch of Bangladeshi flags. Then the camera cuts to a gigantic billboard advertising Robi, a telecommunications company; it displays male and female athletes in red-and-green uniforms. A woman with long flowing hair is shown climbing, and a man is featured with a cricket bat. The sign reads, "Whether on the fields or elsewhere, in all battles, our indomitable spirit ignites." Rijia Begum walks the streets, but she is not necessarily welcomed, let alone celebrated. Her story ends with her standing tall amid the bustle of the city and giving a speech:

> I am not scared of anyone. I might have lost weight [referring to her gaunt physical stature] but my mind hasn't lost its weight, hasn't grown old. My mind is alert. This is my world. I have spent my days in hellish poverty and hardship in this country. I have suffered a lot. But I've watched while playing. I have more left to play. My game is not over yet. I will carry on if I don't find myself in our history. If I am not given a place to belong to any history that's mine.

The camera cuts to an image of graffiti on a brick wall with the words, "VOICELESS BANGLADESHI." Rijia Begum is not celebrated; she does not stride confidently bearing the flags of her nation. Yet, she "carries on" and continues to "play," telling her story and constructing her own history—an alternative mode of being, the narrative arc here is defiant even if submerged—voiceless to the casual observer and in the official archives but eking out an existence nonetheless.

Gender, Oppression, and the Search for Justice

The first story in *Rising Silence* is that of Jharna Basu Halder in Barasat, Kolkata, India. To interview her, filmmaker Gazi crosses the border from Bangladesh to India by train. This imagery broadens the scope of the war beyond Bangladesh and suggests the ongoing repercussions of colonial divisions and the numerous partitions of the Indian subcontinent. Gazi and Halder are on a bed facing each other, reminiscing about the incitement of communal tensions as Hindus and Muslims who had coexisted for decades turned on each other and riots broke out. Halder, of Hindu background, describes her childhood in Bagerhat as "beautiful" yet interrupted by news of communal riots. Their conversation is far ranging: They talk about the student uprisings in 1952, specifically, but also the ongoing protests against the occupation in the 1960s. They discuss the language movement,[1] which was one source of conflict that led to war. They then turn to the other main conflict: West Pakistan's refusal to recognize the results of the election that proclaimed the Awami League as Bangladesh's presiding political party and Sheikh Mujibur Rahman as its elected leader. Mujib's historic speech at Ramna on March 7, 1971, in Dhaka is spliced into the film, declaring, "If one more shot is fired, and any of my people are murdered once again, then this is my request to you. Build a fortress in each and every home. The struggle now is the struggle for our liberation. The struggle now is the struggle for our independence." While images of Mujib's speech are shown to ignite the quest for liberation among the masses in East Pakistan, we hear in the background the news reporting a brutal military assault, "unparalleled in the history of mankind," unleashed by the West Pakistan military. Grainy images of army tanks and soldiers attacking at first unarmed civilians and then guerrilla insurgents appear. "Machine guns, tanks and saber jets against unarmed people. To make this challenge the people have one weapon, an indomitable will." Black-and-white footage of wartime reports relates the grand scale of military violence unleashed on East Pakistan, as Halder tells of her own abduction and rape by the Pakistani army. She complicates the narrative of the Bengali versus Pakistani army by recalling that Bengali razakars, Biharis, and Pakistani soldiers were among the men who raped her at her own home, and that when her father had been shot dead by the Pakistani army, two young Bengali Muslim boys from their neighborhood sat vigil for her Hindu family. Halder identifies one of the men who raped her as a Bihari named "butcher Majid." Postindependence, Halder was haunted by his presence to the degree that she convinced her husband to relocate to India.

While Gazi's primary motivation in *Rising Silence* is to create an archive of silenced stories, Boby's narrators in *Bish Kanta* speak more directly to notions of justice. To that end, it is a film that evokes a response from the spectators, whereas in *Rising Silence* the filmmaking process appears to be part of Gazi's own catharsis and self-actualization vis-à-vis the independence struggle. Boby's film revolves around the stories of three women: Ronjita Mondol, Halima Khatun, and Roma Choudhury. Even though the film centers their three stories, *Bish Kanta* surprisingly opens with an elderly male patriarch commenting on the "scourge" that the Birangona women bear on their lived identities. He leans over conspiratorially and asks the interviewer in the opening scene, "She [referring to Mondol, who is presumed to be mad] is same [as] pros. Don't you know what a pros is?" This comment hearkens back to Saikia's research, where she points out that Birangona women were stigmatized in society as "equivalent to prostitutes" (2011, 56). In an interview about the film, Boby says this about the stigmatization of Mondol:

> The first character in the film is Ronjita Mondol, who also happens to be the first war heroine we got to know after we began our research. I came across her name in a Khulna book on the war of independence, *The Victorious Campaign of 1971*, by Babar Ali. A line in the book referred to Mondol as "crazy" [*pagli*]. I began searching for her. When I found her, I was shocked to see that what was written in the book didn't match reality—when Ronjita was a child, her parents would lovingly call her Pagli, so that was a term of endearment. The politics of morphing her pet name into an inferior label when it crosses into the public realm is perverse. She is crazy because she speaks out. She speaks of her pain.

The film then continues to trace the violence and injustice enacted on the women daily, both during the war and in the postwar period. Boby says she was inspired to make this film—her first solo project—because,

> I like to make films about things that make me uncomfortable. I made this film from a deep sense of discomfort. In early 2011, I had joined filmmaker Rubaiyat Hossain's research on Birangonas and while working on the project I discovered that in everything official—government documents, news, cinemas, photographs, essays—whatever the medium, all post-1971 representations portrayed Birangonas in the same manner: dead or half-dead, distraught, as mostly beggars.

Rubaiyat Hossain, herself a filmmaker who has directed critical woman-centered films including *Meherjaan* (2011), which we studied in the Introduction and Chapter 1, produced *Bish Kanta*; and Boby's work is squarely situated within a trajectory and tradition of progressive activists in Bangladesh. Her work is cross-referenced, and she, in turn, cross-references critical activists in Bangladesh. In a 2016 interview for *Fragments Magazine* with Rahnuma Ahmed, a renowned writer and activist in Bangladesh (and, incidentally, the actor depicting Monika in *Itihaash Konna*), Boby says of her aesthetic choices,

> The difficulty was largely because I didn't want to see them through a 43-year-old lens and didn't want to reproduce the patriarchal prism through which Birangonas are looked at. What I wanted to see, or better still, what I wanted to show was that which Ronjita Mondol, Roma Choudhury, and Halima Khatun wanted to show. This meant that I would have to create an enabling space first. This was the most difficult, and the most time-consuming part.

One can surmise that the creation of an enabling space requires the particular kinds of revelation Boby strives to make, that is, examining the tiered assumptions surrounding categories such as human, Muktijoddha, Birangona, justice. This was particularly true in telling Halima Khatun's story; her role as a freedom fighter—similar to the character Bilqis in Yousuff's *Guerilla*—complicates the gendered recognition of heroism by the Bangladeshi government and society.

Halima Khatun was "13 or 14" when the war broke out. She joined up with her maternal uncle and his contingent at the guerilla camp and soon became part of the resistance movement. Alongside the male Muktijoddhas, she helped blow up three bridges. In one of the battles with the Pakistani army, she and her uncle were captured during a cross fire. The Pakistani army buried her uncle in a shallow pit and took her to their camp, where she was tortured with other women over a period of five months. In the film, she describes her experience during this period as a "goat set loose among tigers." She also speaks to the gendering of male and female experiences of war: "We kept our weapons in the same place, we even slept in the same place. We didn't think of ourselves as men and women. But if any of them came across me now, he would tear me to bits like a tiger." Her voice is juxtaposed with memorials erected in Bangladesh depicting the courageous men with arms marching purposefully to war. One sculpture shows two hands freeing a dove. In another shot in *Bish Kanta*, as Roma Choudhury speaks of her social isolation, the camera looks out through a small window where a farmer herds animals amid lush green fields. Together these shots imply that the women lead isolated and shackled lives, whereas their male counterparts in war are celebrated and free. Halima Khatun brings home this point when she says, "I can't talk about it anymore. All things cannot be said all the time. My kids have grown up. It'll hurt them. They'll feel dishonored." She then goes on to ask, "Why isn't she [the Birangona] respected after what happened to her?" Again, the camera cuts to the war memorials of male soldiers.

After the war, Halima Khatun explains that her father told her not to share her story with anyone lest it hurt her reputation and marriage prospects. "Many people asked me many things. I said no, we weren't hurt, we are all right. Normal." The camera cuts to aluminum pots gathering rain, the ripples coming to a still. An elderly patriarch in the community says in an interview, "We have to find a way of keeping it [Birangona's experiences] hidden. Hiding it means not letting it spread, burying it, concealing it." He closes his two palms together. The stories diverge from time to time, however. Ronjita Mondol's husband says about his wife, "She is not the kind of woman to keep things hidden." He also says that his wife has never done anything to "bother him" and rather it was the community "who was bothered by it." And now as an older woman, he says, she can speak without fear.

Yet the women's stories are not frozen in that singular violence. The violent legacy of the war continues to visit them—an aspect Boby brings into her film with purpose. She speaks of this in her 2016 interview with Rahnuma Ahmed:

> To think that a woman, a raped woman, can be socially hated! One comes across feelings of social hatred when Halima speaks of how people want to spit at her when speaking of her, of how she is not acknowledged as a freedom fighter. One encounters it again when Roma Choudhury speaks of how her son humiliates her, of how she was tricked and cheated by the men she loved. This layer about life in post-independence Bangladesh is present in the film.

In the film, Birangona Choudhury points out that Bangabandhu,[2] the Father of the Nation, called on *Mukijoddhas* to marry Birangona women and then asks indignantly, "Why didn't Bangabandhu get his son to marry a Birangona?" Roma Choudhury is referencing here that the Mujib government attempted to marry off Birangona women with offers of Tk. 5,000 compensation. Not many men came forward to accept such offers, and some who did demanded further compensation (D'Costa 2011). Choudhury continues in the film, "Birangona has to be married to *Bir* [masculine term for Birangona] to be recognized as brave." Choudhury is critical of the government's 2015 policy of granting stipends to Birangona: "Does fifty thousand takas

Figure 4.2 Ronjita Mondol, Muktijoddha Birangona (*The Poison Thorn* [dir. Farzana Boby, 2015]).

compensate for their loss? Maybe they [Birangona women] can buy some betel nut with it." Choudhury condemns the violence of the war altogether and states, "I don't support the war. I don't support it still. I knew the consequences would be disastrous. . . . Why was there a war? I'd predicted that if there was war, the rich would get richer, the poor would get poorer. They'd lose everything. Isn't that what's happening?" Reflecting back on the 1970 election that sparked the war she says, "I lost everything with that one vote in the 1970 elections." In a powerful statement, Mondol says, solemnly, "Nobody has ever asked to be forgiven." We come to learn that she recognized the men—elders in the community—who raped her and that in "liberated" Bangladesh, they roamed around freely. In 1972, Mujib granted amnesty to the Pakistani soldiers; to this, Mondol's husband states, "A general amnesty can only be given to someone who has not directly committed any wrongdoing, whose safety is in jeopardy. But criminals can never be forgiven." Choudhury, too, talks about seeing one of her perpetrators on the streets and that "he would lower his head whenever he would see me." In contrast to Mondol, she offers a surprising hint at absolution: "I think he was remorseful. If he is dead there is nothing to be said, but if he is alive I forgive him."

The theme of political justice—evoked by Boby, the Birangona women, and the activists—is ever present in *Bish Kanta*. Boby highlights individual women's quest for justice:

> If she [Mondol] comes across the *razakars* who raped her and looted their house, she steps forward and questions them. She demands they show remorse. Her defiance and courage are threats to the status quo. Many others are ambivalent about her for crossing religious boundaries and settling down with a Muslim man. The word "pagli" becomes an invective to brush her away, her dreams of justice. It's

like saying that her insistence for justice and reconciliation is abnormal. Villagers also refer to her as a *"beshya"* [prostitute]. These words speak of how deeply entrenched local power structures are. (Rahnuma Ahmed 2016)

Boby sees her film as a call to "reject a patriarchal nationalism that labels a rape victim's resistance as 'abnormal'" and where women's individual as well as comprehensive notions of justice can be gleaned.

The unfinished business of justice for the victims remains an open question, as the women—unlike male Muktijoddhas, who are valorized—are mostly outside the realm of state and even social recognition. The tremendous outpouring of citizens demanding justice for war crimes in the 2013 Shahbag *andolan* (protests)[3] (scenes of which are included in the film), the vociferous chants, the sea of candles on the streets of Dhaka seem a distant movement from the women's isolated existences in the far corners of Bangladesh. Choudhury complicates the justice process as she states: "Catching war criminals is like the Bengali proverb, 'Try to weed imposters and the whole village gets deserted.' They are not a handful. There are hundreds of thousands. There are war criminals even among those demanding their trial." The camera cuts again to the Shahbag *andolan*, streets thronging with thousands of civilians demanding justice for war crimes of 1971.

Woman, Mother, Nature/Nation: Symbolism in *Rising Silence* and *Bish Kanta*

The trope of woman-mother-nature/nation is entrenched in nationalist narratives. Anne McClintock notes, "All nationalisms are gendered; all are invented; and all are dangerous—dangerous . . . in the sense that they represent relations to political power and to the technologies of violence" (1991, 104). In this manner, the nation-state relies on these technologies of violence to punish Others they deem politically subversive, threatening, or deviant. Patriarchal social norms and gendered state violence converge, particularly as notions of proper femininity dictate the manner in which militarized state violence treats the dehumanized populations. According to Cynthia Enloe (2014, 87), women in nationalist stories figure as symbols rather than protagonists or active participants. Women's bodies literally and figuratively become embattled sites—they are "both shaken by crisis" and "actively engaged" by constructing new forms of womanhood. Their bodies are "put on the line" as carriers and resisters/agents and, in the process, contribute to cultural renewal (Sutton 2007, 135). In this section, I trace the ways in which women in *Rising Silence* and *Bish Kanta* enter the nationalist discourse through symbolic associations with nature, animals, and maternal roles, and I explore to what extent these depictions reinscribe/subvert the entrenched narratives.

Much of *Rising Silence* is shot in rural Bangladesh, which evokes images of the shonar bangla[4]—paddy fields, rivers and ponds, lotus flowers. But the bucolic surroundings are often juxtaposed with women speaking of the brutalization of war, as if to mirror how the attainment of "liberty" did not bring peace, dignity, or acknowledgment for women as citizens. Both movies evoke the lush green landscapes of rural Bangladesh, but whereas *Rising Silence* hints at a paradox between the brutalization of women and the attainment of the shonar bangla freedom, *Bish Kanta* uses the landscape—often rainy and ominous, with dark clouds—as the suitable backdrop to the 1971 war and its failure to achieve real liberation for its women citizens. Another scene in *Bish Kanta* shows hibiscus flowers in intense reds and pinks, nestled among the lush landscape, thorny brambles, and swamps—a jarring scene to accompany the stories of sexual torture and ongoing humiliation.

Both films use animal metaphors. In *Bish Kanta*, women's stories are repeatedly juxtaposed with birds—particularly one image where a black bird is trapped in electrical wires, valiantly fluttering to break free—to capture the sentiments of the women's narrations (e.g., Halima Khatun's description of being like a goat set loose among tigers). The film also shows Choudhury living alone with three cats, who are her constant companions. In *Rising Silence*, there are many shots of various animals: cows grazing and at rest, stray dogs sheltered by the interviewees. One scene shows Birangona Rajubala from Shodanandapur, Sirajganj, petting stray dogs at the same time she narrates a painful story about how she distanced herself from her own children to safeguard their reputation. The imagery suggests layered connections between woman and nature, woman and land, and woman and nation—that they are closer to these realms through their pain and spirituality and that they suffered irreversible trauma to birth that shonar bangla. The animals evoke Gazi's opening statement, in which she recalls that in 1971 her father witnessed hundreds of women lined up in convoys of trucks "like sacrificial animals." In "liberated" Bangladesh, Birangona women rear and safeguard the sacrificial animals. On the one hand, referring to women as "sacrificial animals" alludes to the human-animal species divide where the latter are seen as owned property. Animals here are without agency or selfhood in the same way as women—Birangona women—are stripped of their humanity and likened to a "thing" at the mercy of men. Their suffering follows a particular logic of suffering through recurring themes of objectification and captivity. On the other hand, in postindependent contexts, women and animals are shown providing reciprocal care of each other in their continued vulnerability. The exceptional suffering of women during

Figure 4.3 Muktijoddha Birangona Rajubala (*Rising Silence*
[dir. Leesa Gazi, 2019]. Photo credit: Shihab Khan.)

war is also made mundane and domesticated through these scenes depicting animals. Such representations maintain the hierarchy between man-
woman and man-animal as well as the continued suffering of women from
pre- to postliberation Bangladesh.

The connection to the beleaguered women, repeatedly shown as wounded animals, is parlayed through the film *Bish Kanta*'s theme song, written by
Boby, translated by Shahidul Alam, and sung by Priyanka Gope:

Hues in essence of myself
Drift in wonder
Yes they wander
Bird entwined in poisoned thorn
Wings asunder
Entwined in poisoned thorn
De-feathered I float in lilting moat
Speech lost in swirling word
Firefly glows in watery throes
Emptiness in stranded pool
Flutters, flutters, flutters
Entwined in poisoned thorn
Singed soul with fragrance lost

Unending an ode to loss
Deshackled a lost soul
Muted eye bound in black
In black flutters, flutters, flutters
Entwined in poisoned thorn

In *Rising Silence*, the maternal theme comes into play early via Halder, the first Birangona woman who relates her story. Halder has two daughters and shares her traumatic past in a letter to her younger daughter, Prajnadipa. Prajnadipa tells Gazi that her mother's pain was always the "third presence" in her childhood memories with her sister. Both daughters talk about how proud they are of their mother, calling her an "ideal mother" who "lost a lot but . . . was not defeated." Halder appears on-screen sitting between her daughters on a grassy lawn as they sing Tagore's "Why Do You Look at Us." On the train back to Bangladesh, Gazi reflects on her relationship with her own children. She realizes the importance of not being afraid to tell her children "who I am." As the train crosses the border, so, too, does Gazi—from the realm of an interviewer/oral historian/filmmaker to a space that she occupies with the Birangona women as women and as mothers. This crossing of boundaries between interlocutor and filmmaker is a defining characteristic of Gazi's film. She describes in an interview her own transformation, through spending time with the Birangona women, and her realization, "I could have been one of them." This merging of the filmmaker and the subjects of the film, whereby the stories and voice are overlaid, is, however, as I discuss later in the chapter, at times disconcerting.

When Gazi interviews Rajubala from Shodanandapur, Sirajganj, and asks if she can sit next to her, Rajubala answers with a question: "Aren't you my daughter?" She goes on to ask rhetorically, "Who gave birth to you?" Although Rajubala is Hindu, she connects her own spirituality and faith back to the story of Adam and Eve, explaining that both creation stories mean that humans were created to utter God's name. In the course of her encounter with Rajubala, Gazi comes to know from other sources that Rajubala has living children. Earlier, Rajubala had shared how her baby had been brutally killed by the Pakistani army at the time of her abduction. When Gazi interviews Rajubala's daughters, they explained that their mother suffered extreme hardship. She worked, to raise them, as domestic help in other people's homes. They came to know about Rajubala's experiences through other people. Now married with their own families, it seemed they could not put their own family reputation at risk by acknowledging Rajubala. "We could not give her companionship; we have our own families to consider." In turn, Rajubala shared how she keeps a low profile lest her experiences bring shame and undue attention to her family. Her grandchildren are picked on at school and asked, "Did the military take your grandmother?" Her Biran-gona status is poked and prodded. Villagers killed one of her daughters because she protested against these community jeers. Her daughters were harassed and taunted about being fathered and dumped by the Pakistani military. Rajubala explains, "I don't acknowledge my children."

Two other women in *Rising Silence* frame their identities as mothers by highlighting their relationships with their mothers and children: Chaindau Marma talks about having a happy childhood because she had a mother: "I did not have any difficulties, I had my mother." Her adopted son, Kawra Marma, shares that Chaindau raised him with abundant affection, but, upon her return from the military camp, the village was unkind to her. Chaindau talks about her power in the face of trauma and violence by sim-ply explaining, "I didn't die." Her story is narrated against the background of a group of girls playing soccer. The song in the background is, "The Girl Is Goddess Ganga, Jamuna, Saraswati." Juxtaposing the cultural elevation of girls as goddesses, and their potential athletic prowess, with the denigra-tion of Chaindau by her community again is a reminder of the paradoxical gender norms.

Tepri Bewa from Balidara, Thakurgaon, raised her son, Sudhir Roy, a Jud-dhoshishu, among the taunts of the community. She tells Gazi, "My son works hard. Why do people call him names?" Sudhir provides an answer for this question: "Because they [Pakistani army] took my mother, my uncles are alive and my grandparents were saved." Tepri was used as collateral by her own family, who were Hindu and at risk of being killed. By literally giv-ing her to the army, they were able to save themselves. Tepri's granddaugh-ter, Jonota Roy, explains to Gazi that the community tells her, "You don't have any ancestry." But Jonota takes pride in her grandmother's role in the war.

These responses recall Sutton's (2007, 137) assertion of the significance of women's roles in political movements, where they are both engulfed by the crisis and actively engaged in constructing a new society and new sub-jectivities. She discusses women in Latin America who literally "put their bodies on the line/gave their bodies" and, in turn, rebuilt the social body, a form of "sewn up skin" and "renewal." When Rajubala says, "I am a citizen of Bangladesh," it is this sewn-up identity she is referring to. With the newly allocated stipend for Birangona women who have been recognized as free-dom fighters, she promises to "give away to mosques and temples"—the very same mosques and temples that once shunned her but of which she is now a patron. In *Bish Kanta*, Choudhury visits an ashram, holding the arm of a young man, presumably her son. Despite being a Hindu, who are typically cremated, she says that she would like to be buried and lay claim to a piece of land—a form of belonging to the nation, to the land, that she has been otherwise denied. These gendered forms of participation reconfigure women's bodies, maternity, and familial roles beyond the sacrificial to the maternal. Women invoke the metaphor of motherhood often as a form of embodied experience and knowledge that can transform and strengthen their collective identity as citizens.

Filmmaker as Witness, Ally, and Critic

Rising Silence aims to bring awareness about "a forgotten genocide," as Gazi calls it. The film introduces itself as a personal journey of ethical reckoning with the past. It does so through the use of iconic visual and aural signposts and Gazi's voiceover narration, all as backdrop to the stories of the nine featured Birangona women. Bill Nichols (1983, 25) posits that "internal dissonance" is a key characteristic in genre-based documentary "truth productions." Such dissonance allows the voices in the film to compete with and contradict one another. This complicates the stories but also, and importantly, allows them to stand apart from the overarching voice of the film itself. The distinction between the textual voice and the authorial voice prevents the film from simply rubber-stamping a certain truth. This distinction of voice is also accomplished with inserted images and other aural and visual cues. Except for the collective story of Amina, Mukhlesa, and Maleka—three sisters from Rajbari, Ranishoinkul—the women's stories are told in distinct segments. Their backgrounds are varied: they are Muslim, Hindu, Buddhist, tribal; married, widowed, living alone or with children; from loving families who sheltered them and from families who cast them out in shame. Some are destitute, while others have a steady income. Their one unifying theme happens to be motherhood, a point that was made in the previous section.

Rising Silence opens with a quote by African American poet Maya Angelou: "There is no greater agony than bearing an untold story inside you." A civil rights activist, Angelou alludes to the suffering borne of racism and sexism, of rape and segregation, but also the indomitable human spirit of rising above pain and oppression. In helping tell the stories of survivors of wartime rape, Gazi brings to light and assigns meaning to their struggle. Believing that the experiences of women define the Bengali nationalist movement and the blood-drenched birth of the nation, she claims through a cinematic frame that those experiences also transform the women's self, identity, and consciousness. After the Maya Angelou quote, Rising Silence begins with Gazi's voice: "I am Leesa Gazi. I grew up listening to my father telling stories of a forgotten genocide"; then, as if framed between two bookends, it ends with her own self-actualization: "This journey has changed me completely. They have inspired me to understand who I am and what I am capable of as a woman." Alongside the stories of the women she features in

Figure 4.4 Filmmaker Leesa Gazi with Birangona Muktijoddha Mukhlesa Begum (*Rising Silence* [dir. Leesa Gazi, 2019]. Photo credit: Shihab Khan.)

the film, Gazi's own catharsis is just as central to the plot. Indeed, it is somewhat jarring how much screen time is dedicated to Gazi in the film. Her presence is felt in every interview. Evidently, the film memorializes the critical roles of Birangona women in Bangladesh's history, however, pedagogically speaking, the narrator assumes the authorial and authoritative voice.

Styled as a hybrid documentary that makes use of self-reflexive, dialogic, and socially engaged visual and aural narration, Gazi's own background in stage theater and activism shape the film's inception and journey. Gazi traces her interest in Birangona women to the stories her father told her about the 1971 war during her childhood in postindependence Bangladesh. The memory he shared with her about the captive women packed onto trucks like sacrificial animals haunted Gazi; in addition to opening her film with that memory, she shared it in a TEDx talk at the London School of Economics in 2015. "This memory of Birangona women stayed with me forever," she says. Although the government of Bangladesh bestowed the honorific Birangona on the estimated two hundred thousand to four hundred thousand survivors of sexual violence just six days following independence, it has had little effect in granting them an eminent status in society or in integrating them into the nation-building process. Instead, Gazi posits, it relegates the women to a title and a statistic and obscures their lived and individual stories. "They each have a story to tell. And, this is the story of some of these women," she says.

Even as the Birangona women have been seemingly rendered voiceless in history, the film gives them a medium to tell their stories, and Gazi as a filmmaker/interlocutor personifies the contradictions of the documentary medium. The contradiction resonates with Hesford and Kozol's (2001) reminder that films about humanitarian interventions serve both pedagogical and memorial projects in that they offer critical modes of interventions in disrupting monolithic narratives yet may unwittingly contribute to further reification of an entrenched human rights narrative. Cheri Robinson (2017) argues about structures of recognition and recuperation in representing spectacles of transnational violence. She believes that such spectacles/films are a call for empathy, truth, and justice, which, by exposing the audience to the trauma, can educate without being overly didactic. And while contemporary films may not present a call to arms, she says, they do present a compelling call to bear witness.

Gazi (2015) further addresses this need to bear witness and hear these stories:

> I called the film *Rising Silence*, because we, both inside and outside Bangladesh, have enforced this silence, this hushed tone, this ugly secret, this implied blame on to the Birangona. Many times I have been told that this kind of work will help them break the silence. I used to feel pleased about that. Then I found that the Birangona women actually have plenty to say. All of them, in fact, own a towering voice and burning stories. These are the stories that deserve to be told, but are in danger of dying out. We have never cared to listen to them. So there's no scope to break the silence when we collectively have made sure that silence prevails. We have been busy stigmatizing them for generations.

Since 2010, Gazi has met and talked with eighty Birangona women and contributed to an important archive of war stories. In 2014, she and the Komola Collective, a theater group that she founded and runs, produced Birangona: *Brave Woman*, a stage production based on the stories of the survivors she interviewed. They took the show on tour in the UK and Bangladesh. Then, Gazi (2015) relates, "the inevitable happened": One of the women she had interviewed died. She recalls, "That shook me profusely. When a Birangona woman dies, her story dies with her." That became her motivation to make a film about Birangona women: "because they matter."

In a televised interview with Shamim Ara Chowdhury (2019) of TRT World, Gazi relates the connection she felt with the women she interviewed: "I wanted to know them as they are . . . meet them. . . . I see their faces now; I could have been one of them." Gazi shares with Chowdhury that she spent days cultivating trust and friendship with her interlocutors. "I did not want to make them tell me their story. I stayed with them, we cooked together, went shopping together, and gradually they trusted me" (BBC World 2018).

Gazi explains in an interview:

> Filming *Rising Silence* was not an impartial, journalistic sort of exercise—I was already on the side of the Birangona. They had a voice already—even now, some stand on street corners screaming about the horrors of their experience. Others sit and cry in the market places, while those with money and status just pretend it never happened, in order to keep up some show of respectability. I wanted to give the Birangona a microphone, that's all. (quoted in Shah 2019)

In the same interview, Gazi says, "I am an accidental filmmaker, really. I am not formally trained as a director or scriptwriter. Certainly, I did not set out to make *Rising Silence*—I did it simply because I had to." We see Gazi in a hybrid role encompassing activist, director, and interviewer. She is moved by the burden of history and acts on it to bring to light the submerged stories of the Birangona women, yet, at the same time, she reinscribes a victim-savior or a survivor-ally narrative, which goes on to center her as the sympathetic ally and, in the process, diminishes the integrity of the survivors' stories. As noted earlier, unlike Boby, who remains behind the camcorder, Gazi's own center positionality in the film embodies the experiences of Birangona women when she reflects on-screen, "It could have been me." This centering of self does elide certain differences in geographic and class positionality of the film director as an expatriate ally to her interlocutors, a difference that Boby as someone who is more locally based does not necessarily have to traverse through cinematic projection.

Gazi chooses not to be a "behind-the-scene" director/interviewer; she is shown arriving on train, by car, and on foot to the doorstep of each woman she interviews. She casts a lone figure, clad in cotton saris, a teep on her forehead, carrying a tote bag, and meeting each interviewee with an embrace. She sits next to each woman, so both she and the interviewee are centered on the screen. There are two interview segments where she is seated in the center flanked on either side by a Birangona woman. She is certainly not the distant journalist or researcher. She asks each question in a gentle tone, and when the women talk about their trauma, Gazi reaches out to them in a display of compassion. She arrives three days early at Rajbari and is shown walking with Mukhlesa Begum and Amina Begum on either side, as she asks them, "Can I stay with you for three days?" The women readily respond, "You have come here for us; for love."

Figure 4.5 Muktijoddha Birangona Rajubala and Shurjyo Begum with Leesa Gazi (*Rising Silence* [dir. Leesa Gazi, 2019]. Photo credit: Shihab Khan.)

Gazi's involvement in the telling of her interviewees' stories is markedly different from the approach of Boby, who maintains a more traditional behind-the-camera presence. Boby explains her choices in the following manner:

> I wanted to inhabit these women's perspectives. This meant that from the very beginning since shooting started, I needed to develop a method. I chose to shoot with a small Handycam, to have women in the team, to shoot in similar lighting, in the same season, and also, to make use of symbols, not have a commentary, to use visuals and audio in an uninterrupted manner. Instead of working with a predetermined form within which I fitted the documentary material, I allowed the form to emerge from the matter that I shot. It took a long, long time, almost four years. (quoted in Rahnuma Ahmed 2016)

What subsequently stands out to the viewers of these two films are the subtle ways in which Boby directs the arc of the narrative in allowing the form to emerge from the matter—the women's stories directing the unfolding of the narration—in contrast to Gazi's direction, where the story unfolds according to the filmmaker's entrance, engagement, and insertion of self into the stories of the Birangona women. Like in her theatrical presentation of Birangona women in Komola Collective productions, Gazi seems to be interested in an embodied representation in *Rising Silence* where her "journey" from the UK and immersion among interlocutors in Bangladesh is more theatrically weaved into the narrative. It is surprising that, unlike *Bish Kanta*, *Rising Silence* does not draw on other scholars or activists who have worked with Birangona women or are experts on the war and thereby amplifying the argument surrounding the silence and erasure of Birangona from the nationalist memory project. While Gazi's vast archive of stories from a generation of women who are literally dying and taking their stories with them is impressive, certainly she is not the lone voice invested in such recovery projects. On the contrary, a rich archive exists in Bangladesh collected by activists, scholars, and filmmakers and in personal reflections and memoirs of the war (to name a few). Two other films, Catherine and Tareque Masud's *Narir Kotha* (*Women and War*, 2000) and Yasmine Kabir's *Shadhinota* (*A Certain Liberation*, 2003), are excellent examples. Anthropologist Mookherjee (2015, xvi) notes that it is incorrect to assume there is silence about wartime rape in Bangladesh; rather, stories of wartime rape, ironically, exist in both public memory and public secrecy. She talks about the extensive visual and literary representation of Birangona women as well as the ways in which women are often called to testify in human rights and activist platforms. The reification of Birangona representation as silenced, ostracized, and shamed grants the narrator a kind of "narrative license," which then associated wartime rape and its aftermath as rooted in patriarchy, tradition, and culture (156). Silence, as a trope, functions as a shorthand explanation that obscures historical and political contexts as well as differences in experiences among women based on class, race, and social status that may have influenced their positions and negotiations. The filmmaker's assertion, "I could have been one of them" is a case in point that elides her own social location and diasporic position and amplifies a kind of universalized connection to oppression. What is problematic here is the predetermined logic to the enactment of these stories rather than to demystify the singular story and strive for a more ethical narration. Arguably, this is evident in Mookherjee's reading of human rights visual narratives where she often turns to the occlusions and the seeming "non-actors" to shed light on the way trauma is relived within "daily socialities" (108). Mookherjee, thus, in her ethnographic analysis, strives for alternative narratives that do not freeze, demonize, valorize, or "comb over" Birangona women's experiences (23). Importantly, she raises the paradox of human rights stories that highlight a singular trauma yet cannot accommodate the complexities of Birangonas' experiences. As such, they are often subject to authorial co-option (Fitzsimons-Quail 2015, 27). Ethnography, in Mookherjee's opinion, can shift the narrative by engaging in parallel processes of autocritique and reflexivity.

What are we to make of this image of the lone activist filmmaker on a quest to shine light on a forgotten genocide? There are lengthy self-reflections from Gazi throughout the film—she is both visually and aurally omnipresent, even through hushed-voice directing of the flow of conversation while the women are speaking. Yet, how do we process her assertion in the TRT World interview with Chowdhury: "I could have been one of them"? Equally bewildering is the segment she shows at her TEDx talk, which is a dialogue between her and Asia Begum, a Birangona woman, following the theatrical production of their stories in Dhaka. As in *Rising Silence*, this clip shows Gazi and Asia Begum, who had seen the performance, facing each other and holding hands. "Was I able to tell your story?" Gazi asks. Asia Begum responds, "You told them properly, you told them well. Thank you, we are happy." She goes on to say that Gazi's depiction has made the women happier than if they had been compensated monetarily and that the performance had assuaged their pain and would lessen the taunts because the public would have seen the film and, therefore, understood better the women's suffering. There is a particularly painful moment in the clip shown at the TEDx talk, when Asia Begum talks about her entrance in heaven as forbidden: "Our path is cut off. We are violated." There is a valiant effort by Gazi to discourage that thought as both women are shown crying and Gazi comforting Asia Begum: "Sister, sister, sister look at me. It's not your fault." Asia Begum expresses her gratitude and says, "We have nothing to give to you [Gazi, the filmmaker who had made the Birangonas' stories visible]. If we had anything, we would have given it." Gazi responds tearfully, "Only Allah knows what you have given, what you have given to me. . . . You have given a lot. Give me your strength."

This is clearly a sensitive moment, couched in the maternal role that also frames the Birangona and her relationship to the nation, even as it recasts that role with political activism and a political legacy. Women's varied contributions gained Bangladesh its freedom, and yet they were cast away and taunted as pariahs. Gazi—the prodigal daughter/lone activist—returns to make meaning of that trauma and bestows honor through her heroic enactment of the Birangona's story (the theatrical production is a one-woman show where Gazi personifies numerous Birangona women). This return, however, elides the class and transnational location of the director, and the projection of her journey into the lives of Birangona women as a central narrative arc in the film—perhaps to establish an authentic relation to the nation while telling a story about nationhood. Asia Begum thanks Gazi with a collective "we," presumably all Birangona and by association the nation. In the process, Gazi becomes one of them in engulfing their pain within her. Gazi is an approximation of the nation, and, on behalf of it, she asks for the Birangonas' strength, which enabled them to endure the suffering, stigma, and ostracization. Woman, nation, and collective identity merge here in the remembering of embodied knowledge and the configuration of a political consciousness created from loss. It is a curious affirmation of the maternal in the telling of a nation's history and identity. The maternal is also the entry point for the activist who, on behalf of the nation, acknowledges Birangona/mother's venerable contributions and literally gains strength for her own struggles from it.

In a conversation with Frank Wilderson about the positionality of African Americans in United States history, Saidiya Hartman (Hartman and Wilderson 2003) develops the notion of the "sympathetic ally"—in this case, white allies working on behalf of Black subjugated populations—who in their expressions and assertions of support appropriate the suffering of the "actual object of identification" to the extent that the sympathizer becomes the proxy for the enslaved Black bodies. Hartman argues that sympathetic allies can only envision the suffering of the Other if they are subsumed into a common understanding of humanity and thereby displace the condition of the Other. In her words, such expressions of empathy rely on the premise, "Only if I can see myself in that position can I understand the crisis of that position" (189). Only then does the suffering of the Other become meaningful, and, in that process, further violence is done—a kind of insidious and ubiquitous violence—as the sympathetic ally does not comprehend the Other's full humanity. Wilderson cautions that this kind of appropriative solidarity belies "that subjects just can't make common cause with objects" as these are not analogous experiences (190). The question here is whether such consumptive enactments of alliance recognize the desires and positionalities of the Other or fit them into a social order of paternalism. We have to ask: What is accomplished by the filmmaker's ubiquitous presence on the screen—by her tearful embrace of Birangona women, her assertions of being connected to their suffering, her repeated references to her own experience of motherhood?

Marianne Hirsch (2008) writes about memory projects that strive to salvage more distant social and cultural memories by conveying them through individual and familial accounts and aesthetic expression. This revival would then suggest that the individual structures of memory could persist as part of the larger cultural archive, even when those directly involved have passed away. Hirsch believes this enables those without a direct connection to be engaged in the postmemory, even after the generation and its family have died. Part of the purpose for propagating these violent memories would be to transfer the personal back into the political. This argument hearkens back to the discussion around producing disruptive archives of war where women's stories of trauma—however fragmented and partial—are integral to the embodied knowledge-making process necessary to redirect entrenched nationalist, even human rights, narratives. Bringing women's stories into fuller light and beyond a shame-stigma-honor complex reveals the absence of gendered ways the necropolitics of dehumanization unfolds in conflict situations. Thus, the reconstructed personal memories would be reintegrated into the national archive as new official memories, as renewed bonds between community members, and as a means of revitalizing a waning public memory and empathy that, over time, can become

Figure 4.6
Birangona
Muktijoddha
Rajubala (*Rising Silence* [dir. Leesa Gazi, 2019]. Photo credit: Shihab Khan.)

numb due to an overexposure to violence and trauma. Through the mediums of visual texts such as *Rising Silence* and *Bish Kanta*, then, I would argue that the viewer witnesses the personal, which becomes a shared memory. Gazi and Boby, a generation removed from 1971, have created such memories and shared them with regional and global audiences unfamiliar with their history; at the same time, they have created a fresh perspective of the tired masculinist nationalist story.

Conclusion

By telling the story of 1971 through the lens of the Birangona women, *Rising Silence* and *Bish Kanta* contribute to the growing "disruptive archive" of woman-centered visual and literary texts. The suffering—by direct victims and observers—has been reconfigured within a "human rights regime," which has turned it into a "standardized and constructed action" (Givoni 2011). *Rising Silence*, in particular, falls within this reconfiguration, with clearly denoted victims, perpetrators, and saviors and with the filmmaker standing in as activist, sympathetic ally, and curator. Yet, by centering women's submerged histories, both films also contribute to the growing collection of women's voices that may unwittingly stretch our understanding of the "human" on which the regime rests. The differential positionality of Bengali vis-à-vis Pakistani, the necropolitical violence unleashed on male Bengali citizens vis-à-vis women, and the racialized, gendered, and sexualized violence against Bengalis—all of these are illuminated through the vantage point of women (and at times other community members). Among the ways we see this is through the films' use of symbols. For instance, the maternal metaphor both affirms women's roles as mothers and politicizes gender within a nationalist movement. The sacrificial animal trope reflects the vulnerability of women as well as the human-animal, human-woman divide, where the latter of each pair is seen as property—devoid of agency and selfhood—of the patriarchal state and family. Together, the films help create a collective feminine identity and illuminate the politics of a differentially positioned human identity based on embodied knowledge that arises from trauma. The dialogic relationship between Gazi and the subjects of her film challenges official truths and produces a critical cultural text that provides insight into incomplete histories of 1971 and its aftermath. Further, *Rising Silence* recovers women's positions as protagonists and reveals a politics of solidarity. It unearths a feminine perspective even while the filmmaker is central to the creation of a "hospitable memory" and self-referentiality is deployed as a communication strategy (Nichols 1983, 23). In the cinema-of-witness genre (Kaminsky 2006) and through the deployment of "empathetic witnessing" (Hesford and Kozol 2001, 17), the film leaves us with a sense of urgency—that "do something!" response to the lack of justice for war crimes. Together, both *Bish Kanta* and *Rising Silence* call for awareness of the "forgotten genocide" and its "forgotten victims," and they do so in a manner that integrates the filmmakers as activists—more assertively, Gazi, as narrator, director, and friend to her subjects—who are observers and witnesses even as they incite audiences to education and action.

Robinson (2017) comments on the role of the spectator, whose historical knowledge outside of the film requires no action, because the action has become the consumption of the film. By witnessing not only the trauma but its ongoing history, the spectator lifts the trauma from state secrecy and isolation and weaves it back into communal memory. Once it circulates freely in the social sphere, Robinson says, the personal once again becomes political. *Rising Silence* explicitly and *Bish Kanta* implicitly incite the filmmaker/spectator to a disruptive knowledge and empathetic action in the ongoing struggle for justice. In *Rising Silence*, Gazi herself is the actor who is animated into her role of the activist/ally by the very stories she tells. In *Bish Kanta*, on the other hand, activism comes in the form of highlighting the Shahbag *andolan* as a demand for justice, even if the women caution us of the hollowness of gender justice. Van Schendel (2015) argues that 1971 historiographies are reaching a critical juncture where a "second generation" narrative is being constructed that is less reductive, more analytical, and more attuned to the nuance of the multiple wars that unfolded in 1971. Arguably, *Rising Silence* and *Bish Kanta* are at that juncture but may have not quite fully crossed over. Certainly, both films bring to the fore the national contestations and lack of recognition and justice; yet, in so doing, they also reinscribe the politics of shame-silence-stigma, which has been rendered an ambivalent/paradoxical narrative. They further nuance prevailing statist and masculinist versions of the story by drawing attention to the suffering of women and by hinting—through against-the-grain reading—at alternative modes of being survivors. Such a reading can sharpen the analysis of the necropolitics of gendered dehumanization and the differentially constituted humanity of Bengali versus Pakistani, Birangona versus *Bir*, woman versus animal. The stories of Roma Choudhury, Shurjyo Begum, and Rijia Begum depict how they have eked out an existence that embraces survival, a differential agency, and healing—an existence that is borne out of their traumatic past and alludes to a disruption to the nationalist framing of women, violence, and agency. Finally, and importantly, the films question whether such nuanced readings can elide authorial co-options toward nationalist narratives where self-reflexivity of the sympathetic ally can unwittingly add another layer of abstraction to the path of gender justice by foregrounding and fixing Birangona women from a shame-silence stigma to a suffering-sympathy complex.

Muktijuddho Cinema as Human Rights Cinema

> You don't have to privilege the ethical over the aesthetic in art
> if the aesthetic remains the condition of possibility of the
> ethical in art.
>
> —MOTEN, *In the Break*, 249.

The films I discuss in this book have all been materialized within a critical backdrop of the parallel cinema (*Bikalpa Dhara*) movement in Bangladesh, which aimed at drawing out the ethical, political, and aesthetic possibilities in cinema. Shameem Akhtar, with her trilogy on women's Muktijuddho experiences, remains the most prominent and prolific woman filmmaker in Bangladesh, especially within this genre. In addition to *Itihaash Konna* (2000), which we discussed in Chapter 3, two other Akhtar films are set in the war and feature women in central roles. Readers may recall that I began this book with a vignette from one of those two films, Akhtar's *Rina Brown* (2017). The film is based loosely on the 1961 film *Saptapadi*, directed by renowned filmmaker Ajoy Kar. *Saptapadi* is a romantic drama set in preindependence India, where Krishnendu, a Hindu boy, and Rina Brown, an Anglo-Christian girl, are kept apart because of religious differences. In Akhtar's film, the two young lovers are Dara, a Bengali Muktijoddha, and Sandra, his anglicized Christian neighbor, whom, in a nod to *Saptapadi*, he affectionately nicknames Rina Brown. Even though the interfaith relationship raises concern among family and community, the two young lovers push the limits of their own political and cultural beliefs as the war rages around them. Like *Itihaash Konna*, this film is narrated through flashbacks when Sandra returns to an independent Bangladesh to attend a seminar on women and peace, decades after her family left during the war. She seeks out Dara, who is now a corporate executive—a stark contrast to the Tagore-reciting[1] revolutionary she knew in her youth. They spend an afternoon together reminiscing and yearning for the innocence of youth and the love that could have brought them—and by proxy, the nation—"freedom." "War changes everything" is the repeated incantation the setting evokes in the two characters as they look out into the changed cityscape of Dhaka's skyscrapers. Together they gaze at a footbridge in the park that leads to the other side of a lake, perhaps hinting at the freedom that was never realized by either the separated lovers or the nation. However, the encounter frees them from their tortured pasts as they go their separate ways to embark on new endeavors, which are legacies of their shared wartime trauma: Sandra, as a pacifist working toward peace and justice, and Dara, to reconcile with his family. In contrast to *Itihaash Konna*, however, the film does not centralize the Birangona; rather, it narrates the story of war by focusing on another marginal narrative, that of a non-Muslim minority experience.

Yet another of Akhtar's films, *Shilalipi* (*The Inscription*, 2004), tells the true story of female Muktijoddha Selina Pervin, a journalist, writer, and revolutionary in the resistance movement who was abducted and killed by the Pakistani military and Bengali razakars. Narrated in a dual parallel time line, the film traces Pervin's and her son's life trajectories. Pervin's son, Sumon, was raised in an orphanage after the war. The film opens with then eight-year-old Suborno (the fictionalized version of Sumon) witnessing his mother's abduction, and, subsequently, it follows his postindependence pursuit of justice and recognition for his martyred mother. Importantly, we see the grown Suborno—played by actor, cultural activist, and academician Manosh Chowdhury—search for answers to why his mother's contributions had not been properly commemorated in postindependent Bangladesh. Similar to *Itihaash Konna*, *Shilalipi* begins unconventionally, with a prologue—breaking the barriers of fiction, nonfiction, and adapted filmography—as the real Sumon comes on-screen and talks about his mother.

Shilalipi is a particularly remarkable film for shining light on a Muktijoddha who stood out not only for her courageous and critical participation in the nationalist struggle but also as a woman who defied the social and cultural norms of the time. The film is a tribute to this brave combatant, an unsung hero, told through her son's quest for truth and remembrance. It ends with a reminder of the unfulfilled promise of liberation and the undue responsibility placed on the following generations—in this case, the son's need to search for meaning and find acknowledgment for his mother's role in the war. Sumon too is a kind of Juddhoshishu as he is left with the legacy of war that ravaged his mother's generation.

The question of responsibility and justice to and for the children of war is precisely at the heart of Shabnam Ferdousi's feature documentary, *Jonmo Shathi* (*Born Together*, 2016). Ferdousi, filmmaker and journalist at Ekattor Television, narrates her "personal journey"—a quest to find the war babies

Figure 5.1 Sudhir Barman, *Juddhoshishu* (*Jonmo Shathi* [dir. Shabnam Ferdousi, 2016]).

born at Dhaka's Holy Family Hospital on the same day as she, January 14, 1972. Ferdousi grew up hearing stories about her family's experiences during the war. Her mother regaled her with accounts of the fateful night of her birth; she told Ferdousi that she was one of thirteen children born that night, five of whom were born to Birangona mothers. At the hospital, the war babies were separated from the newborns who had civilian parents. Ferdousi was born with a full head of hair, and her parents would tell her that they thought of it as a marker so that she would not get mixed up with the Juddhoshishus. Her mother would tease her in childhood that she was "different" from other children—a tomboy who refused to eat rice, the quintessential Bengali meal. She preferred parathas and rotis, which others thought was a sign that she was likely Punjabi, switched at birth. In a personal interview, Ferdousi (2020) noted the multigenerational trauma caused by war and how she to this day is sensitive to loud noises, particularly gunshots. "I must have heard those noises from my mother's womb during the war." Ferdousi became a mother herself, in 1994, and that experience intensified her desire to locate the Juddhoshishus who she always felt were her companions but on parallel tracks of life. The paths of Ferdousi and the unknown Juddhoshishus unfold through a celebration on Ferdousi's forty-third birthday, which marked the beginning of her journey that led to the film.

Taken together, the films comprising this book highlight socially engaged Muktijuddho cinema, which I also refer to as human rights cinema. I have approached this project with the aim of considering these films and their political and aesthetic contributions to a national quest for healing and justice as well as expanding the quest within a more global arena. Here, I enter the discussion around recuperation, responsibility, and representation by engaging with critical race and feminist frameworks. Anti-racist feminist and critical nationalist approaches evoke the original violence of the nation as well as the ways in which that violence transforms and continues inflecting our ways of seeing, appropriating, and seeking justice against racialized and sexualized dominance. I draw upon Black feminist theory—emerging out of the U.S. context—as a deep and fierce tradition that can shed light on multiple and intersectional racialized and sexualized oppression in disparate sites and at the same time offer a mode of *seeing* and analyzing power that is transnational. In so doing, I am illuminating a conversation about racialized and sexualized oppression in Muktijuddho cinema that is in light of Black feminist theorizing, yet speaking to and expanding it. For, Black Studies, in particular, offers the metanarrative with critical insights in illuminating global frameworks of oppression; this is elaborated at length in Alexander Weheliye's *Habeas Viscus* (2014). Weheliye discusses how the theoretical and methodological protocols of Black Studies illuminate global power hierarchies, in all of their formations, and, namely, advocate for the "radical reconstruction and decolonization of what it means to be human" (4). He lays out this critical protocol in the following way:

> Since blackness has functioned as one of the key signifiers for the sociopolitical articulation of visual distinctions among human groups in modernity, black studies has developed a series of comprehensive analytical frameworks—both critical and utopian—in the service of better understanding and dismantling the political, economic, cultural, and social exploitation of visible human difference. (4)

Weheliye stresses the distinct ways Black Studies has made critical observations about visualizing human difference and the attendant pedagogies for dismantling the mechanisms of exploitation based on visible human difference (4). Of particular significance in studying socially engaged films and their capacity to disrupt foundational narratives is the work of Frank Wilderson (2010), who, addressing the cinematic representation of the suffering of African Americans, points to the unspeakability of that condition despite its inherent "ethical grammar." He asks, "What are we to make of a world that responds to the most lucid enunciation of ethics with violence? What are the foundational questions of the ethico-political? Why are these questions so scandalous that they are rarely posed politically, intellectually, and cinematically—unless they are posed obliquely and unconsciously, as if by accident?" (2). He points to the structural "foundational antagonisms" (6) that undergird the nation—of the exploitation and suffering of Black and indigenous populations that continue within relations of power, hierarchy, domination, and legibility. Delineations of the modes of being Black and indigenous cannot occur on their own terms because it would not make for a "conceptually coherent script"—a condition Wilderson names as the "unthought." Even politically engaged cinematic narratives rely on certain "constituent elements" and "assumptive logic" (7) about the arrangement of power and desire among whites, Blacks, and American Indians such that the positionality of the marginalized cannot be articulated. (The Black subject is always positioned as slave in relation to the white master; the American Indian subject must be positioned vis-à-vis their dispossession and lost heritage.) What this "unthought" hints at are the separate worlds of Black people (unthought) and humans. Even the emancipatory discourses of socially engaged cinematic narrations "cathedralize" slavery as the metanarrative. This is an ontological dilemma undergirding the social death of Black people vis-à-vis forging the notion of humanity. In fact, Wilderson sees cinema as an extension of the technologies of hegemony mobilized to reify (not dissent from) the ruse of civil society—itself also a participant in the continuing legacy of the foundational antagonisms of the nation.

In this chapter, I consider how Muktijuddho cinema, similar to Black and American Indian cinema, articulates and disavows the foundational matrix of violence in the birth of Bangladesh. Here, I delve further into whether Muktijuddho cinema can labor imaginatively and disrupt ethical dilemmas predicated on the formation of the nation and its gendered categories, such as Muktijoddha and Birangona. Or, alternatively, does it reiterate the ethical "scaffolding" of the heroic masculinist integrity of the nation and citizen? How does the positionality of socially engaged directors and the work of political cinema manifest the ethics, politics, and aesthetics of Muktijuddho film? What narrative strategies can lend themselves to disrupting the trope of heroism and sacrifice—what Wilderson calls the "moves from equilibrium to disequilibrium to equilibrium" within filmic narratives, which cannot ultimately emplot the narrative of the oppressed (26)?

While not claiming to cover the genre of Muktijuddho cinema comprehensively, I have chosen to analyze in this book films that have consciously attempted to engender dialogue around pressing issues of women's victimization and dared to imagine different ways of being/seeing within and against a Muktijuddho imaginary. As socially engaged films, to what extent do they push the structure of Muktijuddho ideology? My project explores the possibilities of film as a site to articulate an ethics that acknowledges this "foundational violence"; recuperates it even if in fragments; imagines differently the irreconcilable relationship between humanity, freedom, and the conceptual, multifaceted prism of the Birangona; and examines the linked concepts of Birangona, Muktijoddha, and Juddhoshishu. In this final chapter, I explore three dimensions essential to a consideration of Muktijuddho cinema as human rights cinema: (1) building on material from the Introduction, I contextualize the political economy of infrastructure and aesthetics that imbricates Muktijuddho cinema; (2) I explore the asymmetrical constructions of subjectivity and humanity within the regime of human rights that inflects its visual narration; and (3) I consider the possibilities for agency and healing that implicate at once the narrator, performer, and spectator in a quest for political justice. Together these dimensions exemplify the humanitarian impulse at the heart of Muktijuddho cinema.

Aesthetics and Infrastructure of Muktijuddho Cinema

The cinematic dramatization of the Muktijuddho in socially engaged films depends as much on filmic infrastructure as on the visual narrative. Infrastructures of production and exhibition tend to be restricted by national and global regimes of finance and of knowledge. Furthermore, the aesthetic form of presenting the narrative through moving images, replete with shooting and editing mechanisms, guides the viewer's "directionality of observation" (Fuhrmann 2017, 253). Like *Bish Kanta* and *Rising Silence*, Ferdousi's *Jonmo Shathi* is also a hybrid documentary. Sponsored jointly by Ekattor Television and Liberation War Museum, Ferdousi completed *Jonmo Shathi* within one year. She attributes this speed to the support she received from the sponsors, alluding to both the necessity and urgency of the topic and its past erasures in national history. The film premiered simultaneously at Star Multiplex in Dhaka and at important film festivals throughout Bangladesh, including the Dhaka International Film Festival, and internationally at festivals in Mumbai, Kerala, and Patna. It won the National Film Award in 2016, the same year it was released.

Ferdousi's film joins those of Akhtar and Boby, discussed in previous chapters, in falling within the art cinema trajectory; their production and exhibition are linked to and determined by the infrastructure of socially engaged cinema in Bangladesh. In production and distribution, *Jonmo Shathi* stands out among these films because of the infrastructural support it received. For the most part, these films are entrepreneurial endeavors. They are made in 16 mm, or using a Handycam Camcorder, in the case of Boby. They follow a realist aesthetic, and they were screened primarily at film festivals and on television. Their democratic production and distribution prioritize the dual importance of accessibility and authenticity. Meghna Guhathakurta (2003), feminist scholar, activist, and daughter of martyred intellectual Jotirmoy Guhathakurta, writes about Akhtar's *Shilalipi*, "The effectiveness of the film lies much in the creative imagination of the director and the sincere and hard work of most of the actors." In this statement,

Guhathakurta affirms the Muktijuddho aesthetic of the film, which includes Akhtar's casting choices—cultural activists and members of the intelligentsia, many of whom have direct experiential links to Muktijuddho—who give credence to the film's weighty content and place it within the genre of national- and film society–movement inspired cinema. The film is part of a broader epistemological and historical project of political justice, and its aesthetic choices and format attest to it.

The same characteristics of realism are at work in Akhtar's *Rina Brown*, whose title character is played by Akhtar's own daughter, Proma Paboni. In a reflection of the film the reviewer quotes Akhtar: "I will not be satisfied until I have a film that perfectly captures the essence of '71, which the next generation can look at as the definitive film." There is a disjuncture here of course between the realist pedagogy that Akhtar alludes to and a more critical approach to the relationship between realism, nationalism, and creating a decolonizing record of violence. For as we have seen in earlier chapters, the notion of the "essence of '71" (*shadhinotar chetona*) can be deployed and coded as an elite class consciousness even as Akhtar's Muktijuddho films engender a more nuanced rendering of gender and sexuality and one that is evident in the traumatic realist aesthetic and pedagogy of her films (Dabashi, 2006, 21). The reviewer adds:

> What she [Akhtar] said echoed in the voice of Proma Paboni, her daughter playing the lead role in "Rina Brown." "The young generation is honestly tired of the numerous cash-grabs in the guise of patriotic films. To us, what happened in '71 is not as important as it should be. We tend to look forward to the future rather than the past and the facts being politically misused does not help either." Proma, while having worked in films before, is making her first appearance in a lead role in a film. ("Team Rina Brown" 2017)

Although many of the aesthetic decisions made in filming, casting, and distribution of socially engaged films about the Muktijuddho were originally driven by finances, these decisions often imprint the films as critically important. A documentary about Alamgir Kabir, the monumental figure in the Bangladeshi freedom struggle and cinema, and recognized as a founder of the film society movement in Bangladesh, reveals how he frequently lacked funds to complete projects and the staff and crew worked without compensation (Kawsar Chowdhury 2015). Another review of Akhtar's filmography states, "Despite the obstacles faced during the making of the film, including not raising funds and being able to solely cast seasoned actors, Shameem Akhtar feels this has enriched the overall experience. Describing the newcomers in the film she said, 'Some of these people have never been

filmed before, and they have brought fresh perspectives to their characters'"
(Bhuiyan 2016). Taken together, it is clear that experiencing critical Muktijuddho cinema requires a more nuanced understanding and engagement
with the intersection of infrastructure, production, circulation, and mode
of "seeing."

In writing about early postindependent Africa, Larkin (2019) shows that
media production and circulation were maintained by local governments
and international donors who influenced the production of higher-quality
cinema for elite international audiences. This trend was followed by small
entrepreneurs and NGO professionals, whose low-budget productions were
distributed locally through informal networks. Larkin demonstrates that
the history and impact of African cinema is layered—that is, the emergence
of these nationalist, auteurist, NGO-driven cinema genres defies identification as a linear progression and instead coexists in a composite and diverse
ecology (113). Film in Bangladesh followed a similar layered evolution and
one on which I elaborated in the Introduction. The appetite for more weighty
and cultural nationalist films that appealed to the urban elite overlapped but
was somewhat supplanted by increasing commercial, auteurist, NGO, and
entrepreneurial productions becoming available to wider audiences. Several factors were at work here. Tax policies benefited cinema halls in rural
areas, leading to a wider distribution in those regions that previously had
had limited access to film. Concurrently, cinema halls in the cities found
themselves competing with modes of home entertainment that were becoming ubiquitous in the late 1970s and early 1980s—satellite television, VHS,
VCDs, and DVDs. The films emerging from the alternative cinema genre in
the 1980s and beyond were sometimes shown in the cinema halls but also
in private screenings in cultural and educational institutes or select gatherings. These films were considered more genteel and artistic renderings of
what Hoek (2014) calls a "national modernity for the Bengali middle class"
(19). By the 1980s, however, that gentility had simultaneously given way to
a wider popular and more commercial tradition whose aim was to appeal to
the masses. An article in the popular film magazine *Chitrali* (1977), featuring interviews with leading actors of the time, captures the sense of melancholy that accompanied this (d)evolution. Stars of popular cinema in Bangladesh lament the loss of the golden age yet celebrate the possibilities of
Muktijuddho cinema. Golam Mostafa in this article points to early high-
nationalist cinema such as *Titas Ekti Nodir Nam* (*A River Called Titash*, 1973),
Dhire Bohe Meghna (*Quiet Flows the Meghna*, 1973), and *Shurjokonna* (*Daughter of the Sun*, 1975) as reflecting national pride in the industry. Akhter Hossain expresses pride in the industry's development in a free country liberated
from West Pakistan colonial dominance, where free thinking and expression
could lead to boundless possibilities. In contrast, renowned actor Ujjal points

out how the commercial aspect to cinema has overrun the artistic possibilities and that free thinking has been replaced with imitation of more commercially successful Indian and Western filmography. Actors Sohel Rana and Rosy Samad agree with Ujjal's criticisms and express hopes for better days for the industry—better stories, writers, and directors. Film critic Anupam Hayat affirms these criticisms and argues that the degradation of the industry—largely due to "new money" investors lacking culture or critical aesthetic/moral sensibility—is linked to capitalist consumption and erosion of not only skill, talent, and training but also the "true spirit" of nationalist struggle (2011, 42).

This shift from the golden age of Bengali cinema also marks the emergence of the parallel cinema movement in Bangladesh, which is distinct from industry cinema and the FDC establishment. It is associated with Alamgir Kabir and the film appreciation courses he inaugurated in the Bangladesh Film Archive in 1981. Inspired by great Bengali filmmakers, Italian neorealists, and the French New Wave, Kabir made a mark through his own modernist and realist style of art cinema. His students started to make 16 mm films outside of the FDC bureaucracy. This format was cheaper and allowed for more innovation, and these films screened outside at cultural programs and institutions. One such program is the Goethe-Institut Bangladesh's "Through Her Eyes—A Space to Watch and Discuss Films with Women Filmmakers of Bangladesh," produced in collaboration with the International Film Initiative of Bangladesh (IFIB). "Through Her Eyes" screens films monthly and provides an opportunity for discussion between the filmmakers and film enthusiasts, students, academics, film professionals, funding agencies, broadcasters, rights groups, and journalists. It was at one of these events that Akhtar's *Shilalipi* premiered. A review of the event praises the film and its screening:

> The screenplay of the film is beautifully written. . . . The whole war depicted from a young and independent single mother's perspective living in urban Bangladesh back in the '70s has not only set standards for upcoming female filmmakers of Bangladesh, but for the whole war filmmaker community of our country. After the film was screened Akhtar came onto the stage and answered questions from the audience. She shared what challenges she faced as a female filmmaker who started her career in the '90s, how she did not have enough funding to shoot this film on 35mm film, and how hard it is to get financing and sponsors for films. She told Dhaka Tribune's Showtime that she wants to keep making films and is currently working on another film which is based on rape victims of the 1971 Liberation War. (*Dhaka Tribune* 2019)

Here, again, the composite ecology of cinematic infrastructure to production and exhibition becomes evident. Ferdousi echoes these sentiments in a personal interview about her own work and position as a woman filmmaker (Ferdousi 2020). She states that despite her training and skill she had to work doubly hard to prove herself as a filmmaker. The recent government grants have certainly helped entrepreneurial filmmakers, she says, and she has the support of Ekattor Television, where she is employed. She maintains that there is a pedagogical market and demand for films about the Liberation War, and her inspiration came precisely from that desire: to educate the Bangladeshi people about their own nationalist history and its erasures/silences. The inspiration, infrastructure, screening, and viewing cultures indelibly shape the genre of Muktijuddho cinema and its liberatory and humanistic pedagogy.

Articulating the Human in Muktijuddho Cinema

Socially engaged films by and about women share a rubric with the infrastructures and visual narratives of "human rights cinema." In this section, I explore how Muktijuddho cinema about women extends beyond nationalist and becomes part of the broader transnational discourse of human rights. Human rights discourse traditionally has been under the purview of disciplines such as legal studies, political science, and international relations. Increasingly, scholars in the humanities have joined the conversation, asking about the aesthetic, visual, and cultural renderings of human rights principles, rhetoric, and politics. Current discourses of human rights also make use of the language of moral superiority, protection, and benevolence. Instead, I highlight that in cinematic realms human rights is a diverse repertoire with multiple relationships to power and critiques, violence, and memory. This section looks at the production and circulation of visual cultures and elucidates critical perspectives on differential renderings of human lives, subjectivity, social desire, and agency. I explore how human rights narrations tend to emplot questions of women's victimization and suffering and how those perspectives map onto structures of political power and action.

The disciplinary tensions between art and science, subjectivity and objectivity, and the aesthetics and pedagogical value of the filmed subject have been long standing, particularly in visual anthropology. Calling for disciplinary rigor, El Guindi (2004, 186–187) concludes that anthropologists must do anthropology, including visual ethnography, whereas filmmakers should do film with all its attendant technologies. Humanists, on the other hand, blur the distinctions between aesthetics and politics by suggesting that the condition of the political—which, as we have seen in the previous discussion, also encompasses the infrastructural—sometimes is what enables or disables artistic expression (Moten 2003; Mengesha 2017). This leaves us with critical questions that strike at the heart of this book: How can we conceptualize the ethicopolitics of human rights in such a way that it cannot be reduced to a humanitarian "right to intervene" in the affairs of others? What political interests drive state, civil society, artist, and activist demands for representation over various narrations of human rights? How do filmic practices provide a space for critical reflection on human rights institutions and practice? How might memorials and narrations have an immediate effect on minority groups affected by human rights atrocities? While in the global intellectual arena the scope of human rights seems to prioritize a "crisis narration," rethinking its historic, aesthetic, and political abstractions not only offers us a new avenue to imagine its many layers but also can provide us with a productive scope to frame art, politics, and varied modes of suffering and living.

Critical feminist scholars such as Parikh (2017) and Schaffer and Smith (2004) have probed the so-called binary between aesthetics and politics and have added the moral, aesthetic, and ethical aspects of culture in our understanding of "the human" and "the political." They trace human rights discourses and practices as multidimensional domains that intersect at critical points, intertwining one another in an ethical relationship that illuminates and frames claims for recognition, inclusion, dissent, and social justice. At the same time, such embodiments present deep problems: That suffering and trauma must have occurred, have been visually displayed, and have been verbally testified to—often in graphic terms—for the recognition of that suffering to elicit an organized response is a troubling set of criteria for human rights discourse.

Black feminist scholars have been critical in tracing the evolution of concepts such as human rights, suffering and justice, bringing particular emphasis to the historical double standard in institutionalizing such discourses when the majority of the world's populations—emphatically Black people—were considered to be in the purview of neither the human nor the rights (Hartman 1997; Wynter and McKittrick 2015; Spillers et al. 2007). Based on her readings of slave narratives, and regarding the condition of Black people in human rights discourse, Hartman posits:

The discourse of humanism at the very least was double-edged since the life and liberty they held in esteem were racial entitlements formerly denied them. In short, the selective recognition of humanity that undergirded the relations of chattel slavery had not considered them men deserving of rights or freedom. Thus in taking up the language of humanism, they seized upon that which had been used against and denied them (1997, 5).

Following this line of thinking, Weheliye has called for "a recalibration" of our understanding of "the category of the human in western modernity" (2014, 5).

The dual standard in recognizing humanity is laid bare in *Jonmo Shathi*, when Ferdousi locates her first birth companion—Sudhir, son of Birangona Tepree Barman, in Thakurgaon. Curiously, Tepree and Sudhir are also featured in Gazi's *Rising Silence*; yet, methodologically and pedagogically, Ferdousi's representation of self and interlocutors are quite different. Visually, the lush landscapes of rural Bangladesh, the long road symbolizing the journey to get to the subjects of the film, and the shots of stormy skies contrasted with sunny blue ones ring familiar to a Muktijuddho cinema aesthetic. The driving narrative of *Jonmo Shathi*, however, remains the journey, the search. Unlike in *Rising Silence*, we do not witness the researcher/filmmaker/activist participating in the storytelling act; neither is the story about Tepree's encounters with the Pakistani army or the razakars central to the plot. Rather, her surroundings tell the story of her marginalization, isolation, and destitution. Even though the current government in Bangladesh instituted a stipend for Birangona women, neither Tepree nor her family have been able to draw on it. Ramesh Barman, her brother, tells Ferdousi that the stipend is "gobbled up by the chairman of their village." Tepree— the war heroine—is introduced first inside her meager living arrangement, a small bamboo hut with a tin roof. She is seated on a makeshift wooden bed, wearing a faded green cotton sari, and her gray hair is shorn close to her scalp, reminiscent of instances where women's hair is cut off in an act of humiliation. The camera pans to her bare, scuffed feet with a broken toenail. She looks out at the door, which is ajar, letting sunlight stream in. The cinematic framing of Tepree underscores her degraded humanity. Evidently, she has been neither recognized nor valued for her heroism.

Gradually, Ferdousi introduces us to the family members with whom Tepree resides: her brother Ramesh, son Sudhir, daughter-in-law Basanti, and granddaughter Jonota. As Ferdousi talks to Tepree and her family members, the story of Sudhir and his mother is patched together. Tepree was held in a Pakistani army camp for six to seven months during the war as collateral in exchange of the safety of her family, who, as part of the Hindu minority, was more vulnerable to attack by the Pakistani army. When she returned to her family, however, her husband refused to take her back. Ferdousi asks how Tepree felt when, soon after her return, Sudhir was born. She replies, "I felt really good when I saw him the first time; I love him a lot." Despite the

Figure 5.2 Tepree Barman at her home (*Jonmo Shathi* [dir. Shabnam Ferdousi, 2016]).

community's hatred toward babies born of wartime rape, Tepree's own father felt differently. He said to Tepree, "Daughter, don't kill this child. After I die, he will look after you. This child will feed you. It will be your future."

Sudhir is seen as a lone figure, a community outcast, in the film. He describes himself as living hand to mouth, driving a *van gaari* ten hours a day. He tells of a lonely childhood full of hardship, working in the homes of rich families in exchange for food. "We did not have that kind of a family; people hated me. They called me 'son of Punjabi.'" Long shots of him staring emptily across the lush green landscape, looking deep into the sunset, punctuate his conversations with Ferdousi. The patriotic song "Ek Shagor Rokter Binimoye" ("Freedom Gained through an Ocean of Blood Spill"), by Sabina Yasmin, is the ringtone of his cell phone. Another scene depicts Sudhir's daughter Jonota doing schoolwork. Ironically, she reads from a textbook, "Those who love and devote themselves to the welfare of their country and nation, they are the true representatives of mankind." Ferdousi is not subtle in the use of cultural codes to denote Sudhir's outsider status. Sudhir shares how he cannot eat fish because he is repulsed by the smell. This refers to the saying, "*maach e bhaat e Bangali*" (fish and rice are the essence of a Bengali)—in contrast to a common cultural knowledge in South Asia that Punjabis do not eat or cook fish, whereas it makes up an important part of the diet of Bengalis/East Pakistanis. Sudhir eats all kinds of meat—even beef, despite being raised Hindu. He shares that he was always seen as resembling Punjabis rather than Bengalis, given his wheatish complexion, impressive height, muscular build, and angular facial features.

The precarious conditions of the survivors of sexual violence and the Juddhoshishus born to them is further reinforced in *Jonmo Shathi* by Barrister Dr. Tureen Afroz, a prosecutor for the international criminal tribunal. "There was a time when war babies were killed. The sentiment was, 'I can't catch the Pakistani father, or the *razakars*, the child is theirs, result of rape, let's finish them off.' That is why the government was forced to send these children abroad." It is interesting that Ferdousi—in what may reveal a certain pro–Awami League tone—chooses to omit mention of Sheikh Mujib's pronouncement that Juddhoshishus had tainted Pakistani blood and, therefore, needed to be flushed out of the nation.

Ferdousi's film furthers the conversation about the aesthetic, visual, and political renderings of human rights principles and rhetoric. Following Weheliye's cue about understanding alternate modes of the category of the human in Western modernity, the film helps in centralizing critical questions shrouding the intersections of aesthetics, politics, and responsibility. With a critical perspective, *Jonmo Shathi* and the other woman-centered Muktijuddho films we have discussed articulate other ways of being human outside of institutionalized codifications. More explicitly, they illuminate the differential humanity (or, specifically, human and Muktijoddha, human and Juddhoshishu, human and Birangona) outside of institutionalized legal and political frameworks, which seem to foreground notions of crisis narrative or put it within a framework of resistance/agency. At the same time, these films help us think about what constitutes the human; they open us up to different modes of being, through other frameworks, that advance a racialized, gendered reading—and the possible intellectual and political implications of those differences. They help generate an ethical or disruptive archive for victims of the 1971 war and encourage potentially noninterventionist viewing practices and calls for justice and responsibility for the victimized.

Method, Pedagogy, and Grammar of Muktijuddho Cinema

In *Scenes of Subjection*, Hartman (1997) writes about how routine descriptions of the bodily violence inflicted on slaves can leave readers/viewers, perhaps, too familiar with the foundational violence of slavery. She draws attention to the schematic ways audiences are "called upon to participate in such scenes" (3). "Are we witnesses who confirm the truth of what happened in the face of the world-destroying capacities of pain, . . . or are we voyeurs fascinated with and repelled by exhibitions of terror and suffering? What does the exposure of the violated body yield?" Questioning whether such routine representations are depicted merely to give spectators the opportunity for self-reflection, she draws attention to "the precariousness of empathy and the uncertain line between witness and spectator" (4). Of course, this begs the question of how one gives expression to such mass atrocities without further sensationalizing the suffering of Black people, numbing the spectators, and facilitating the attendant narcissistic identification. In her own work, Hartman states that she chooses to look "elsewhere" and to defamiliarize what has become routine. Her purpose is to illuminate the terror of the mundane and the quotidian rather than exploit the shocking spectacle. She shows the terror and the violence in many registers, including the normalized and the celebrated. For instance, she suggests that "benevolent correctives and declarations of slave humanity intensified the brutal exercise of power upon the captive body rather than ameliorating the chattel condition" (5). A recognition of humanity in certain grand and small gestures led to further oppression, she asserts; instead of reckoning with the constitution of the slave humanity, it has served to reinforce the paternalist master-slave relationship.

Hartman asks, "How does one tell the story of an elusive emancipation and a travestied freedom?" (10). In posing this question, she, in part, draws attention to the process by which historical narratives emerge, particularly regarding stories of subalterns. Archives, conditional as they are, can determine the narration of history, a national past, and a representation of power relations. Citing the provisional nature of archives, Hartman claims to read them against the grain, hoping to provide a different account of the past yet remaining cognizant that the circumstances in which she works are limiting. A full recovery of the slave experience is never possible, and the danger of reproducing the authorial narrative is ever present. Her work entails "excavations at the margins" and acknowledges silences and exclusions. "In this regard, the effort to reconstruct the history of the dominated is not discontinuous with dominant accounts or official history but, rather, is a struggle within and against the constraints and silences imposed by the nature of the archive—the system that governs the appearance of statements and generates social meaning" (11). It is a resistant reading within a circumscribed history and context that hints at something aberrant even as it complies with dominant modes of reading. Like narratives of slaves, those of war victims are overdetermined, yet the work of reconstruction highlights relations of power, voice, and the authority of speech in public performances of trauma. The end of the war, the gaining of independence, failed to bring freedom; instead, flawed reconstruction practices stand for presumed emancipation and its failures. Nevertheless, these imperfect glimpses and interpretations offer some semblance of the experiences of the survivors and forge paths, however uncertain, for a "just responsibility"—a term coined by feminist philosopher Brooke Ackerly, who defines it as responsibility rooted in the principles of human rights. Just responsibility intertwines location, mode, and the action of political actors (who are "we" in a political community?) within a global landscape for transformation (2018, xii). Women-centric Muktijuddho cinema, such as Akhtar's trilogy, and others discussed in this book is both justice-driven as well as deploying an architecture of regenerative humanistic encounter that is decidedly different from an interventionist, or voyeuristic, human rights praxis.

In the realm of cinematic representation of gendered violence, the environments in which rape stories are told are often settings that yield a social life of their own, scripting and enfolding the narratives within a racialized and gendered visual grid. As the work of Nayanika Mookherjee (2015) has shown, stories of rape are continually invoked in public formats that can feel exploitive. She wrote of the betrayal of exposure when human rights activists asked a group of Birangona women to travel to Dhaka under the impression that they were going to meet with the prime minister. Instead, the women were made to provide testimonials to a UN committee. The testimonials are meant to stamp their authenticity and are held up as displays of agency and resistance, but Mookherjee sees them as instrumental or transactional social interactions, whereby the stories are consumed and appropriated by social justice institutions and larger audiences. It has given rise to an economy that traffics in morality, respect, and expectations regarding Birangona status in society; it commodifies their stories and conducts business with their reenactments of trauma. Mookherjee traces how rehabilitation of Birangona women has historically served as a trope of modernity for the new nation of Bangladesh. It arguably continues now, within development regimes denoting women's empowerment, dispersing sovereign power among social workers and development agents to carry on the work of rehabilitating/empowering. Mookherjee suggests these reenactments of victimhood masculinize the Birangona by ascribing heroism, as opposed to the failure to enact (i.e., remaining inactive), which feminizes them. The visual grid enables a narration that frequently characterizes the Birangona by way of her departure, such that she remains the specter, the ghost, the absent-present. There is a mechanical reproduction and circulation of these audiovisuals within a savior paradigm, a characteristic of human rights discourse. Mookherjee asks the critical question: Do human rights stories "have space to accommodate complexities of birangonas' experiences?" (2015, 262).

A case in point involves Sudhir Barman, from *Jonmo Shathi*, who was asked to escort his mother, Tepree Barman, to an event called "Rising Path of War Heroines." This event, organized by Bangladesh Nari Shangbadik Kendro at the Jatiyo Press Club Auditorium, took place on December 13, 2014—the middle of the month that celebrates Bangladesh's Victory Day, which is always filled with commemorations, memorials, seminars, and festivals, often recognizing wartime survivors. Tepree was on the schedule to be honored for her sacrifice for the nation. *Jonmo Shathi* follows the mother and son to the event, where we witness the excess of the nationalist narrative, the limits/fragility of its construction, and the differential granting of humanity to the liberated Bangladeshis, specifically the Birangona and the Juddhoshishu. Sudhir is wearing a lungi with a jacket—it is winter in Bangladesh. The lungi denotes his working-class background, whereas the jacket alludes to the solemnness of the event. Sudhir's ghostlike figure wafts through the Jatiyo Press Club. He looks perplexed, uncomfortable. He is seated alone in a sea of empty chairs, toward the back of the room. The camera pans to the abyss of his empty eyes. It seems Ferdousi has arranged for him to speak at the event even though he is hesitant to do so, unsure what the program even entails. Eventually he takes the podium—again, a lone figure among the polished, well dressed, presumably articulate experts seated on stage poised to make important remarks. He narrates:

> My mother has brought me up since I was a child. My grandfather died when I was little. I couldn't continue with my studies after his death. I had to work in other people's homes in exchange of rice. It was impossible for me to continue my studies. Most people are aware of their father's identify but not me. I do not know who my father is—I cannot tell you who he is because I do not know. When the question was posed everyone could answer—but not I. What else is there to say?

His voice trails off; his eyes are misty as he slowly exits the stage, walking behind the long table where the experts are seated. Visually, this is a dramatic scene, bringing into sharp relief the histories of inequality and who constitutes the human, the citizen. An against-the-grain reading of the constitutive narrative illuminates Sudhir—the so-called subject of the justice project of 1971—in his peripheral status. His voice matters only when called on; he is not seated with the "experts" on stage, and he does not fit within the contours of the human rights event. He is granted agency and voice only upon being summoned and is swiftly stripped of it upon return to his village, where he disappears again from the political life of "human rights advocacy" in Dhaka. His voice does not fit the assertive narrative of resistance/agency; in fact, his speech is despondent and self-effacing. There is no conversation, no engagement surrounding his question—"What else is there to say?" There is only an uncomfortable transition that accompanies his exit.

In the landscape of urban, neoliberal, and genteel human rights advocacy, a newer hierarchy has emerged: that of the experts in relation to those

Figure 5.3 Sudhir Barman at the Jatiyo Press Club Auditorium, December 13, 2014 (*Jonmo Shathi* [dir. Shabnam Ferdousi, 2016]).

who are called on to testify at the will of the experts. In a comparative vein, Hartman (2020) examines how the discourse of rights within the context of slavery has been used to facilitate newer relations of domination. She points to the construction of the proprietorial self vis-à-vis the pedagogical and legislative efforts to remake the former slave into "rational, acquisitive, and responsible individuals" (6). Instead of liberation, these efforts sandwich former slaves between "modes of servitude and racial subjection" (6). The glaring questions here are whether the enslaved population's rights can possibly be realized and whether the term "human" can be applied to all. Can a Birangona still be human if she does not reenact her trauma in a scripted manner? Can the Juddhoshishu integrate into the nation if his story does not resonate with its forward-looking mission? Tepree was summoned to signify a certain commemoration of her emancipation and Sudhir to testify about his belonging to the liberated nation. But rather than place them into triumphant scripted roles, the efforts to remake both into free citizens only illuminates newer registers of subjection as these so-called free citizens disrupt the nationalist and human rights archive.

In an interview with Hazel Carby about her 2019 book *Imperial Intimacies*, Hartman reiterates the methodological value of excavation and interpretation of archival materials. She speaks to specific scenes in Carby's book that are written in the third person that address experiences she may have had in her childhood. "The narrative advances on dual tracks and the story oscillates between 'the girl' and the 'I' of the adult narrator, a scholar and researcher, in search of the pieces of her past and reckoning with what it means to be black and British" (Hartman 2020). By moving from the auto-biographical to the third person, then, Carby is able to tell the experiences of a Black British subject growing up with the weight of colonialism and slavery tracing its roots and subsequent webs across geographies. Hartman asks, "These distinct narrative perspectives are related to issues of withholding and disclosing stories and with disassociation and traumatic memory. Where does pain lodge and who is responsible for narrating it?" Carby's response to Hartman is as follows:

> There was one moment when I was writing about something I discovered in the National Archives and you said to me, "Why don't you dwell on that moment, the moment when you actually found that? Put yourself there, what were you thinking?" Oh, I knew what I was thinking! But I hadn't written about any of that. So when you said to me, "dwell," you were also asking me to think about my own investment. You were asking me to think about how I was shaped by the history and by the act of finding out what I was finding out, by hearing stories I wasn't meant to hear. It opened the floodgates, in some ways. So I decided to begin the book there, with what I call "the question." (Carby quoted in Hartman 2020)

Similar to Carby's narrative choice, Ferdousi enters the story of 1971 through a dual first- and third-person encounter—that of her own birth, which is part of the legacy of trauma, and that of her search for birth companions. Ferdousi, too, seems called to mindfulness, to "dwelling"—and it is these moments of encounter that make *Jonmo Shathi* so compelling and that reveal the impossibility of recuperation yet, at the same time, the value of attempting it, however fragmentary. Sudhir's speech disrupts the business as usual narration of survivor stories at the Victory Day celebration; and in his unanswered question and exit from the frame there is a hint of what an alternative seeing of the Juddhoshishu might look like.

Entering the story as a companion, someone on a parallel yet vastly different life circumstance from the Juddhoshishus, Ferdousi opens up the structural marginalization of the victims of war and the possibilities of their humanity. Methodologically, she stitches together a narrative for her birth companions by following the leads she excavates through visits to hospitals, orphanages, law offices, NGOs, and research institutions and by talking to activists and witnesses to the atrocities committed in 1971. *Jonmo Shathi* is the rendition of a search, a quest to recover the stories of the children and to elaborate on their forgotten, rejected, missing, cast out status in postindependence Bangladesh. Each "recovery" is a dwelling—a pause, an elaboration of the underside of the glorious independence story. The film serves as an archive into glimpses of an incomplete and erased history of a foundational national antagonism. *Jonmo Shathi* opens with images of the Bangladeshi flag and the iconic National Parliament House , contrasted with war footage. The film's first interviewee is Ferdousi's own father, who narrates the trauma endured by the family and the nation and points out that, unlike pre-1971 generations, Ferdousi was "born a free citizen." As we learn in the course of the film, that is clearly not the case for the three birth companions she locates.

Ferdousi's quest takes her first to Holy Family Red Crescent (then Red Cross) Hospital. She meets with its director, who informs her that "no real information is available" because all records are discarded four years after birth. Nevertheless, the neonatal ward is still there, and we witness the camera spanning the white halls and neat row of beds. It is a haunting scene of absence and loss as Ferdousi recalls her missing birth mates. She is able to locate a nurse, Shanti D'Costa, who worked at Holy Family during and after the war and had more recently moved on to a private clinic. D'Costa reveals that she witnessed the birth of forty-five hundred Juddhoshishus at Holy Family. "They were kept separate from normal babies," she explains, emphasizing the distinction made at the time between children of war, and children born to civilians. These babies were also kept apart from their mothers and not breastfed. The nurses fed them separately per the orders of the hospital management, who arranged for their adoptions abroad.

Ferdousi's next interview is with a researcher, Shahina Hafiz, at her home. Hafiz shares the whereabouts of a living Birangona and her son in Mymensingh. Hafiz discusses the rejection this child experienced from the wider community and, in turn, his own rejection of his mother out of humiliation. Each encounter we witness between Ferdousi and her interviewees unfolds as an archive of information, where she, along with her audience, discovers, excavates, and interprets. The infrastructure of the film and its visual narrative together offer up this pedagogical opportunity for the viewers to go on a collective journey of political transformation.

The camera continues to follow Ferdousi, who travels by rickshaw to the Chotomoni Nibash (Baby Home) Orphanage in Azimpur, Dhaka, which had aided in adoptions of Juddhoshishus post-1971 until the practice was halted in 1975. There she meets with the subcaretaker, Selina Akhter. Neither Akhter nor the current director (whom Akhter calls on the phone) are able to verify any information. Ferdousi, though despondent, refuses to admit defeat and continues on her quest. Her next stop is Dr. M. A. Hassan, freedom fighter and researcher for the War Crimes Fact Finding Committee. He talks about three children of war he came across at Dhaka University campus. In

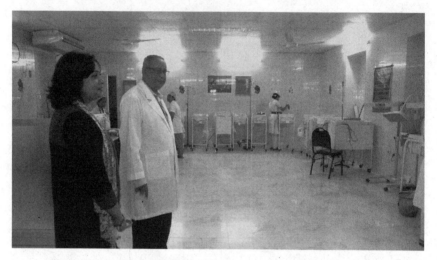

Figure 5.4 At the Holy Family Red Crescent Hospital neonatal ward
(*Jonmo Shathi* [dir. Shabnam Ferdousi, 2006]).

two different families, the mothers had kept their daughters' identities as
Juddhoshishus secret because they feared ostracism, particularly in marriage prospects. The third converted to Christianity, perhaps hoping to escape the social scrutiny of dominant Muslim cultural norms. In all instances, however, Hassan opines that the families did not accept the children. "In
the post-war reconstruction era, the question of the war babies was dumped
to the back-burner, rendered inconsequential among other bigger social problems."

We follow Ferdousi next to the social service agency Caritas, where she
meets with volunteer and pastor Richard William Timm, affectionately
known as Father Timm. He narrates stories about the adoptions of fifty-odd
Juddhoshishus arranged by the Mymensingh District Commissioner. The
Birangonas were placed in an old building in Dhaka; Ferdousi visits the site,
and we see the large, airy, empty rooms. Even though abortion was (and is)
illegal, under the special provision granted by the government, many pregnancies—even later term—were aborted. Sisters of Charity, a wing of Mother Teresa's Catholic institution, intervened and worked side by side with
International Planned Parenthood facilitating adoptions. When Ferdousi
visits the offices of Sisters of Charity in Old Dhaka, she is informed that no
figures could be released due to some concerns in the postwar period that
orphanages were "selling babies" abroad.

Leaving no stone unturned, Ferdousi takes us to meet with renowned
activist Maleka Khan at the Women's Rehabilitation Center, the first organization established for the rehabilitation of the survivors of the war's sex-

Figure 5.5 At the Shirajganj Women's Rehabilitation Center
(*Jonmo Shathi* [dir. Shabnam Ferdousi, 2006]).

ual violence. Khan talks about the activists and cultural icons Begum Sufia Kamal and Begum Badrunnessa Ahmed, who formed this organization. She shares that women who were without children or were separated from their children found it easier to recover from the trauma and reintegrate into society. "They felt relieved that danger had been evaded." In the Sirajganj Women's Rehabilitation Center, Ferdousi meets with three female staff members—who, again, are not able to offer any specific information about the children but reiterated that the whole experience was shrouded in secrecy and shame and that "no one [Birangona women or the staff] disclosed any information about the children of the Pak army because it was a matter of dignity, a matter of survival for the women."

Lilian Mengesha (2017), a critical race and feminist scholar, also addresses the notion of "dwelling in the moment" in research related to past trauma that cannot be fully recovered. Mengesha discusses the work of Guatemalan artist Regina José Galindo, who, through dramatic performance, evokes the mass rape and genocide of Mayan women and the more recent femicide against Latin American women who are considered "disposable." In her 2005 video performance, PERRA (bitch), Galindo inscribes the word *PERRA* on her own body with a blunt paring knife, thereby evoking the continuum of violence against some women and the "remnant of an embodied archive of injury." The femicides of the early 2000s to present, Galindo elucidates, are connected to the violent history against Mayan women. By staging this historical continuum, the artist crystallizes the temporal possibilities and connections between spectatorship and violence.

When Mengesha meets Galindo in 2013, eight years after the making of *PERRA*, the scar from those incisions symbolizes "a wound of the past," denoting that the historical and the social event are coeval. The scar now takes the form of a ghost, suggests Mengesha, citing the work of Avery Gordon: "Something lost, or barely visible, or seemingly not there to our supposedly well-trained eyes, makes itself known or apparent to us, in its own way" (1997, 8). Conjuring this ghost is reminiscent of the way Sudhir appears at the Victory Day event, wafting in and out of view, ill-fitted like his jacket in the landscape of urban NGO-based human rights advocacy experts and clients, disrupting the regimen of the human rights speech with his ephemeral presence and swift exit.

The metaphor of the ghost recurs in Mengesha's commentary on *PERRA*. Using the work of Dominick LaCapra, Mengesha reads the video performance as a mode for secondary witnesses of "working-through" and "acting out" historical trauma involving "mourning and melancholy" and a "relation to the past that recognizes its difference from the present—simultaneously remembering and taking leave of or actively forgetting it" (LaCapra 1999, quoted in Mengesha 2017, 142). In doing so, Mengesha offers a way for spectators and performers to be coevally implicated in a productive relation to the performance/viewing of trauma. Mengesha develops the important concept of "defecting witness," which encompasses this measurement of time in one's own viewing practices of trauma and recognizes one's own partialities in reinterpreting the visual enactment. Mengesha draws on the work of art historian Amelia Jones on a queer feminist theory of durationality, which "destabilize[s] meanings, assumptions, and binaries in favor of uncertainty, dispersal, and disorientation" (142). Durationality is about slowing down our interpretations of the visual and paying attention to process and embodiment. Importantly, this theoretical framework "resists dualities of subject/object and audience/performer such that conditions of desire, repulsion, and vulnerability are neither evacuated nor unidirectional but rather diffused" (142). Spectators and performers become one in the process through an affective mutuality, yet the distance to the past and the relationality between the two entities are not obscured. Spectators are defecting witnesses as they shape an ethical mode of viewing difficult art/visual enactments, and rather than passively or aggressively consuming and intervening, they shift to a more ethical shared responsibility. Mengesha suggests that this shift from the certainty of details toward an "ethical uncertainty" allows the viewer to walk alongside another's pain and share the burden (144). This shift that is enabled by the process of defection is "the [affect] of witnessing difficult performance as part of an act of falling away from one allegiance toward another," she says. The performance inspires viewers/performers to (re)experience the weight of the historical suffering but with an awareness of the distance from it. Mengesha cautions that the performance is not a copy of the trauma but an enactment of it; it can project an aura of the gravity but cannot replicate it. "Defecting offers an alternative heuristic for how one might emotionally engage with the residues of excessive violence, or bear what feels unbearable" (145).

This notion of the defecting witness is relevant to our viewing/reading of Monwara Clark, another birth companion to Ferdousi. Clark is a Canadian citizen who returns to Bangladesh to search for her birth records and possibly her birth mother. Per the Bangladesh Abandoned Children (Special Provisions) Order 1972, the first flight taking Juddhoshishus to Canada arrived on July 15, 1972. It carried fifteen children. Clark does not know much about her birth mother other than she was attacked with a bayonet while Clark was in utero. Remarkably, Clark carries an imprint of that attack on her skin. She tells Ferdousi and the other cultural activists present, "I was never born, I don't have a birth certificate." The absence of the birth certificate continues to map trauma in her life as Clark goes through a contentious divorce and her partner claims sole custody of their daughter, Juha, on the grounds that Clark has no family lineage. Clark responds to these challenges with anger and defiance; she stands in stark contrast to the melancholic and ghostlike Sudhir, who asks, "What is the point of thinking and desiring to know about my identity—what will that yield anyway?" Clark is poised—wearing a fuschia *kameez*, a yellow flower tucked into her flowing black tresses—as she demands answers and accountability from bureaucrats and activists she encounters in her search for answers:

Why am I here? Why did this happen? There is no answer, right? For the longest time, I was really angry. I was angry at Bangladesh. I was angry because I am alive. . . . I was angry because they gave me away. Bangladesh gave me away. They could have raised me. They could have given me the same things as your kids have. Why didn't you guys take me? Why am I in Canada? Why couldn't I be like your kids?

Her questions are directed to the filmmaker, the activist, the viewer connecting and implicating all to the process of pedagogical performance and production. Clark literally carries a scar imprinted on her in utero; the visceral and social consequences of it have haunted her whole life with pain and a sense of nonbelonging. Her birth companion, Ferdousi, and the collective community gathered around her on-screen—as well as the off-screen witnesses—are implicated in her demand for answers.

The notion of the defecting witness is akin to Hartman's concept regarding the epistemological limits in writing of the unspeakable and the unknown (2008). In *Scenes of Subjection* (1997), Hartman reveals that while

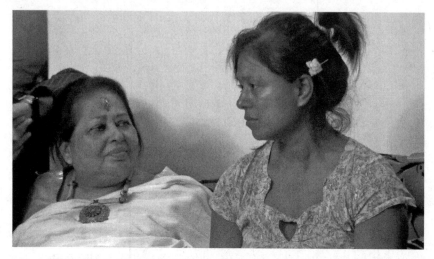

Figure 5.6 Juddhoshishu Monwara Clark with Ferdousi Priyobhashini
(*Jonmo Shathi* [dir. Shabnam Ferdousi, 2006]).

she recognizes "the political utility and ethical necessity of historical fiction," such stories—trafficking between fact, fiction, and fable—afford a
"way of living in the world in the aftermath of catastrophe and devastation"
(3). The essential question she poses about stories that endeavor to represent
the lives of slaves is, "Who does that narrative enable?" (Hartman and Wilderson 2003, 184). Unpacking the notion of "empathic identification," Hartman
points to the ways that slave voices are rendered silent or diminished, dis-
cernable only through appropriation by narrators. "On the one hand, the
slave is the foundation of the national order," she writes. "On the other, the
slave occupies the position of the unthought" (184–185). She calls this trend
"the metanarrative" that attempts "integration into the national project, and
particularly when that project is in crisis, black people are called upon to affirm it" (185).

This selective turn to integrate victims of 1971 who are also otherwise
outcast is noticeable in *Jonmo Shathi*'s illumination of the children of war
in the story of the nation. Specifically, this is illustrated by the story of Shamsunnahar from Habiganj, Madhabpur, the last of Ferdousi's three birth
companions, whom Afroz, the prosecutor for the international criminal tribunal, introduced to Ferdousi. Shamsunnahar's mother, Majeda, gave witness testimony in the trial of Syed Mohammad Kaiser, a convicted war criminal. When Ferdousi arrives in Habiganj, she learns that she cannot meet
Shamsunnahar or Majeda in their home because their identities as Birangona and Juddhoshishu are kept secret from the community—signifying

their inability to publicly acknowledge their true identities and simultane-ously occupy public space or garner recognition in the nation. They meet instead in a secluded bungalow in one of the tea gardens, where Majeda dis-cusses testifying to Kaiser's role as a perpetrator of violence during the war. Years later, Majeda recognized him when he was campaigning to run for political office. He was the razakar who had rounded up Bengalis for mass murder and taken Majeda's father hostage, and he was in the group that ab-ducted her. Majeda was held and tortured in a camp for seven to eight days. Two months later she realized she was pregnant. She shares, "I can't express the pain and suffering of that time." When Ferdousi asked whether she want-ed to have the baby, she poses the question back, "Did I want the baby?" The camera cuts to stormy skies. Majeda returned to her husband a few years later with Shamsunnahar. After marriage, Shamsunnahar's own husband left her when he discovered her identity as a Juddhoshishu. "These things don't remain secret; people talk behind our backs. They say, 'She is a Pun-jabi's child.'"

Ferdousi calculates that Shamsunnahar would have been born in May 1972. Her birth companion's heartrending story unfolds. "I am depressed most of the time. I can't eat [she suffers from goiter]. I am enjoying a cup of tea with you after two years. I don't like my life, I don't like anything. I have never been in love." She continues, "I am not at peace with myself. I can bare-ly think of others." She is barely able to maintain herself, she tells Ferdousi, and cannot even think of having children. Ferdousi probes about whether she ever wanted to know about her birth father. Shamsunnahar looks at flies swarming on a pool of stagnant water. "What do you want from this coun-try?" Ferdousi asks. "I don't want anything," says Shamsunnahar, staring at a pool of pink lotuses—the national flower. She talks about the routine threats of violence she encounters from the community because she accom-panied Majeda when she testified against Kaiser. Her mother is unable to pro-tect her, as she must keep her own identity of Birangona and her daughter's as Juddhoshishu secret for Shamsunnahar to remain within her family and community and to keep her honor intact. Ferdousi extends an invitation to Shamsunnahar—her birth companion—to live with her. Shamsunnahar declines and says she wants to leave the country. It is another sign that there is no space in Bangladesh for Juddhoshishu—not for Sudhir, who quietly exits the stage; not for Clark, who has been exiled to Canada; and not for Sham-sunnahar, who longs to find another place to call home. The film draws to a close with shots of the setting sun in the horizon, gathering clouds. The screen alternates between a melancholic Sudhir gazing into the distance, Sham-sunnahar walking alone across a vast rural landscape, and Clark looking downward, defeated by the system in her efforts to locate a birth certificate.

Figure 5.7 *Juddhoshishu* Shamsunnahar with her mother, Majeda (*Jonmo Shathi* [dir. Shabnam Ferdousi, 2006]).

Conclusion

Hartman's acknowledgment of the limitations of archives presents a tension about her own investment in writing narratives that preserve stories. She says:

> For me, narrating counter-histories of slavery has always been inseparable from writing a history of present. . . . As I understand it, a history of the present strives to illuminate the intimacy of our experience with the lives of the dead, to write our now as it is interrupted by this past, and to imagine a free state, not as the time before captivity or slavery, but rather as the anticipated future of this writing. (2008, 4)

Jonmo Shathi offers reminders of Hartman's caution about narrating counterhistories of captivity and anticipated freedom. In a particularly intense moment in the film, Ferdousi asks Sudhir about growing up without legitimacy (i.e., without a father) in Bangladesh. Sudhir explains that he sought to marry into a family where he could experience the affection of a father. In the next scene, Ferdousi talks about not being able to visit Shamsunnahar at her own home. "I have to meet her at the tea garden, or inside the bungalow in the garden where she arrives covered in a burqa. We meet by the railway tracks or in the paddy fields in secret, in trepidation of the public eye." The camera cuts to a thunderous gray sky. Monwara Clark leaves for Canada empty-handed and with no trace of a birth certificate or family. The anticipated future is always interrupted by its past.

Hartman's methodological clarity in writing a partial yet critical narrative of loss is of great interest to me in my study of the pedagogical and political value of Liberation War cinema by and about women. Hartman and Wilderson discuss specifically the privileged position the visual narratives seem to hold within extant racially classified schema in society. In this arena, they underscore the way the racialization process has operated: Technologies of racialization dispose of bodies, appropriate them as products, and fix them within a visual grid. These optics are at work in reenacting a Muktijuddho ideology that also narrates gendered and sexualized categories that allow only certain visualizations in the service of the nation. Turning to the pedagogical value of films such as *Jonmo Shathi* is a way to read and see against the grain of that classified visual schema and visualize alternative modes of living, suffering, being, witnessing, and sharing pain.

Jonmo Shathi, *The Poison Thorn*, and *Rising Silence* grapple with the past to raise a critical awareness and shared responsibility for those who suffered in the birth of Bangladesh. This suffering has not ended but lives in an ongoing legacy; neither has freedom appeared in its full glory to embrace the survivors of a liberated country. Appropriating their stories to bolster the progress of the nation does further violence in which we—readers, viewers, activists—are all implicated. Yet, we must tell the stories in anticipation of a future where we can imagine alternate modes of being human, a future in which Birangona and Juddhoshishu do not have to "exit" or reenact their trauma on cue.

Mengesha effectively pushes the self-referential and narcissistic undertone of "empathic identification" by deploying LaCapra's notion of "empathic unsettlement" (1999) and Jill Bennett's articulation of "empathic vision" (2005)—both frameworks eliciting a secondary witnessing, where one strives to see the other's position but, at the same time, recognizes the incongruity of that position and consequently moves away from an appropriation/consumption intent. Bennett's empathic vision, in particular, suggests a move away from the interpersonal to the political sphere. In this space of interconnections, even despite the incongruity of experience, a fragmented link may be forged. Mengesha reiterates how the notion of the defecting witness is not about knowing or feeling the pain of the Other but rather "an impulse to carry the burden alongside: a politics of rage, a sense of injustice, and an approximation to the unimaginable" (2017, 156). Perhaps that is the critical legacy of this genre of woman-centered films about the Muktijuddho—an attempt by filmmakers to contribute to the fragmented elaborations of a silenced and instrumentalized history; and in the process, carry the burden—in whatever small, minimally successful measures across time and space—of those in the margins of history. In doing so, these films may hope to conjure a legacy of injustice and, perhaps, a just responsibility among readers, viewers, and actors.

Hartman writes that the archive of slavery is built on a "founding violence," and the same is true for the archive of sexual violence in the founding of Bangladesh. "This violence determines, regulates and organizes the kinds of statements that can be made about slavery and as well it creates subjects and objects of power" (Hartman 2008, 10). Regarding the tension between the ethical and the political, particularly in relation to the aesthetic, Hartman evokes the work of Fred Moten, who discusses the "terrible beauty" that exists at the scene of subjection and asks, "Do the possibilities outweigh the dangers of looking (again)?" (4). The question remains open about what kind of story can be told about the dead, the lost, the subaltern, and the "romance of resistance." The telling of such impossible stories must also emphasize the impossibility of their telling.

Such impossibility is embedded in all of Akhtar's films, which as Guhathakurta (2017) notes emphatically, are known for their affective power: *Shilalipi*, for instance, ends with Suborno and his friend viewing the monument for the martyred intellectuals in the killing fields of Rayer Bazaar, where his martyred mother Selina Pervin's body was found. On the foundation stone laid by Projonmo 1971, an organization founded by the children of martyrs, is a question for all who visit: *"Tomra ja bolecchiley. bolcchey ki ta Bangladesh?"* (Does independent Bangladesh reflect what you had intended?) A gentle tune of a flute, written by Akhtar and with lyrics and vocals by Moushumi, plays as the camera pans the swaying green rice fields of Bengal. The music accentuates the loss, struggle, and sacrifice of martyrs such as Pervin. It is a scene whose sights and sounds linger in the memory long after the film is over. Akhtar has quite effectively used the "silences" to express the impossible—for example, news of Pervin's brother's death in battle finds expression in images of Pervin's fingers tightly clenching the iron bars of the window and of a dilapidated building with incense sticks burning on the veranda. The visual effect Akhtar is able to achieve through such images hearkens back to the sensibility of "traumatic realism"—a term coined by Hamid Dabashi to describe the "visual vocabulary" of Palestinian cinema, which I discussed in the Prologue (2006, 21). This sensibility of traumatic realism inheres in the woman-centered films highlighted in this book, which strive to illuminate the specter of loss, even if capturing it remains incomplete, elusive, and fragmented. This sensibility inflects the different modes of seeing and being that the films gesture toward, and it is in imagining these differences that we are pushed to bear witness to the tormented, differential, yet promisory liberation of 1971. Importantly, these films disrupt unequivocal narrations of freedom, subjectivity, and justice.

· A performance of past violation "stretches time and space of violence into the present," Mengesha says, allowing it to "recursively bear witness in the present." Such performance leaves the witness/viewer with scarring that is "living and moving proof of violence's affective remains" (2017, 152). Hartman calls this telling the "recombinant narrative," pointing to the excess, that which belies verification. Ontologically, this narrative exists in the space between social and physical death. It also leaves us to account for the "precarious lives which are visible only in the moment of their disappearance" (2008, 12). Birangona and Juddhoshishu are put on stage and then made to exit, the specter of their ghostlike appearance remaining as an absent-presence. The dramatization of trauma in Mengesha's work focuses on the corporeal enactment of trauma within a social space and reveals the multitudes implicated in the process—witness, performer, narrator, political actors. What lingers in this moment can be generative for envisioning a narrative of the future even as the ghost of the past continues to haunt.

Epilogue

Why does human rights discourse collect narratives of pain, and why do viewers need them in order to prove harm was done? These seemingly cynical questions elicit a generative conversation about limits, containments, and ruptures of human rights cinema. Colonial ideology relies on the visibleness of pain and suffering of the oppressed in order to summon them into humanity. Following suit, the subjugation and pained existence of the oppressed is seen as grounds for recuperation of subjectivity, even as it solidifies a self-Other foundation to a politics of recognition. In *Scenes of Subjection* (1997), Saidiya Hartman elucidates how recognizing the personhood of the slave by amplifying suffering and cruelty, not only by slaveholders but also by liberal abolitionists, enhanced the humanity [of the slave] in abjection. This logic of domination that reifies suffering as the source of recognition and assimilation gets taken up, even if unwittingly, as the rationale for representation of a victimized humanity where the wounded and injured being is a more enthralling subject of human rights.

The underlying beliefs of such authoritarian representational traditions bestow authenticity and verifiability to a pained existence, even when the wounded do not benefit materially or politically from the victimized subjectivity. Tuck and Yang (2014) call for a refusal of such modes of knowledge that bolster the voice of the oppressed through an articulation and display of pain. Even as an integration of the silenced/erased voice is critical, these authors remind us to acknowledge the patronizing view involved in the

Figure E.1 Gurudasi Mondol (*Shadhinota* [dir. Yasmine Kabir, 2003]).

process that secures legitimacy through a reiteration of subjugation. Calling these narratives reflective of a "pain and damage-centered research," Tuck (2009, 2010) theorizes alternatively a "desire-based research" that, without denying the pain and trauma, also positions such narratives as yielding a kind of knowing that is wise. "Utilizing a desire-based framework is about working inside a more complex and dynamic understanding of what one, or a community, comes to know in (a) lived life" (Tuck and Yang 2014, 231). Desire framework refuses teleological self-centering representation, shifting the gaze to the workings of power, to possibilities outside of hegemonic logics but not necessarily through a reactive stance. Desire is both a methodological and an epistemological shift, repositioning the Other as an intellectual, generative, creative subject as opposed to an instrumental or anthropological one. As a methodology, this refusal strives toward an encounter with the subject through a representational process that humanizes and particularizes the subject as well as the viewer and the researcher (filmmaker) to engage them in an ethical and political relationship.

In this book, I have engaged with woman-centered films about the Muktijuddho that trouble a certain nationalist sentiment around gender in which women are relegated to codified and instrumentalized roles. In various ways and to certain degrees, these films—both documentary and narrative—break out of the mold of the absent-presence of women with their entrance into the plot relegated to sacrificial and supplementary roles. They exit from these tragic frames whereby they cannot be integrated into a liberated Bangladesh in their full subjectivity, often instrumentally called on—in voyeuristic depictions of suffering—to bolster a glorious war narrative yet be cast away as tainted afterward. The newer genre of Muktijuddho cinema discussed in this book aspires to tell different stories that offer a different modality of belonging and becoming for women survivors of war. These retellings rehistoricize the masculinist Muktijoddha (Man/Human) category by delinking from the discursive production of it and move in a different direction: "Toward the Human, after Man" (Wynter quoted in Mignolo 2015,

122). Drawing on the critical work of Black feminist scholar Sylvia Wynter, Walter Mignolo suggests that the teleological construction of Human in human rights discourse is predicated on assumptions about that which is not human—those who have been, and are, excluded from this imaginary. In the Muktijuddho genre, that Man/Human has been presumed masculine, valiant, honorable, brave, and fitting of national commemoration, whereby displacing women as lesser, expendable, and only assimilable through a display of suffering. The films discussed in previous chapters break out of the mold of nationalist cinema that puts a woman on a pedestal even as she is peripherally accepted as Human/Muktijoddha and/or ejected from the visual frame. A newer human rights cinematic tradition that these films gesture toward, foregrounds an aesthetic of traumatic realism (Dabashi 2006) yet evokes a new feminist political vision that enfolds the viewer, the subject of representation, and the filmmaker within an ethically symbiotic relationship. Yasmine Kabir's *Shadhinota* is a powerful example of this regenerative humanistic encounter.

The chapters of *Ethical Encounters* approach films from interdisciplinary critical Black and women of color feminist perspectives and illustrate that cinema—constituting what Nasreen Rehman (2020, 97) calls a "multisensory archive"—is potent for studying a struggle for self-determination laden by colonial, regional, and national contestations yet immanently intertwined through global cinematic discourses of war and trauma. Rehman sees art and aesthetics not as mere reflections of political struggle but as its very terrain. Trauma cinema in Bangladesh, for instance, challenges historical oblivion by carving out a transnational common ground of political recognition, avoiding a parochial historical approach. For filmmaking is susceptible to opposite trends of boundary formation and of rupture as in border-crossing filmmaking like *Meherjaan*. While film production tends to be restricted by national and global regimes of finance and knowledge, as a collaborative and often demotic medium of producing meaning in multiple sensory forms, cinema also is open to competing social and political claims staked by its makers, financiers, and target audiences. The form could well be animated in ways that exceed or critique cognitive categories, be they nationalist, regional, or global (Chowdhury and De, 2020, 4).

The documentary films of Bangladeshi filmmaker Yasmine Kabir cover human rights topics ranging from the interventions, failures, and excesses of development to migrant and child labor, to war victims and gender violence. With a minimalistic, poignant, and yet direct style, she captures her subjects' voices with intense close-up shots, and employs an aesthetic that disrupts visual frames of recognition. It is a technique that strategizes making suffering legible within humanitarian regimes of intervention and care. It also validates particular forms of agency as valid and recognizable. This style is exemplified in *Shadhinota* (*A Certain Liberation*, 2003), which follows Gurudasi Mondol, a survivor of the Bangladesh Liberation War, as she wanders through the streets of her small town (mofussil) Kopilmoni in Khulna District, Southern Bangladesh. The disruptive narration of Gurudasi's personhood illuminates "border spaces" of knowing and inhabiting (Khoja-Moolji 2016) that contest and rewrite the dominant discourse of women's (human) belonging, recovery, healing, and justice.

Shadhinota is a story about a woman survivor of Pakistani military and Bengali collaborators' (razakars) violence during the Bangladesh Liberation War in 1971. Notably, the title Birangona is never mentioned in the film although we come to learn Gurudasi Mondol was held captive and tortured by the Pakistani army and its collaborators. Furthermore, a confluence of poverty, patriarchy, military, and state violence is seen to shape her daily existence. Wartime violence and its affects are framed within a cascading continuity of structural violence. My analysis of the film contends that transnational and Black feminist frameworks provide a reading beyond a story of trauma and survival that challenges colonial heteronormative and heteropatriarchal assumptions of what recovery, reintegration, and resilience should look like for women. I focus on the ways in which Gurudasi Mondol is embedded in a particular set of relations with kin and community in her hometown and illuminate the gendered agency and desire she articulates as a survivor, which is, in turn, nurtured by the kin and community as a demonstration of nonnormative and nonregulative care. The film's aesthetic draws on a ghostly/haunting narrative of past pain that imbricates the present and brings attention to Gurudasi Mondol's resilience and adaptation to trauma rather than emphasizing a modality of autonomous agency and resistance. In highlighting the impossibility of a resolution to trauma, the film opens up deeper questions about repair, healing, justice, and witness. As such, it offers a new epistemological genealogy of subjectivity borne out of trauma that is resistant to a binary liberal framework of just being human and just being victim. It delinks from the spatial-temporal framing of the linear progression of human rights discourse, performative of an "epistemic disobedience" (Mignolo 2015, 106) that opens up new directions in analyzing the feminist struggle for justice and accountability.

Yasmine Kabir's *Shadhinota* offers a vision of her engagement with multiple forms of expression as well as her struggles with various forms of normalized governmentalities, including those of militarized, statist, and patriarchal social formations. In this epilogue, I draw from the aesthetics and politics of Kabir's film and explore her feminist contributions to thinking about expression, personhood, subjectivity, and humanity within the Muktijuddho woman-centered genre. The human rights industry offers only regulative discourses of trauma, healing, and reconciliation. These dissolve in the face of Kabir's bold confrontation with history as she delves into the strange condition of freedom for women in postwar independent Bangladesh. A figure bearing the marks of the many ways society has inflicted violence, Gurudasi's movements signify life clashes and combust of body with war, haunting with presence, freedom with abjection, memory with forgetting. Kabir guides viewers through the ordinary and extraordinary violence that imprints and structures women's lives, fueled by histories of betrayal through prevalent institutions of patriarchy, nationalism, and even human rights. The mundane intersects with the political in Kabir's films—inherent within the relations of women and family, kin and community, in the ways one navigates social norms, or in the very ways one imagines the world. It generates urgent questions: How do we live in the wake of catastrophe? How do we dispense with trauma? What does it mean to be a victim and/or human?

The film opens with historic footage from Victory Day 1971 and Sheikh Mujib's return to Bangladesh. *Joy Bangla* chants and massive jubilations on the streets fill the screen. In quick succession, and in black-and-white, camera shots chronicle subsequent military rulers General Ziaur Rahman and General Hossain Mohammad Ershad. These are followed by short, in-color clips of speeches by democratically elected prime ministers Sheikh Hasina (daughter of assassinated president Sheikh Mujib) and Begum Khaleda Zia (widow of assassinated president Ziaur Rahman). Their speeches proclaim the freedom struggle as the peoples' victory and lay claim to the nation along their party line, which is then contrasted with Gurudasi Mondol's appearance on the screen, wielding a lathi (bamboo rod) at the viewer and speaking derisively, "A kick in your faces." The kick could very well also be directed at the litany of political leaders preceding her appearance on the screen. Certainly, her cryptic comment, "Sheikh Mujib broke my leg but gave me this stick," is emblematic of her ambivalence to authority, be it the founding president of the nation or the local district commissioner or chairman she later goes on to admonish in the film. She has pet names for the Bangladesh Rifles, the paramilitary force tasked with guarding the borders of Bangladesh, and the Bangladesh Navy, institutions she refers to as "mangy cats" and "Camay" (perhaps a reference to the bar soap owned by Unilever and widely available in Bangladesh). The community also has names for her: "free woman," "mad woman," "a woman with a history," "well known," and "a good person." "I am not a good girl," says Gurudasi to the camera in one of the opening shots as she asks the interviewer, "Who sent you? Khaleda Zia? Hasina? Newspapers?" She mocks the film crew, "Dhaka Faka (empty)" perhaps alluding to the empty rhetoric of the human rights advocates who routinely come from the city.

Figure E.2 Gurudasi
Mondol wielding
a bamboo stick
(*Shadhinota* [dir. Yasmine
Kabir, 2003]).

A methodology that reads against the grain and shifts toward a more imaginative interpretation of a historical presence might be the way to tell an impossible story yet, at the same time, illuminate the impossibility of its telling. By articulating through critical fabulation, Saidiya Hartman (2008) offers an alternative method of inquiry and politics—one that might allow for a different way of encountering, inhabiting, and disrupting the epistemologies of being human. This alternative opens up an imaginative horizon where racialized, sexualized bodies enact waywardness to make meaning of their haunted presence in a world that was not meant to recognize their humanity. It centers the experience of the disenfranchised and helps demolish the neat disciplining of knowledge and experience. Not merely confined to "counter-histories"—an important observation made by feminist film scholars about women's cinema—it also provides a "history of the present . . . the incomplete project of freedom . . . [which is] a condition defined by the vulnerability to premature death and to gratuitous acts of violence" (4). Critical fabulation—a speculative history that at once rejects the possibility of recuperation—nevertheless offers a tentative reckoning with a ghostly past. Hartman's methodology fleshes out my own tentative reflections about what it means to "retell" or animate trauma through cinema as a gendered and "multisensory archive" (Rehman 2020) of 1971. Its intent is not "to give voice" in the face of a silent archive but to demonstrate "narrative restraint, the refusal to fill in the gaps and provide closure . . . which are always in excess of legibility" (Hartman 2008, 12).

Critical fabulation or speculative reading of Yasmine Kabir's film thus elicits both caution and possibility. Offering both a counterhistory and a history of the present, Kabir's methodology powerfully brings to the fore the "incomplete project of freedom" (Hartman 2008, 4). Critical fabulation is a mode of narration that reflects on a practice of telling and retelling, listening and relistening, that helps expand the prevailing methods of making visible and audible. It is a reworking of stories that illuminate submerged histories. Cinematic narrations can aid the retracing of women's stories—and be a tool with which to narrate a certain impossibility (Hartman and Wilderson 2003, 184). A conceptually aligned project, it listens and imagines to be able to produce knowledge against the grain of prevailing systems and gestures toward an alternative and anticipatory mode of knowledge. *A Certain Liberation* is a rich resurrection of a sometimes neglected and at times instrumentalized Birangona history. Kabir examines haunting erasures and silences—the disruptive and aberrant enunciation of war and its long reverberations. Identifying moments of defiance and joy in the life of her subject, Kabir is simultaneously wary of the impossible project of revising or recovering a history and trauma that insists on agency or autonomy where instead there may be adaptation or survival. Gurudasi's movements hold the horrors of wartime past even as they represent, fleetingly, a future wayward defiance of authority and categorization. "I am not a good girl," she says to the camera, and "Who listens to you?" she also says, mocking the women in the community who try to rein in her unrestricted mobility into bazaars and other public spaces. She does not conform to an imagined social order and hierarchy of society. She dances suggestively to loud *filmy* songs for the camera as well as for an audience of community members, defying the norms of conduct both for older women and for women who are marked by the war's horror. Regulative discourses of victimhood constrain the reception of women as victims; Gurudasi is not reducible to those, nor to her suffering.

This reading of the film gives us a deeper, nuanced understanding of Gurudasi Mondol's survival as an Other—a category of being human constituted through the violence of occupation, militarism, and heteropatriarchy. Yasmine Kabir's narrative is nonlinear, choppy, and disjointed, jumping from past to present, using spatial shifts that disavow a linear narrative that assumes an obtainable resolution or expected trajectory for healing. Tuck and Yang (2014, 231) question the developmental hierarchy in colonial representation that posits a linearity where pain and oppression are set on a path toward wholeness and a victim can reach a level of humanization through neoliberal empowerment attachments and therefore develop a "closeness" with the whole human (Man/Human). *Shadhinota*'s nonlinear and disruptive narrative, on the other hand, reflects Grace Cho's (2008, 30) theorization of haunting and ghostliness that insists we see the violences of the past existing in traces of the present. The temporality of haunting disrupts time as a linear progression, where the silenced past is not left in the past; instead, the erasure of past violence shapes the present.

The haunting reverberation of past trauma is palpable in the film's rei-magination of love, family, and community in Gurudasi Mondol's life in the face of heteropatriarchal militarism and domestication. From her neighbors and community members, viewers learn that Gurudasi's family, including her husband and four children, were brutally murdered in front of her by the razakars in 1971. She was held captive in an army camp and eventually rescued by freedom fighters. Her husband was a tailor, and she used to work as a peon in the army officers' barracks. Apparently, the strike against her family was retaliation for Gurudasi's defiance of orders in the office. Postin-dependence, Gurudasi seems to have received meager support from the state; she shows the viewers her humble living conditions, a small room with a leaky tin-shed roof and patched-up walls of bamboo, covered by a plastic tarp. A single wood cot (chauki) with a thin jute covering and an altar for the Gods are the only furniture. A neighboring family watches after her daily needs, provides her with meals, and takes care of her when she is ill. The lighting in the room is always dim, making the red hibiscus she offers to the Gods in prayer at her alter seem all the more intense and fiery.

Gurudasi embraces a maternal role in the community and calls herself "Mother of Bengal." "All the children are mine," she tells the viewers. We see a close up shot of her tear-drenched face and hear her voice heavy with emo-tion saying, "If I could only hear the call of Ma. If you don't [call me Ma], who will? Otherwise, I'll hang myself." This is immediately followed by the women in the community talking about the freedom Gurudasi has to move about in the public spaces. The contrasting of freedoms—that of the nation to the war victim, the survivor's to the women in the community—is woven together in seamless juxtapositions. One interviewee says, "She [Gurudasi Mondol] has freedom. She has no husband, no children, she can go any-where." She refers to her own limited mobility in contrast: "If I did that, people would very likely say to my husband 'what's your wife doing in the bazaars?'" Another female interviewee points out that Gurudasi roams the community as a way of earning money, referring to her own limitations in contrast: "If I did that, my daughters could not marry." Children adore Gu-rudasi. One little boy is shown saying, "I find her very beautiful. Better than the Prime Minister is my maashi." Several others relate their admiration by also calling her "maashi" (maternal aunt) and urge the filmmaker to name the film after her, styled as "Queen of the Jungle" or "Queen of the Village."

Stories abound from the community about her love and watchful affec-tion for babies, toddlers, and youths. She has breastfed many of the children in the community and takes an active role in their rearing. Several scenes in the film depict her admonishing the youths with her ubiquitous wood stick when she finds them roaming about aimlessly on the streets instead of attending school. The same playful admonishing is reserved for adult men

in the community whom she routinely "harasses" for money, food, or ciga-
rettes. Several men comment about the extreme suffering Gurudasi has endured and encourage the filmmakers—whom they take for "NGO workers,"
journalists, and human rights advocates—to arrange funds for her mainte-
nance. "One cannot survive such grief," they tell the filmmaker as an explanation of Gurudasi's unconventional behavior. A surviving male freedom
fighter, part of the group that had rescued Gurudasi from the Pakistani
army barracks, informs the interviewer that they had even taken her to the
Mental Hospital in Pabna; however, she had escaped from there. Another
male community member quotes Tagore to refer to Gurudasi's "wayward"
behavior: "God will not keep me in this pit of illusion. Instead, He has gift-
ed me the entire world."

The first half of the film establishes Gurudasi within the sociality of her
community. Interestingly, the camera follows her rapid movements from
the streets, to alleyways, to restaurants, to peoples' homes, creating a dizzy-
ing effect for the viewers as they try to keep up with her seemingly erratic
movements. Accompanying the quickly shifting shots are narratives pointing to her liminality as an elder, as a survivor of unspeakable trauma, as a
war heroine, as a maternal figure garnering love, reciprocity, and mutuality
from the community. They speak of the "chaos of the war" parallel to the
chaotic movements of the camera, talking about a time when all social norms
broke down. Gurudasi as a victim and survivor of that chaos is afforded a
liminality, a border-crossing subjectivity, to traverse norms and cross boundaries that otherwise would not be permissible in society. Gurudasi's aggressive, in-your-face persona and defiance of authority challenge the normative
grammar of survival from heteropatriarchal, nationalized, and militarized
violence. Her associations with the community—whose children she breast-
feeds and rears, who feed and take care of her even as far as to change their
own dietary habits to respect her religious observances by abstaining from
cooking beef in the house—expand the normative views of family bonds. In
the characterization of Gurudasi, her survival is fully embodied as a mother, with the love and nurturing of her nonnormative and nonregulative kin
and community. Gurudasi's neighbor, who is also a surrogate family, tells
the filmmaker, "We are all human beings. If you cut us, you will see blood.
What difference does it make who is Hindu or Muslim? Bhagwan—Allah?
It's the same." Yasmine Kabir is interested in how her subject navigates abject trauma through improvised kinship and community networks. Indeed,
Kabir's film pushes beyond nonnormative constructions of kinship through
an elaborate reading of family formation, motherhood, caretaking, and
other-mother figures as they are mapped onto the body of Gurudasi.

The second half of the film takes a quieter, more intense tone. The camera movement is not so rapid nor erratic. There are more close-up shots of

Gurudasi's face, eyes, feet, and hands, which seem to denote the intensity of her emotions. Her body literally embodies her suffering. The viewer is made to "see" her and reckon with her pain as it implicates the audience, filmmaker, and the subject of the film. The pain is a ghostly presence, as articulated by Avery Gordon: "Ghosts are never innocent: the unhallowed dead of the modern project drag in the pathos of their loss and the violence of the force that made them, their sheets and chains" (1997, 22). Yasmine Kabir presents an alternative form of agency and empowerment outside the normative definitions of redress or recognition of wrongdoing or agency. We can interpret Kabir's film as a narrative of resilience and survival where the past and present are blurred by the haunted presence of trauma. This moves toward a feminist methodology to be seen and recognized, to gesture toward a generative memory that encompasses healing. In the final moments of the film, Gurudasi relates the story of the massacre of her family, and the camera is very still. Perhaps her own liminality is further portrayed by her position with the crew suspended on water, on a boat away from the security of the land that also betrayed her ("My leg broke when Bangladesh was liberated," she says twice in the film). "In this life what did I get?" The playful, always moving, cackling with laughter, harassing-the-community-for-money persona is deeply contrasted with the quiet, still, and reflective Gurudasi as she shares the story of her loss. The film's ending makes this poignant point as Gurudasi steps off the boat, onto the riverbank, turns around, and faces the camera. The interviewers are still seated inside the boat, and she summons them with a wave of her hand, as if to say "come with me, what are you waiting for?" It is a call for an ethical engagement with the present. It evokes the question: What would real repair or justice look like? Kabir's narrative reveals how reparations are impossible in a present-day structure that is built on and perpetuates the violences of the past, yet that must be embedded in a recognition of injustice, harm, and wrongdoing by the state, and also serve as a meaningful plan to disrupt the structures that perpetuate ongoing violence and injustice. The haunting in Gurudasi challenges heteronormative assumptions confronting patriarchy and state power, while centering Gurudasi's resilience as a nonlinear reclamation of her life, body, and desires. As a methodology, such witnessing presents possibilities for pushing heteronormative assumptions of what survival looks like.

Gurudasi is embedded in relations of kin and community, and this emerges in the comment from a male member, "She is my uncle's daughter." In fact, the community in her hometown responds to Gurudasi with affection, mild exasperation, admiration, and respect. The women in the community are in awe of Gurudasi and the ways in which she is free of societal constraints. The narrative of *Shadhinota* does not present Gurudasi as an archetypical war survivor, reflecting how the violence and trauma are unresolvable. Indeed, trauma is ubiquitous in the first half of the film when Gurudasi is seen wandering everywhere, owning the streets, defying normative characterizations of women victims as silenced or erased. However, we learn this ubiquity is not necessarily of assimilation into the national narrative but rather at once mockery (of authoritarian regimes), derision, and deep despair. A much more nuanced and complex personhood complicates the overdetermination of women's bodies with the national body. Gurudasi cannot be contained into a nationalized patriarchal embarrassment that leads to shame. The uncomfortable silence belongs to the powers that be in their failure to make any meaningful redress to the victim.

Further, *Shadhinota* highlights the formation of subjects constituted through the violence of occupation and militarism as well as the silencing of that violence through attempts to control its remembrance through narrow definitions of national victory and state-based redress. The film eschews such linear narratives of violence and jubilation as firmly in the past and remediable by redress and, instead, posits a disruptive mode of recalling and addressing the legacies of violence that highlight, rather than erase, the persistence of gendered, sexualized, and classed oppression in the present. At the same time, *Shadhinota* disrupts regulative formations of family and the state as the providers of care and makes visible the nonnormative alternative narrative of structures of kin, community, and survival.

The national-level processes underway for redress, restitution, criminal trials, and apology are not within the purview of the film's alternative framings of justice. That the state can issue an apology and make a restitution agreement assumes that victims of such crimes are reparable and the enemy state forgiven. Gurudasi Mondol names the person who shot her husband: "Mozhair, that evil bastard who made me a widow." What would justice look like to Gurudasi? In answer to that, she lists capturing Mozhair, the government providing her with social security, and a meeting with the prime minister where she could share her experience. None of these have been realized despite the *faka* (empty) narratives of the state. Instead, Gurudasi's voice and remembrances point to the unforgivable stamp of such crimes, an irreparableness that presents a nonlinearity where the violence persists in the present. What is freedom after the smothering brutality of war after all, particularly for women? "I am at peace in this jungle," says Gurudasi. "This in itself is peace—to talk to you." Her yearning to share her burden is also exemplified by her narration of a story involving the Prime Minister Sheikh Hasina. We see a still image of Gurudasi looking through a barred window at the camera. She is adorned in red and green, the colors of the Bangladesh flag, with a baseball hat askew on her head, the words "Joy Bangla" across the front flap. The image is from the time Sheikh Hasina had come to town for an event commemorating Bangladesh's independence, when Gurudasi had tried to arrange a meeting with her, but the police barred her from entering the venue.

Curiously, Gurudasi tells the interviewer she would rather be buried and memorialized with a monument where the community could bring alms and gifts in her memory. This is accompanied by shots of Gurudasi offering flowers and alms to the altar in her room and at the temple. If she were to be cremated, like Roma Choudhury also says in *Bish Kanta*, as I elaborated in Chapter 4, no trace of her would remain and no one would remember her. Perhaps her wish to be buried is in order to leave traces of her story, to make hers and thus all those other narratives more *visible* or audible, more accessible, to enable readers, viewers, and others to engage those narratives with a deeper sense of the present. *Shadhinota* ought to be seen as a confluence of genres: women's countercinema with an oppositional standpoint, narrating submerged histories (White 2015); human rights cinema engaging an aesthetic that emerges from and under duress of sublated violence (Dabashi 2006); and a vision offered of an alternate mode of being human and becoming human (Weheliye 2014; Mignolo 2015). The film offers a regenerative memorialization (Ahad-Legardy 2021, 88), at once acknowledging the trauma, injury, and loss, while deploying a creative process to narrate a revivification or a "new relation" to the historical past toward a healing response.

Glossary

Andolan—Protests.

Atar—Perfumed oils.

Bangabandhu—Translated as "friend of Bengal," this was a popular title for Sheikh Mujibur Rahman.

Baul—A group of mystic minstrels with mixed traditions from Sufism and Vaishnavism.

Beshya—Prostitute.

Bideshi—Foreigner.

Bikalpa Dhara—Alternative cinema.

Birangona—Brave woman or war heroine; it was an honorific bestowed, by the government of Bangladesh, on women survivors of sexual violence during the Liberation War.

Boromama—Eldest maternal uncle.

Chachi—Aunt.

Dhoti—A wraparound garment worn by men in the Indian subcontinent, often associated with Hindus.

Faka—Empty.

Ghazal—A poetic form of Persian origin, invoking love, longing, and melancholy. It is sung most famously by artists in the Middle East and South Asia.

Hijra—The transgender, intersex, or third-gender people of South Asia.

Insan—Human beings.

Insaniyat—Humanity.

Juddhoshishu—War child; a child of wartime rape.

Kameez—A tunic, typically worn over trousers.

Khanelaga—Touched by a Pakistani (i.e., raped).

Khota—Scorn.

Korbaan—Sacrifice.

Laathi—A bamboo rod.

Lungi—A long skirtlike garment worn mostly by men and less frequently by women across South Asia. Although men of all social classes wear lungi at home, the garment can be a marker of social class as it is associated with physical laborers.

Mofassil— Small town.

Muktijoddha—Freedom fighter.

Muktijuddho—The Bangladesh Liberation War of 1971.

Mut'a—A short-term contractual marriage.

Nanajan—Grandfather.

Pakisongom—A union between Bangladesh and Pakistan.

Panjabi—A long shirtlike garment worn by men in the Indian subcontinent.

Punjabi—A native of the region of Punjab, the language spoken in the region.

Parathas—Layered flatbread eaten across South Asia.

Razakar—East Pakistani paramilitary force organized by West Pakistani military, and composed of anti-Bangladesh and Pro-Pakistan groups. Members of this group are referred to as war collaborators.

Roti—Unleavened flatbread.

Shadhin Bangla Betar Kendro—Independent Bengal Radio Center.

Shadhinota—Liberation.

Shadhinotar chetona—"The spirit of '71," the frame enacted to further the grand narrative of Bangladesh's liberation.

Shonar Bangla—Golden Bengal, a discourse and imagery derived from the national anthem of Bangladesh.

Shothik dharona—Correct understanding.

Shurma—Kohl.

Sindhoor—Red-colored cosmetic powder worn by women along the part of their hair. It is traditionally associated with married Hindu women.

Tasbeeh—Prayer beads used by Muslims.

Teep—Dot worn on the forehead by women, traditionally connoting Bengali ethnicity and aesthetic.

Topee—Skullcaps worn by Muslims.

Van gaari—A form of cycle rickshaw that carries passengers or goods.

Notes

PROLOGUE

1. The partition of British India in 1947 created two new nation states: India and Pakistan. Pakistan was formed along religious lines, with the two most populous Muslim regions of the subcontinent becoming its Western and Eastern Wings. The Western Wing of the new Islamic Federation of Pakistan exercised political, cultural, and economic domination over East Pakistan. In March 1971, long-standing political discontent and cultural nationalism led to a military assault by the West Pakistani army and the declaration of East Pakistan's independence, signified by its new name, Bangladesh. The Bangladesh Liberation War was supported by India. In December 1971, Bangladesh became an independent nation after a nine-month war. The relatively lesser-known history of the creation of Bangladesh, as a continuum of the partition's unresolved legacy, can be found in D'Costa 2011.

2. Following the Liberation War, he would become the first president of the People's Republic of Bangladesh.

3. Jagannath Hall was a residence hall at Dhaka University that housed minority students, including Hindus, Buddhists, and Christians. The Pakistani army targeted its students and staff that night, in a military strike known as Operation Searchlight, and murdered its former and current provosts at the time, Professors Govinda Chandra Dev and Jyotirmoy Guhathakurta.

4. The popularly shortened name of Sheikh Mujibur Rahman. He was also known affectionately as *Bangabandhu*, which translates to "friend of Bengal."

5. An invocation commonly uttered by Muslims at the beginning of any undertaking. It translates to "In the name of Allah." The military assault in 1971 was legitimized by the West Pakistani administration as being necessary to bring the Bengalis back to the path of proper Islam, an essential undertaking in the name of religion.

6. The first of the four pillars of Islam, asserting faith in Allah and Muḥammad as his prophet.

7. After the Pakistani army surrendered, Bengali men are reported to have targeted those who had collaborated with the Pakistanis in wartime killings. Such excesses of war may be hidden in statist narratives; however, filmic representations have brought to the fore the marginal stories. Tareque Masud's 2009 film *Noroshundor* (*The Barber Shop*) is a case in point, as a sensitive and compassionate narrative of a Bengali Muslim boy, running from the Pakistani army and local collaborators, who is surprisingly sheltered by Biharis in a barbershop.

INTRODUCTION

1. A state in eastern India that abuts Bangladesh and prior to 1947 was one contiguous province of Bengal.

2. Shonar Bangla discourse is derived from the national anthem of Bangladesh, which is titled "Amar Shonar Bangla" ("My Golden Bengal"). The song is an extract of a longer lyric written by Rabindranath Tagore in 1906. The song describes the Bengali landscape as verdant, idyllic, and as a place of abundance and stunning beauty. Overtly masculinist language alludes to the devotion of male inhabitants to revere and protect the fertile motherland. See Siddiqi 2003 for a nuanced critique of the shonar Bangla discourse and the many contestations over it.

3. *Birangona* means brave woman or war heroine. Following independence, the term was bestowed on the survivors of sexual violence by Sheikh Mujibur Rahman and the government of Bangladesh to honor the women for their role in the freedom struggle. However, the label frequently served to further ostracize the women as reintegration into society remained incomplete. On October 23, 2015, the Bangladesh government for the first time declared forty-three Birangona as freedom fighters; the Bangladesh parliament previously recognized the proposal in January 2015. The depiction of Birangona women in cinema is taken up at length in the following chapters of the book.

4. A form of cinema produced with an urban setting and audience in mind. It is associated with having "an international standard" and mirroring an elite life style of a global middle class. For a detailed discussion, see Larkin 2019, 108.

5. The Bangladesh Film Censor Board, under the "immorality and Obscenity" clause prohibits explicit sexual scenes. Haque notes in his study that hardcore rape scenes can be found in the "cut pieces" that had been written about by Lotte Hoek (2014).

6. Numbers are contested with regard to the genocide in East Pakistan in 1971. Reportedly, between one million and three million lives were lost, two hundred thousand to four hundred thousand women were victims of sexual violence, and twenty-five thousand forced pregnancies occurred during the war.

CHAPTER 1

1. Committee formed in 1971 by occupying forces of West Pakistan to aid in the process of crushing the Bengali resistance.

2. The Lahore Proposal was a formal political statement presented by A. K. Fazlul Huq and adopted by the Muslim League at its three-day general session, March 22–24, 1940. It called for the creation of "independent states" for Muslims in British India. The constituent units of these states were to be autonomous and sovereign. This was later interpreted as a demand for a separate Muslim state, Pakistan.

3. Baloch soldiers are portrayed in most historical depictions of the Pakistani army during the Liberation War as brutish Pathans (i.e., Pashtuns). Ongoing insurgency in the

southwestern province for greater economic and political power has contributed to the minoritized status of this ethnic group in Pakistan. Considered an Other, their weaker status in the national context is likened to the marginalization of Bengalis in East Pakistan.

4. For a detailed review of this book, see Elora Chowdhury 2012.

5. More information is available at http://www.khonatalkies.com/meherjaan.php .Accessed June 1, 2021.

6. I draw from Judith Butler's notion of the "precariousness" of life and how we are conditioned to recognize the differential treatment of lives within certain epistemological frameworks with regard to war and conflict. Butler encourages an ethical rethinking of waging violence without refuting the violent formation of the nationalist subject. Choosing nonviolence, she contends, is an ethical practice that is fallible and experimental yet attending to the grievability, precarity, and vulnerability of all lives. For a fuller discussion of this concept, see Butler 2009.

7. Sufi bauls connote both a religious sect and a musical tradition in Bengal. They are known for their syncretic beliefs, which incorporate Vaishnava Hindu and Sufi Muslim traditions. They are an important cultural force in Bengal and are distinct in their clothing and musical instruments.

8. The director's decision here to feature a Baloch soldier is noteworthy. As mentioned in endnote 3, the weaker status of Balochistan renders it an Other within the national context of Pakistan. Some scholars have pointed out that Baloch regiments, even though a minority in 1971, unleashed terrible violence, particularly in the killings of the night of March 25, 1971. On that night, army units directed by West Pakistan launched a military operation called Operation Searchlight in East Pakistan against Bengali civilians, students, intelligentsia, and the armed personnel who were demanding that the military honor the first-ever democratic elections in Pakistan, won by an East Pakistan party, or allow East Pakistan to separate from West Pakistan. There is historical evidence, however, that a Baloch soldier from Quetta named Asgar Baluch defected from his regiment during the war and was sheltered by a Bengali family in a village in Comilla. In time, he began dressing like the Bengali men in the village and appreciating their local foods and livelihoods, and he changed his name to Nabi Baksh. He married the daughter of the man who gave him shelter and lived his remaining life in Bangladesh (Sajjad 2012).

9. A short-term contractual marriage with the same obligations as *nika*, the Islamic permanent marriage contract. The practice of *mut'a* marriage was more prevalent in pre-Islamic Arabia. Sunni Muslims believe this practice was abolished by the Prophet Muḥammad and later confirmed by Caliph Umar. Shia Muslims, however, contest the authority of Umar's abolition.

10. Although the Indian national anthem is Tagore's "Jana gana mana"—an ecumenical lyric—the more Hindu-imagery-centric "Bandemataram" by Bankim has displaced the former in Hindutva vocabulary. The term "Bandemataram" brings up the classic masculine nationalist issue of territorial defense through invoking what has become the primary national anthem of the Hindutvavadis. In addition, the blog writer engaged in a diatribe against the *lungi*-clad man—here, we encounter vile anti-Muslim imagery of the kind common in partition parlance. This kind of defiling and infantalizing of the Muslim male body is riddled with Hindutva masculinism.

11. Available at www.sachalayatan.com. Accessed June 1, 2021.

12. Comfort women were women and girls forced into sexually serving soldiers by the Imperial Japanese Army in occupied countries and territories, most notably South Korea, before and during World War II. The name "comfort women" is a translation of the Japanese *ianfu*, a euphemism for "prostitute."

13. Admittedly, *Meherjaan* makes no attempt to address this question, but other scholarly works are raising these questions in powerful ways. See, for example, Siddiqi 2013.

14. The author is grateful to Dr. Liz Philipose for illuminating this point.

CHAPTER 2

1. Bengali Muslim is an ethnic, linguistic, and religious identification that is understood to have emerged as a synthesis of Islamic and Bengali cultures. The Bengali Muslim population make up the majority of Bangladesh's citizens. After the partition of India in 1947, they were the majority group in Pakistan until the independence of East Pakistan in 1971. The ethnolinguistic and religious components of this identity, which Bengalis claim to be fluid, have been alternatively seen as contradictory to one another by West Pakistani statist perspective and subsequently this sentiment was mobilized for political gains. The trajectory of middle-class Bengali Muslim women's identity integrates the sociocultural, economic, political, religious, and chronological histories of the Muslim population in Bengal. It can be traced to 1918 with the founding of *Sougat*, a liberal reformist periodical that pioneered the women's weekly *Begum* a few weeks before the 1947 partition. For a more comprehensive discussion of the trajectory of Bengali Muslim women's identity, see Amin 1996.

2. Altaf Mahmud was a musician, cultural activist, and martyred freedom fighter of the Bangladesh Liberation War. He was also an activist of the Language Movement in 1952 and composer of "Amar Bhaier Rokte Rangano," the famous song written to commemorate the killing of Bengali student protesters on February 21, 1952, by the Pakistani army.

3. Ziaur Rahman (January 9, 1936–May 30, 1981) was the seventh president of Bangladesh; he served from 1977 to 1981. During the Liberation War, he was the sector commander of Sector 1, then Sector 11, then brigade commander of Z Force. As deputy and later army chief of staff and major general, he dissolved the parliament and instituted a state of emergency under martial law following the assassination of Sheikh Mujibur Rahman. He later founded the Bangladesh Nationalist Party in 1978 during his tenure as President of Bangladesh. He was assassinated in 1981. Begum Khaleda Zia, spouse of the Late Ziaur Rahman, served as Prime Minister of Bangladesh from 1991 to 1996, and then later from 2001 to 2006.

4. *Shadhin Bangla Betar Kendro* (Independent Bengal Radio Center) was the clandestine radio station in Kalurghat, north of the city of Chittagong, Bangladesh. Soon after the Pakistani army took over the Dhaka Radio Center on March 26, 1971, *Shadhin Bangla Betar Kendro* began broadcasting and became the media center of the Bengali nationalist force. The station transmitted the declaration of independence of Bangladesh and played a vital role in the Liberation War.

5. An outer garment worn by some Islamic women. It covers the body and the face in public and is commonly worn in Asia, Africa, Europe, and, especially, the Middle East.

6. Skullcaps associated with Islamic dress in the subcontinent.

7. Hindus are geographically, culturally, ethnically, and religiously identified as indigenous to South Asia. As of this writing, there are about 1.03 billion Hindus worldwide. They adhere to a wide array of religious beliefs and practice.

8. A burial rite in Greek culture, where the concept of the physical body incorporates the political economy of prosperity after death. Sophocles's *Antigone*, ca. 441 B.C.E., exemplifies the importance of the customs and culture of honoring the deceased. Traditions include public mourning, a funeral, and offering rituals before burying the body.

9. Kazi Nazrul Islam is the national poet of Bangladesh and is recognized as the rebel poet, after the title of this poem. "*Bidrohi*," published in 1922 in *Bijli* (*Lightning*) magazine, is his most famous work. It criticized the British Raj and called for revolution.

10. The term refers to the transgender, intersex, or third-gender people in South Asia. Several South Asian countries, including the government of Bangladesh, legally recognized *Hijra* as the third gender in 2013. Despite this legal recognition, *Hijras* continue to struggle for their social and political rights as citizens.

CHAPTER 4

1. The Bengali resistance to Urdu's being declared the state language and the demand for Bengali to be recognized as an official state language.

2. Translated as "friend of Bengal," this was a popular title for Sheikh Mujibur Rahman.

3. On February 5, 2013, protests began in Shahbag, Bangladesh, following what many considered to be lenient sentencing of those convicted of war crimes—especially Abdul Quader Mollah, who had been convicted on five of six counts and was sentenced to life imprisonment rather than death. Tens of thousands of people joined the demonstrations, which spread across the country. Later demands included banning the Bangladesh Jamaat-e-Islami party from politics, including elections, and a boycott of institutions supporting (or affiliated with) the party.

4. Literally, "golden Bengal," this is also the title of the national anthem of Bangladesh.

CHAPTER 5

1. Rabindranath Tagore (1861–1941) was a Bengali writer, poet, composer, and artist. He is sometimes referred to as the Bard of Bengal. Tagore was awarded the Nobel Prize in Literature in 1913.

References

Abar Tora Manush Ho. 1973. Directed by Khan Ataur Rahman. Dhaka, Bangladesh: Janata Chitra Prakalpa.

Ackerly, Brooke A. 2018. *Just Responsibility: A Human Rights Theory of Global Justice.* New York: Oxford University Press.

Agami (The Next). 1984. Directed by Morshedul Islam. Dhaka, Bangladesh: Chalachitram Film Society.

Aguner Poroshmoni. 1994. Directed by Humayun Ahmed. Dhaka, Bangladesh: Nuhash Chalachittra.

Ahad-Legardy, Badia. 2021. *Afro-nostalgia: Feeling Good in Contemporary Black Culture.* Urbana: University of Illinois Press.

Ahmed, Irfan. 2012. "Modernity and Its Outcast: The Why and How of India's Partition." *South Asia: Journal of South Asian Studies* 35, no. 2: 477–494.

Ahmed, Rahnuma. 2016. "Voices Unbound." *Fragments Magazine*, October 20, 2016. Available at http://fragmentsmagazine.com/2016/10/20/voices-unbound/.

Ahmed, Rubaiyat. 2012. "Bangladesher Cholochitre Narir Ongshogrohon (Nobboy Doshok Porjonto)" (Women's Participation in Bangladeshi Cinema [Until 1990s]). *Bangladesh Film Archive Journal* 5 (June): 56–74.

———. 2013. *Tareque Masud.* Dhaka: Bangladesh Film Archive.

Ahmed, Sara. 2004. *The Cultural Politics of Emotion.* New York: Routledge.

Akhtar, Shaheen. 2018. *The Search.* New Delhi: Zubaan Books.

Akhter, Fahmida. 2015. "The Construction of the 'New Bengali Woman' in Nasiruddin Yousuff's *Guerilla* (2011)." *South Asian Popular Culture* 13, no. 3: 199–216.

———. 2020. "Zahir Raihan's *Stop Genocide* (1971): A Dialectical Cinematic Message to the World." In *South Asian Filmscapes Transregional Encounters*, edited by Elora Halim Chowdhury and Esha Niyogi De, 233–249. Seattle: University of Washington Press.

Akram, Tanweer. n.d. "Bangladesh and Pakistan." Virtual Bangladesh. Accessed November 25, 2021. Available at http://www.virtualbangladesh.com/history/overview _akram.html.

Alamgir, Jalal, and Bina D'Costa. 2011. "The 1971 Genocide: War Crimes and Political Crimes." *Economic and Political Weekly* 46, no. 13: 38–41.

Alor Michil (Procession of Lights). 1974. Directed by Narayan Ghosh Mita. Dhaka, Bangladesh.

Amar Jonmobhumi (My Motherland). 1973. Directed by Alamgir Kumkum. Dhaka, Bangladesh: Films International.

Amin, Sonia Nishat. 1996. *The World of Muslim Women in Colonial Bengal, 1876–1939*. Leiden: E. J. Brill.

Anam, Tahmima. 2007. *A Golden Age*. New York: HarperCollins.

———. 2011. *The Good Muslim*. New York: HarperCollins.

Annis, David B. 1987. "The Meaning, Value, and Duties of Friendship." *American Philosophical Quarterly* 24, no. 4: 349–356.

Aristotle. 2012. *Aristotle's Nicomachean Ethics*, translated by Robert Bartlett and Susan Collins. Chicago: University of Chicago Press.

Atikuzzaman, Abul Khaer Mohammad, and Priyam Pritim Paul, eds. 2018. *Chalachitra O Jatiya Mukti: Alamgir Kabir Rochona Shangraha 1 (Cinema and National Freedom: Collected Works of Alamgir Kabir Vol I)*. Dhaka: Agami Publishers.

Bagha Bangali (The Fierce Bengali). 1972. Directed by Anondo. Dhaka, Bangladesh: Anondo Kothachitro.

BBC World. 2018. "Hearing the Stories of Bangladesh's 'Birangona' Women." December 18, 2018. Available at https://www.bbc.co.uk/programmes/p06vww7m?ocid=social flow_facebook&fbclid=IwAR0Ks3nGqC3lNZLzodTDZ6lneXMdIm897XI0ECf _o6Etz2UzrGrjzOmQJMg.

Behula. 1966. Directed by Zahir Raihan. Dhaka, Bangladesh.

Bennett, Jill. 2005. *Empathic Vision: Affect, Trauma, and Contemporary Art*. Stanford, CA: Stanford University Press.

Bhabha, Homi. 1990. "Introduction." In *Nation and Narration*, edited by Homi Bhabha, 1–7. London: Routledge.

Bhaumik, Subir. 2011. "Book, Film Greeted with Fury among Bengalis." *Aljazeera*. April 29, 2011. Available at http://www.aljazeera.com/indepth/features/2011/04/20114291 74141565122.html.

Bhowmick, Bikash Chandra. 2009. *Women on Screen: Representing Women by Women in Bangladesh Cinema*. Dhaka: Bangladesh Film Archive.

Bhuiyan, Robina Rashed. 2016. "Rina Brown: More Than Another Film." *Daily Star*, June 3, 2016. Available at https://www.thedailystar.net/arts-entertainment/film/rina-brown -1233556.

Bose, Brinda. 1998. "In Desire and in Death: Eroticism as Politics in Arundhati Roy's 'The God of Small Things.'" *Ariel: A Review of International English Literature* 29:59–72.

Bose, Sharmila. 2011. *Dead Reckoning: Memories of the 1971 Bangladesh War*. London: Hurst.

Brown, Brene. 2012. *Daring Greatly: How the Courage to Be Vulnerable Transforms the Way We Live, Love, Parent, and Lead*. New York: Gotham.

Brown, Wendy. 2004. "'The Most We Can Hope for. . .': Human Rights and the Politics of Fatalism." *South Atlantic Quarterly* 103, nos. 2–3: 451–462.

Brownmiller, Susan. 1975. "Against Our Will: Men, Women and Rape." Accessed June 1, 2021. Available at https://web.archive.org/web/20050205160345/http://drishtipat .org/1971/war-susan.html.

Bueno-Hansen, Pascha, and Sylvanna M. Falcón. 2018. "Indigenous/Campesina Embodied Knowledge, Human Rights Awards, and Lessons for Transnational Feminist Solidarity." In *Decolonizing Feminism: Transnational Feminism and Globalization*, edited by Margaret A. McLaren, 167–195. New York: Rowman and Littlefield.

Butler, Judith. 2009. *Frames of War: When Is Life Grievable?* London: Verso.

Carby, Hazel. 2019. *Imperial Intimacies: A Tale of Two Islands*. New York: Verso.

Chakravarty, Sumita. 2003. "The Erotics of History: Gender and Transgression in the New Asian Cinemas." In *Rethinking Third Cinema*, edited by Anthony Guneratne and Wimal Dissanayake, 79–100. London: Routledge.

Chatterjee, Sushmita. 2016. "What Does It Mean to Be a Postcolonial Feminist? The Artwork of Mithu Sen." *Hypatia: Journal of Feminist Philosophy* 31 (Winter): 22–40.

Chitra Nadir Paare (Quiet Flows the River Chitra). 1998. Directed by Tanvir Mokammel. Dhaka, Bangladesh.

Cho, Grace M. 2008. *Haunting the Korean Diaspora: Shame, Secrecy, and the Forgotten War*. Minneapolis: University of Minnesota Press.

Choudhury, Babul. 1971. *Innocent Millions*. Bangladesh: Bangladesh Government.

Chowdhury, Afsan. 2011. "Meherjaan Controversy: It's Not about the Film, but about Us and Our History." *bdnews24.com*, February 6, 2011. Available at http://opinion .bdnews24.com/2011/02/06/meherjan-controversy-it%E2%80%99s-not-about-the -film-but-about-us-and-our-history/.

———. n.d. "The Bewas Village." Accessed June 1, 2021. Available at https://web.archive .org/web/20050205160824/http://drishtipat.org/activists/Afsan/bewas.htm.

Chowdhury, Apon. 2017. "Amader Cholochitrey Muktijuddho: Asha, Prapti Ebong Prottasha" (Muktijuddho in Our Cinema: Expectations, Realization and Inspiration). Dhaka: *Bangladesh Film Archive Journal* 12 (June): 59–67.

Chowdhury, Elora Halim. 2012. "Debunking 'Truths,' Claiming Justice: Reflections on Yasmin Saikia, *Women, War and the Making of Bangladesh: Remembering 1971.*" *Human Rights Quarterly* 34, no. 4: 1201–1211.

———. 2016. "The Space between Us: Reading Umrigar and Sangari in the Quest for Female Friendship." In *Dissident Friendships: Feminism Imperialism and Transnational Solidarity*, edited by Elora H. Chowdhury and Liz Philipose, 160–181. Urbana: University of Illinois Press.

Chowdhury, Elora Halim, and Esha Niyogi De, eds. 2020. *South Asian Filmscapes: Transregional Landscapes*. Seattle: University of Washington Press.

Chowdhury, Kawsar. 2002. *Tales of the Darkest Night (Shei Raater Kotha Bolte Eshechi)*. Dhaka, Bangladesh.

———. 2015. *Protikuler Jatri Alamgir Kabir* (Counter Image). Available at https://www .youtube.com/watch?v=6OEZVlorXb0.

———. n.d. *Protikuler Jatree (Counter Image)*. Bangladesh: Prova-Sruti-Obokolon.

Chowdhury, Shamim Ara. n.d. *Interview with Leesa Gazi*. Accessed June 1, 2021. Available at https://www.trtworld.com/video/showcase/rising-silence-in-conversation-show case/5d2ebc9fb9fa6764a9a59038.

The Clay Bird (Matir Moyna). 2002. Directed by Tareque Masud. Dhaka, Bangladesh: Audiovision.

Cocking, Dean, and Jeannette Kennett. 1998. "Friendship and the Self." *Ethics* 108, no. 3: 502–527.

Collins, Patricia Hill. 2004. *Black Sexual Politics: African Americans, Gender, and the New Racism.* New York: Routledge.

Dabashi, Hamid., ed. 2006. *Dreams of a Nation: On Palestinian Cinema.* London: Verso.

Daily Star. 2017. "Ayesha Jalal Interview: Separating a Once Historically Indivisible People." August 25, 2017. Available at https://www.thedailystar.net/star-weekend/sepa rating-once-historically-indivisible-people-1453531.

Daiya, Kavita. 2008. *Violent Belongings: Partition, Gender, and National Culture in Post-colonial India.* Philadelphia: Temple University Press.

———. 2011. "Visual Culture and Violence: Inventing Intimacy and Citizenship in Recent South Asian Cinema." *South Asian History & Culture* 2, no. 4: 589–604.

Das, Veena. 2007. *Life and Words: Violence and the Descent into the Ordinary.* Berkeley: University of California Press.

D'Costa, Bina. 2000. "(Dis)Appearing Women in Nationalist Narratives: Interview with Respondent A (Part 1)." Available at https://web.archive.org/web/20040626053736 /http:/www.drishtipat.org/1971/docs/interview1_bina.pdf.

———. 2002. "(Dis)Appearing Women in Nationalist Narratives: Interview with Dr. Geoffrey Davis (Part 2)." Available at https://web.archive.org/web/20040521042616 /http:/www.drishtipat.org/1971/docs/interview2davis_bina.pdf.

———. 2004. "War Babies: The Question of National Honour." May 21, 2004. Available at https://web.archive.org/web/20050205020353/http://drishtipat.org/1971/war.htm.

———. 2005. "Coming to Terms with the Past in Bangladesh." In *Feminist Politics, Activism and Vision,* edited by Luciana Ricciutelli, Angela Miles, and Margaret H. McFadden. London: Zed Books.

———. 2011. *Nationbuilding, Gender and War Crimes in South Asia.* New York: Routledge.

Derrida, Jacques. 1994. *Specters of Marx: The State of the Debt, the Work of Mourning, and the New International.* Translated by Peggy Kamuf. New York: Routledge.

Dey, Saurav. 2016. "Jonmo Shathi: A Quest for Identity." *Daily Star,* March 24, 2016. Available at https://www.thedailystar.net/arts-entertainment/film/jonmo-sathi-quest-iden tity-1198555.

Dhire Bohe Meghna (*Quiet Flows the River*). 1973. Directed by Alamgir Kabir. Dhaka, Bangladesh: Bangladesh Films International.

Dring, Simon. 2021. "Despite Threats, I Stayed. The Truth of What Happened Had to Be Told." *Daily Star,* March 25, 2021. Available at https://www.thedailystar.net/opinion /news/despite-threats-i-stayed-the-truth-what-happened-had-be-told-2066161.

Ekattorer Michil (*Procession of 1971*). 2001. Directed by Kabori Sarwar. Dhaka, Bangladesh.

El Guindi, Fadwa. 2004. *Visual Anthropology: Essential Method and Theory.* Walnut Creek, CA: Altamira.

Enloe, Cynthia. 2004. *The Curious Feminist: Searching for Women in a New Age of Empire.* Berkeley: University of California Press.

———. 2014. *Bananas, Beaches, and Bases: Making Feminist Sense of International Politics.* 2nd ed. Los Angeles: University of California Press.

Ethirajan, Anbarasan. 2011a. "Bangladesh Finally Confronts War Crimes 40 Years On." *BBC News.* November 19, 2011. Available at http://www.bbc.co.uk/news/world-asia -15794246.

———. 2011b. "Bangladeshi War Film Meherjaan Rekindles Old Enmities." *BBC News.* April 19, 2011. Available at http://www.bbc.co.uk/news/world-south-asia-13034953.

Ferdaus, Rubaiyat, Mahmuduzzaman Babu, Kaberi Gayen, and Ferdousi Priyobhashini. 2011. "Meherjaan: An Insult to the Liberation War and Women." *Prothom Alo.* January 26, 2011.

Ferdousi, Shabnam. 2020. Interview by the author. Dhaka, Bangladesh. January 8, 2020.

Fitzsimons-Quail, Alice. 2015. "Who Is Speaking? Co-option, Authority, and Envisioning the Nation: Women and Narratives of Sexual Violence in Conflict." *South Asianist* 3, no. 2: 24–52.

Fleetwood, Nicole R. 2011. *Troubling Vision: Performance, Visuality, and Blackness.* Chicago: University of Chicago Press.

Fox, Nicole. 2019. "Memory in Interaction: Gender-Based Violence, Genocide, and Commemoration." *Signs: Journal of Women in Culture and Society.* 45, no. 1: 124–148.

Franco, Jean. 2013. *Cruel Modernity.* Durham, NC: Duke University Press.

Friedman, Marilyn. 1995. "Feminism and Modern Friendship: Dislocating the Community." In *Feminism and Community,* edited by Penny E. Weiss and Marilyn Friedman, 187–208. Philadelphia: Temple University Press.

Fuhrmann, Arnika. 2017. "*This Area Is [NOT] under Quarantine*: Rethinking Southeast/ Asia through Studies of the Cinema." In *Area Studies at the Crossroads: Knowledge Production after the Mobility Turn,* edited by Katja Mielke and Anna Katharina Hornidge, 251–268. New York: Palgrave Macmillan.

Gandhi, Leela. 2006. *Affective Communities: Anticolonial Thought, Fin-de-Siecle Radicalism, and the Politics of Friendship.* Durham, NC: Duke University Press.

Gayen, Kaberi. 2013. *Construction of Women in the War Films of Bangladesh* (*Muktizuddher Cholochchitre Naree Nirman*). Dhaka, Bangladesh: Bengal.

Gazi, Leesa. 2015. TEDx Talk. London School of Economics. May 7, 2015. Available at https://www.youtube.com/watch?v=Fr5UJMG5DGc.

Gendercide. n.d. "Case Study: Genocide in Bangladesh, 1971." Accessed June 1, 2021. Available at https://web.archive.org/web/20050204185006/http://gendercide.org/case _bangladesh.html.

Gilson, Erinn Cunniff. 2016. "Vulnerability and Victimization: Rethinking Key Concepts in Feminist Discourses on Sexual Violence." *Signs: Journal of Women in Culture and Society* 42, no. 1: 71–98.

Givoni, Michal. 2011. "Witnessing/Testimony." *Mafte'akh.* 2nd ed. (Winter): 147–169.

Goldberg, Elizabeth Swanson. 2007. *Beyond Terror: Gender, Narrative, Human Rights.* New Brunswick, NJ: Rutgers University Press.

Gordon, Avery. 1997. *Ghostly Matters: Haunting and the Sociological Imagination.* Minneapolis: University of Minnesota Press.

Guerilla. 2011. Directed by Nasiruddin Yousuff. Dhaka, Bangladesh: Ashirbad Cholochitra, Impress Telefilm.

Guerin, Frances, and Roger Hallas. 2007. "Introduction." In *The Image and the Witness: Trauma, Memory and Visual Culture,* edited by Frances Guerin and Roger Hallas, 1–20. London: Wallflower.

Guhathakurta, Meghna. 2003. "War and Woman: Tears Engraved in Stone." *South Asian Citizens Wire.* January 23, 2003. Available at http://insaf.net/pipermail/sacw_insaf .net/2003/001468.html.

———. 2005. "War of Symbols: How Today's Generation Remembers 1971." February 5, 2005. Available at https://web.archive.org/web/20050205160119/http://drishtipat.org /1971/war-meghna.html.

———. 2017. "Film Review Shilalipi." Available at https://www.academia.edu/8377324 /Film_review_Shilalipi.

Haq, Fahmidul, and Pronob Bhowmick. 2014. *Tareque Masud, Jatiotabad O Cholochitro* (*Tareque Masud, Nationalism and Cinema*). Dhaka, Bangladesh: Agami.

Haque, Muhammed Shahriar. 2015. "Discursive Legitimization of Rape-Discourse in Bangladeshi Popular Cinema." Proceedings of 2nd Research World International Conference, New York, USA, December 26: 14–19.

Hartman, Saidiya V. 1997. *Scenes of Subjection: Terror, Slavery, and Self-Making in Nineteenth Century America*. New York: Oxford University Press.

———. 2008. "Venus in Two Acts." *Small Axe* 12, no. 2: 1–14.

———. 2020. "Errant Daughters: A Conversation between Saidiya Hartman and Hazel Carby." January 21, 2020. Available at https://www.theparisreview.org/blog/2020/01/21/errant-daughters-a-conversation-between-saidiya-hartman-and-hazel-carby/.

Hartman, Saidiya V., and Frank B. Wilderson III. 2003. "The Position of the Unthought: An Interview with Saidiya V. Hartman Conducted by Frank B. Wilderson III." *Qui Parle* 13, no. 2 (Spring/Summer): 183–201.

Hayat, Anupam. 2011. *Bangladesher Muktijuddhobhittik Cholochitro (1971–2007)*. (*Muktijuddho-centered Films of Bangladesh (1971–2007)*). Dhaka: Bangladesh Film Archive.

Hesford, Wendy S., and Wendy Kozol, eds. 2001. *Haunting Violations: Feminist Criticism and the Crisis of the "Real."* Chicago: University of Illinois Press.

Hill, Glen, and Kabita Chakma. 2020. "Silencing Films from the Chittagong Hill Tracts: Indigenous Cinema's Challenge to the Imagined Cultural Homogeneity of Bangladesh." In *South Asian Filmscapes: Transregional Encounters*, edited by Elora Halim Chowdhury and Esha Niyogi De, 77–96. Seattle: University of Washington Press.

Hirsch, Marianne. 2008. "The Generation of Postmemory." *Poetics Today* 29, no. 1: 103–128.

Hobson, Janell. 2008. "Militarizing Women in Film: Toward a Cinematic Framing of War and Terror." In *Security Disarmed: Critical Perspectives on Gender, Race, and Militarization*, edited by Barbara Sutton, Sandra Morgen, and Julie Novkov, 231–243. New Brunswick, NJ: Rutgers University Press.

Hoek, Lotte. 2014. *Cut Pieces: Celluloid Obscenity and Popular Cinema in Bangladesh*. New York: Columbia University Press.

Hoffman, Eric. 1997. "Love as a Kind of Friendship." In *Sex, Love, and Friendship: Studies of the Society for the Philosophy of Sex and Love, 1977–1992*, edited by Alan Soble, 110–119. Amsterdam: Rodopi.

Hooliya. 1984. Directed by Tanvir Mokammel. Dhaka, Bangladesh: Kino-Eye Films.

Hossain, Hameeda. n.d. "The Lessons We Never Learn." Available at https://web.archive.org/web/20040331153243/http://www.drishtipat.org/1971/docs/war-hameeda.htm.

Hossain, Naomi. 2018. "The Geopolitics of Bare Life in 1970's Bangladesh." Paper presented at the Association for Asian Studies Conference in Washington, DC.

Innocent Millions. 1971. Directed by Babul Choudhury. Bangladesh: Bangladesh Government.

Islam, Kajalie Shehreen. 2012. "Breaking Down the Birangona: Examining the (Divided) Media Discourse on the War Heroines of Bangladesh's Independence Movement," *International Journal of Communication* 6. Available at https://ijoc.org/index.php/ijoc/article/view/874/787.

Itihaash Konna (*Daughters of History*). 2000. Directed by Shameem Akhtar. Dhaka, Bangladesh: Mrittika.

Jaikumar, Priya. 2007. "Translating Silences: A Cinematic Encounter with Incommensurable Difference." In *Transnational Feminism in Film and Media*, edited by Katarzyna Marciniak, Aniko Imre, and Aine O'Healy, 207–226. New York: Palgrave Macmillan.

Jankovic, Colleen. 2014. "Houses without Foundations: On Belonging in Palestinian Women's Cinema." E-cadernos CES 22. Available at https://journals.openedition.org/eces/1827.

Jibon thekey neya (Glimpses of Life). 1969. Directed by Zahir Raihan. Pakistan: Zahir Raihan.

Jonmo Sathi. 2016. Directed by Shabnam Ferdousi. Dhaka, Bangladesh: Liberation War Museum and Ekattor Media.

Joy Bangla (Victorious Bengal). 1972. Directed by Fakhrul Alam. Dhaka, Bangladesh.

"Juddhho Shishuder Niye Jonmoshathi" (Born Together Screened with the War Children). 2016. *Prothom Alo*. Available at https://www.prothomalo.com/amp/entertainment/article/808090/%E0%A6%AF%E0%A7%81%E0%A6%A6%E0%A7%8D%E0%A6%A7%E0%A6%B6%E0%A6%BF%E0%A6%B6%E0%A7%81%E0%A6%A6%E0%A7%87%E0%A6%B0-%E0%A6%A8%E0%A6%BF%E0%A7%9F%E0%A7%87-%E2%80%98%E0%A6%9C%E0%A6%A8%E0%A7%8D%E0%A6%AE%E0%A6%B8%E0%A6%BE%E0%A6%A5%E0%A7%80%E2%80%99.

Junaid, Naadir. 2020. "Cinema That Raises a Critical Consciousness: The Films of Alamgir Kabir." In *South Asian Filmscapes Transregional Encounters*, edited by Elora Halim Chowdhury and Esha Niyogi De, 266–282. Seattle: University of Washington Press.

Kabir, Ananya Jahanara. 2005. "Gender, Memory, Trauma: Women's Novels on the Partition of India." *Comparative Studies of South Asia, Africa and the Middle East* 25:177–190.

Kaminsky, Amy. 2006. "Marco Bechis' Garage Olimpo." *Jump Cut: A Review of Contemporary Media*. Accessed June 1, 2021. Available at https://www.ejumpcut.org/archive/jc48.2006/GarageOlimpo/text.html.

Kanon, Rukhsana Karim. 2015. "Our Liberation War on Celluloid." *Bangladesh Film Archive Journal* 9 (December): 75–81.

Kaplan, E. Ann. 2005. *Trauma Culture: The Politics of Terror and Loss in Media and Literature*. New Brunswick, NJ: Rutgers University Press.

Karim, Lamia. 2004. "Democratizing Bangladesh: State, NGOs, Militant Islam." *Cultural Dynamics* 16, nos. 2–3 (October): 291–318.

Khan, Salimullah. 2018. "Bhumika: Alamgir Kabirer Oggyan Othoba: 'Ami Muktijuddhoke Bujhte Parini'" (Introduction: The Bewilderment of Alamgir Kabir: "I Did Not Understand the Muktijuddho"). In *Cholochitro O Jatiyo Mukti: Alamgir Kabir's Rochona Shongroho (Cinema and National Freedom: Collected Essays of Alamgir Kabir)*, vol. 1, edited by Abul Khayer Mohammad Atiquzzaman and Priyam Pritam Pal, 13–38. Dhaka, Bangladesh: Agami Prokashoni.

Khan, Zeeshan Rahman. 2006. "The State We Are In." *Star Weekend Magazine* 5, no. 90: April 14, 2006. Available at http://archive.thedailystar.net/magazine/2006/04/02/pers.htm.

Khoja-Moolji, Shehnila. 2016. "The Making of Humans and Their Others in and through Transnational Human Rights Advocacy: Exploring the Cases of Mukhtar Mai and Malala Yousafzai." *Signs: Journal of Women in Culture and Society* 42, no. 2: 377–402.

LaCapra, Dominick. 1999. "Trauma, Absence, Loss." *Critical Inquiry* 25, no. 4: 696–727.

———. 2001. *Writing History, Writing Trauma*. Baltimore: Johns Hopkins University Press.

Laclau, Ernesto. 2006. "On the Names of God." In *Political Theologies: Public Religions in a Post-secular World*, edited by Hent de Vries and Lawrence E. Sullivan, 137–147. New York: Fordham University Press.

Langerova, Viera. 2018. "Bangladesh: The Rising National Cinema: In 16th Dhaka International Film Festival." Available at http://fipresci.org/report/bangladesh-the-rising-national-cinema/.

Larkin, Brian. 2019. "The Grounds of Circulation: Rethinking African Film and Media." *Politique Africaine* 153, no. 1: 105–126.

Laub, Dori, and Shoshanna Felman. 1992. *Testimony: Crisis of Witnessing in Literature, Psychoanalysis, and History.* New York: Routledge.

Le Monde. 2002. "Interview with Tareque Masud." *Le Monde*, May 15, 2002. Available at http://ctmasud.web.aplus.net/filmmakers/interview_LeMonde.htm.

Liberation Fighters. 1971. Directed by Alamgir Kabir. Bangladesh: Bangladesh Government.

Lindsey, Treva B. 2013. "Complicated Crossroads: Black Feminisms, Sex Positivism, and Popular Culture." *African and Black Diaspora* 6:55–65.

Lugones, Maria, in collaboration with Pat Alake Rosezelle. 1995. "Sisterhood and Friendship as Feminist Models." In *Feminism and Community*, edited by Penny E. Weiss and Marilyn Friedman, 135–146. Philadelphia: Temple University Press.

Lynch, Sandra. 2005. *Philosophy and Friendship.* Edinburgh, UK: Edinburgh University Press.

MacManus, Viviana Beatriz. 2020. *Disruptive Archives: Feminisst Memories of Resistance in Latin America's Dirty Wars.* Chicago: University of Illinois Press.

Mansbridge, Jane. 1995. "Feminism and Democratic Community." In *Feminism and Community*, edited by Penny E. Weiss and Marilyn Friedman, 341–366. Philadelphia: Temple University Press.

Mascarenhas, Anthony. 1972. *The Rape of Bangladesh.* Delhi: Vikas.

Masud, M. 2017. "They Are Not the Result of Anyone's Sin" (*Ora karo paaper foshol na*). *Prothom Alo*, December 16, 2017. Available at http://www.prothomalo.com/entertainment/article/1387871/%E2%80%98%E0%A6%93%E0%A6%B0%E0%A6%BE-%E0%A6%95%E0%A6%BE%E0%A6%B0%E0%A6%93-%E0%A6%AA%E0%A6%BE%E0%A6%AA%E0%A7%87%E0%A6%B0-%E0%A6%AB%E0%A6%B8%E0%A6%B2-%E0%A6%A8%E0%A6%BE%E2%80%99%3E.

Maswood, Manzur H. 2019. "Morshedul Islam: The Maestro of Independent Cinema." *New Age*, April 19, 2019. Available at http://www.newagebd.net/article/70267/morshedul-islam-the-maestro-of-independent-cinema.

Mbembé, Achille. 2003. "Necropolitics." Translated by Libby Meintjes. *Public Culture* 15, no. 1: 11–40.

McClintock, Anne. 1991. "'No Longer in a Future Heaven': Women and Nationalism in South Africa." *Transition* 51:104–123.

McHugh, Kathleen. 2009. "The World and the Soup: Historicizing Media Feminisms in Transnational Contexts." *Camera Obscura: Feminism, Culture, and Media Studies* 24, no. 3: 111–150.

McKittrick, Katherine, ed. 2015. *Sylvia Wynter: On Being Human as Praxis.* Durham, NC: Duke University Press.

McWilliams, Sally E. 2009. "Intervening in Trauma: Bodies, Violence, and Interpretive Possibilities in Vyvyane Loh's *Breaking the Tongue*." *Tulsa Studies in Women's Literature* 28, no. 1: 141–163.

Megher Onek Rong. 1976. Directed by Harunur Rashid. Dhaka, Bangladesh: Rotna Kothachitra.

Meherjaan. 2011. Directed by Rubaiyat Hossain. Dhaka, Bangladesh: Era Motion Picture.

Meherjaan Debate 1. 2011. Arts. *bdnews24.com*, February 17, 2011. Available at http://arts.bdnews24.com/?p=3417.

Meherjaan Debate 7. 2011. Arts. *bdnews24.com*, June 2, 2011. Available at http://arts.bdnews24.com/?p=3710.

Meherjaan Press Kit. 2011. Available at http://www.khonatalkies.com/meherjaan.php.

Meherjaan Screening and Panel Presentations. 2011. Harvard University, November 3, 2011. Cambridge, Massachusetts.

Meherjaan website. n.d. Available at http://www.khonatalkies.com/meherjaan.php.

Mengesha, Lilian G. 2017. "Defecting Witness: The Difficulty in Watching Regina Jose Galindo's PERRA." *Drama Review* 61, no. 2: 140–157.

Mignolo, Walter D. 2015. "Sylvia Winter: What Does It Mean to Be Human?" In *Sylvia Wynter: On Being Human as Praxis*, edited by Katherine McKittrick, 106–123. Durham, NC: Duke University Press.

Mohaiemen, Naeem. 2011. "Women on the Verge." *Himal Southasian* (March): 83–84.

Mokammel, Tanvir. 2017. "Bangladesher Bikolpo Cinemar Andolon a Kichu Obhiggota." (Bangladesh Film Society Movement and Some Experiences). *Bangladesh Film Archive Journal* 12 (June): 54–58.

Mookherjee, Nayanika. 2003. "Ethical Issues Concerning Representation of Narratives of Sexual Violence of 1971." Available at http://www.drishtipat.org/1971/docs/war_nayanika.pdf.

———. 2008. "Gendered Embodiments: Mapping the Body Politic of the Raped Woman and the Nation in Bangladesh." *Feminist Review* 88, no. 1: 36–53.

———. 2011. "Love in the Time of 1971: The Furore over *Meherjaan*." *Economic and Political Weekly* 46, no. 12: 25–27.

———. 2015. *The Spectral Wound: Sexual Violence, Public Memories, and the Bangladesh War of 1971*. Durham, NC: Duke University Press.

Moraga, Cherrie. 1983. "Refugees of a World on Fire: Foreword to the Second Edition." In *This Bridge Called My Back: Writings by Radical Women of Color*, edited by Cherrie Moraga and Gloria Anzaldúa. 2nd ed. New York: Kitchen Table/Women of Color.

Moten, Fred. 2003. *In the Break: The Aesthetics of the Black Radical Tradition*. Minneapolis: University of Minnesota Press.

Mukh O Mukhosh (*The Face and the Mask*). 1956. Directed by Abdul Jabbar Khan. Dhaka, Bangladesh: Iqbal Films.

Muktir Gaan (*Song of Freedom*). 1995. Directed by Catherine Masud and Tareque Masud. Dhaka, Bangladesh: Audiovision.

Muktir Kotha (*Words of Freedom*). 1999. Directed by Catherine Masud and Tareque Masud. Dhaka, Bangladesh: Audiovision.

"Mumbai Utshobe Jacchhe Jonmoshathi" (Born Together Going to Mumbai Film Festival), 2018. banglatribune.com, January 20, 2018. Available at https://www.banglatribune.com/entertainment/284499/%E0%A6%AE%E0%A7%81%E0%A6%AE%E0%A7%8D%E0%A6%AC%E0%A6%BE%E0%A6%87-%E0%A6%89%E0%A7%8E%E0%A6%B8%E0%A6%AC%E0%A7%87-%E0%A6%AF%E0%A6%BE%E0%A6%9A%E0%A7%8D%E0%A6%9B%E0%A7%87-%E2%80%98%E0%A6%9C%E0%A6%A8%E0%A7%8D%E0%A6%AE%E0%A6%B8%E0%A6%BE%E0%A6%A5%E0%A7%80%E2%80%99.

Murphy, Ann V. 2011. "Corporeal Vulnerability and the New Humanism." *Hypatia* 26: 575–590.

Nagar, Richa, and the Sangtin Writers. 2006. *Playing with Fire: Feminist Thought and Activism through Seven Lives in India*. Minneapolis: University of Minnesota Press.

Narayan, Uma. 1988. "Working Together across Difference: Some Considerations on Emotions and Political Practice." *Hypatia* 3, no. 2: 133–140.

———. 1995. "Colonialism and Its Others: Considerations on Rights and Care Discourses." *Hypatia* 10, no. 2: 31–47.

Narir Kotha (*Women and War*). 2000. Directed by Catherine Masud and Tareque Masud. Dhaka, Bangladesh: Audiovision.

Nash, Jennifer. 2008. "Strange Bedfellows: Black Feminism and Antipornography Feminism." *Social Text* 97, no. 25: 51–77.

Netto, Priscilla. 2005. "Reclaiming the Body of the 'Hottentot': The Vision and Visuality of the Body Speaking with Vengeance in *Venus Hotentot 2000.*" *European Journal of Women's Studies* 12, no. 2: 149–163.

Nichols, Bill. 1983. "The Voice of Documentary." *Film Quarterly* 36, no. 3: 17–30.

Niloy, Suliman. 2016. "Shabnam Ferdousi's 'Born Together' Attempts to Document Lives of Bangladesh War Children." *bdnews24.com*, March 22, 2016. Available at https://bdnews24.com/film/2016/03/22/shabnam-ferdousis-born-together-attempts-to-document-lives-of-bangladesh-war-children.

Ora Egaro Jon. 1972. Directed by Chashi Nazrul Islam. Dhaka, Bangladesh: Parvez Films.

Orunodoyer Ognishakkhi. 1972. Directed by Subhash Dutta. Dhaka, Bangladesh: Shatodal Kothachitra.

Panjabi, Kavita. 2005. *Old Maps and New: Legacies of the Partition.* Calcutta: Seagull.

Parikh, Crystal. 2017. *Writing Human Rights: The Political Imaginaries of Writers of Color.* Minneapolis: University of Minnesota Press.

Perry, Imani. 2018. *Vexy Thing: On Gender and Liberation.* Durham, NC: Duke University Press.

Pettman, Jan Jindy. 2006. "Women, Colonisation, and Racism." In *Beyond Borders: Thinking Critically about Global Issues*, edited by Paula S. Rothenberg, 142–149. New York: Worth.

The Poison Thorn. 2015. Directed by Farzana Boby. Bangladesh: Khona Talkies. DVD.

"Post-independence Bangladeshi Cinema: Through the Lens of the Film Stars." 1977. *Chitrali.* March 25, 1977.

Puri, Jyoti. 2016. "Juxtaposing 'Antipolice' Rhetorics: Policing, Race, Gender, and Sexuality across Southern Contexts." Paper presented at *National Women's Studies Association Annual Conference: Decoloniality.* Montreal, Quebec. November 10–13, 2016.

Raju, Zakir Hossain. 2002. "Bangladesh: A Defiant Survivor." In *Being and Becoming: The Cinemas of Asia*, edited by Aruna Vasudev, Latika Padgaonkar, and Rashmi Doraiswamy, 1–25. Delhi: Macmillan.

———. 2015. *Bangladesh Cinema and National Identity: In Search of the Modern?* London: Routledge.

Rehman, Nasreen. 2020. "Pakistan, History, and Sleep: Hassan Tariq, a Progressive Patriarch, and Neend." In *South Asian Filmscapes: Transregional Encounters*, edited by Elora Halim Chowdhury and Esha Niyogi De, 97–116. Seattle: University of Washington Press.

Rich, Adrienne. 1995. "If Not with Others, How?" In *Feminism and Community*, edited by Penny E. Weiss and Marilyn Friedman, 399–406. Philadelphia: Temple University Press.

Richlin, Amy. 1997. "Foucault's History of Sexuality: A Useful Theory for Women?" In *Rethinking Sexuality: Foucault and Classical Antiquity*, edited by David H. J. Larmour, Paul Allen Miller, and Charles Platter, 138–170. Princeton, NJ: Princeton University Press.

Rina Brown. 2017. Directed by Shameem Akhtar. Dhaka, Bangladesh: Mrittika.

Rising Silence. 2019. Directed by Leesa Gazi. Bangladesh: Komola Collective.

Robinson, Cheri. 2017. "Representations of Transnational Violence: Children in Contemporary Latin American Film, Literature and Drawings." PhD diss., UCLA, Los Angeles. Available at https://escholarship.org/uc/item/86c996hr.

Roktakto Bangla (Blood Stained Bengal). 1972. Directed by Momtaz Ali. Dhaka, Bangladesh: Momo Kothachitro.

Rothe, Ann. 2011. *Popular Trauma Culture: Selling the Pain of Others in the Mass Media.* New Brunswick, NJ: Rutgers University Press.

Roy, Sandip. 2004. "A Boy, a Nation, and a Clay Bird." *India Currents*, June 14, 2004. Available at http://www.indiacurrents.com/news/view_article.html?article_id=1a1ef52726 2e67c758fd3.

Rummel, R. J. 1997. *Death by Government.* New York: Routledge.

Saikia, Yasmin. 2011. *Women, War, and the Making of Bangladesh: Remembering 1971.* Durham, NC: Duke University Press.

Sajjad, Lt. Col. 2012. "Asgar Baluch: A Baluchi Soldier." *Daily Star: Independence Day Special*, March 26, 2012. Available at http://www.thedailystar.net/suppliments/2012/26 _march/pg11.htm.

Sajjad, Tazreena. 2009. "The Post-Genocidal Period and its Impact on Women." In *Plight and Fate of Women During and Following Genocide*, edited by Samuel Totten, 219–248. New York: Routledge.

Sangster, Joan. 1994. "Telling Our Stories: Feminist Debates and the Use of Oral History." *Women's History Review* 3, no. 1: 5–28.

Saptapadi. Directed by Ajoy Kar. 1961. India: Alochhaya Productions Pvt. Ltd.

Schaffer, Kay, and Sidonie Smith. 2004. *Human Rights and Narrated Lives: The Ethics of Recognition.* New York: Palgrave MacMillan.

Shah, Subi. 2019. "The Filmmaker Bringing Survivor Stories to Light." *New Internationalist*, July 25, 2019. Available at https://newint.org/features/2019/06/19/mixed-media -spotlight-leesa-gazi.

Shaikh, Nermeen. 2004. "Interview with Tareque Masud." *Asia Source*, June 1, 2004. Available at https://asiasociety.org/interview-tareque-masud-director-clay-bird.

Shilalipi (The Inscription). 2004. Directed by Shameem Akhtar. Dhaka, Bangladesh: Mrittika.

"'Shilalipi' to Be Screened at Goethe Institut on Sunday." 2019. *Dhaka Tribune*, March 17, 2019. Available at https://www.dhakatribune.com/showtime/2019/03/17/shilalipi -to-be-screened-at-goethe-institut-on-saturday.

Shimana Periye. 1977. Directed by Alamgir Kabir. Dhaka, Bangladesh.

Shohat, Ella. 2003. "Post-Third-Worldist Culture: Gender, Nation, and the Cinema." In *Rethinking Third Cinema*, edited by Anthony Guneratne and Wimal Dissanayake, 51–78. London: Routledge.

Shongram. 1974. Directed by Chashi Nazrul Islam. Dhaka, Bangladesh: Anupam Kothachitra.

Shongram 71. 2014. Directed by Munsur Ali. London: Spotlight UK.

Shorot'71 (Autumn '71). 2000. Directed by Morshedul Islam. Dhaka: Bangladesh: Bangladesh Shishu Academy.

Shurjokonna (Daughter of the Sun). 1977. Directed by Alamgir Kabir. Dhaka, Bangladesh: Alamgir Pictures.

Siddiqi, Dina. 2003. "In Search of Shonar Bangla." *Himal Southasian.* Available at http:// www.himalmag.com/component/content/article/146/1811-In-Search-of-Shonar-Bangla.html.

———. 2013. "Left Behind by the Nation: 'Stranded Pakistanis' in Bangladesh." *SITES: New Series* 10, no. 1: 150–183.

———. 2017. "Ghosts of 1947." Available at https://www.thedailystar.net/star-weekend /ghosts-1947-1452604.

Sobhan, Zafar. 2011. "The Pakistani Patient." *Sunday Guardian*, February 1, 2011. Available at http://www.sunday-guardian.com/analysis/love-in-the-time-of-civil-war.

Sophocles, Aeschylus, Euripides. 2017. *The Greek Plays*, edited by Mary Lefkowitz and James Room. New York: Modern Library.

Spillers, Hortense J. et al. 2007. "'Whatcha Gonna Do?' Revisiting 'Mama's Baby, Papa's Maybe: An American Grammar Book'; A Conversation with Hortense Spillers, Saidiya Hartman, Farah Jasmine Griffin, Shelly Eversley, and Jennifer L. Morgan." *Women's Studies Quarterly* 35, nos. 1–2: 299–309.

Spivak, Gayatri. 2008. *Other Asias*. New York: Wiley Blackwell.

Srinivas, Lakshmi. 2005. "Communicating Globalization in Bombay Cinema: Everyday Life, Imagination and the Persistence of the Local." *Comparative American Studies* 3, no. 3: 319–344.

Stillman, Sarah. 2007. "The Missing White Girl Syndrome": Disappeared Women and Media Activism. *Gender and Development* 15, no. 3: 491–502.

Stone-Mediatore, Shari. 2003. *Reading across Borders: Storytelling and Knowledges of Resistance*. New York: Palgrave Macmillan.

A State is Born. 1971. *A State Is Born*. Directed by Zahir Raihan. Bangladesh: Bangladesh Government.

Stop Genocide. 1971. Directed by Zahir Raihan. Bangladesh: Bangladesh Chalachitra Shilpi-O-Kushali Swahayak Samity and Bangladesh Liberation Council of the Intelligentsia.

Sutton, Barbara. 2007. Poner el cuerpo: Women's Embodiment and Political Resistance in Argentina. *Latin American Politics and Society* 49, no. 3: 129–162.

Tawil-Souri, Helga. 2005. "Coming into Being and Flowing into Exile: History and Trends in Palestinian Film-Making." *Nebula* 2, no. 2: 113–140.

"Team Rina Brown." 2017. *Daily Star*, January 21, 2017. Available at https://www.thedailystar.net/showbiz/cover-story/team-rina-brown-1348345.

Titas Ekti Nodir Naam (*A River Called Titash*). 1973. Directed by Ritwik Ghatak. Dhaka, Bangladesh.

Torchin, Leshu. 2007. "Since We Forgot: Remembrance and Recognition of the Armenian Genocide in Virtual Archives." In *The Image and the Witness*, edited by Frances Guerin and Roger Hallas, 82–97. London: Wallflower.

Tripathi, Salil. 2016. *The Colonel Who Would Not Repent: The Bangladesh War and Its Unquiet Legacy*. New Haven, CT: Yale University Press.

Tuck, Eve. 2009. "Suspending Damage: A Letter to Communities." *Harvard Educational Review* 79, no. 3: 409–427.

———. 2010. "Breaking Up with Deleuze: Desire and Valuing the Irreconcilable." *International Journal of Qualitative Studies in Education* 23, no. 5: 635–650.

Tuck, Eve, and K. Wayne Yang. 2014. "R-Words: Refusing Research." In *Humanizing Research: Decolonizing Qualitative Inquiry with Youth and Communities*, edited by Django Paris and Maisha T. Winn, 223–247. Thousand Oaks, CA: Sage.

Van Schendel, Willem. 2015. "A War within a War: Mizo Rebels and the Bangladesh Liberation Struggle." *Modern Asian Studies* (October): 1–43.

Wasserman, Tina. 2007. "Constructing the Image of Postmemory." In *The Image and the Witness: Trauma Memory and Visual Culture*. Edited by Frances Guerin and Roger Hallas, 159–173. London: Wallflower.

Weheliye, Alexander G. 2014. *Habeas Viscus: Racializing Assemblages, Biopolitics, and Black Feminist Theories of the Human*. Durham, NC: Duke University Press.

Weiss, Penny, and Marilyn Friedman, eds. 1995. *Feminism and Community*. Philadelphia: Temple University Press.

White, Patricia. 2015. *Women's Cinema, World Cinema: Projecting Contemporary Feminisms*. Durham, NC: Duke University Press.

Wilderson III, Frank B. 2003. "The Prison Slave as Hegemony's (Silent) Scandal." *Social Justice* 30, no. 2: 18–27.

———. 2010. *Red, White, and Black: Cinema and the Structure of US Antagonisms*. Durham, NC: Duke University Press.

Williams, Patricia J. 1998. "What's Love Got to Do with It?" *The Nation* 23 (November):10.

Woolf, Virginia. 1963. *Three Guineas*. New York: Harvest Books.

Wright, Melissa W. 2011. "Necropolitics, Narcopolitics, and Femicide: Gendered Violence on the Mexico–U.S. Border." *Signs* 3, no. 36: 707–731.

Wynter, Silvia. 2003. "Unsettling the Coloniality of Being/Power/Truth/Freedom: Towards the Human, after Man, Its Overrepresentation—An Argument." *CR: The New Centennial Review* 3, no. 3: 257–337.

Wynter, Silvia, and Katherine McKittrick. 2015. "Unparalleled Catastrophe for Our Species? Or, to Give Humanness a Different Future: Conversations." In *Sylvia Wynter: On Being Human as Praxis*, edited by Katherine McKittrick, 9–89. Durham, NC: Duke University Press.

Young, Iris Marion. 1995. "The Ideal of Community and the Politics of Difference." In *Feminism and Community*, edited by Penny E. Weiss and Marilyn Friedman, 233–258. Philadelphia: Temple University Press.

Yusuf, Ananta. 2014. "Between Politics, Cinema and Art." *Daily Star*, January 31, 2014. Available at https://www.thedailystar.net/between-politics-cinema-and-art-9139.

Zaman, Nadeem. 2018. *In the Time of the Others*. New Delhi: Picador.

Zamann, Mustafa. 2006. "Women against the Odds." *Star Weekend Magazine* 5, no. 81 (February 3, 2006).

Index

Page numbers in italics refer to illustrations.

Elora Halim Chowdhury is Professor of Women's, Gender, and Sexuality Studies at the University of Massachusetts Boston. She is the author of *Transnationalism Reversed: Women Organizing against Gendered Violence in Bangladesh,* which won the National Women's Studies Association's Gloria E. Anzaldúa Book Prize. She is the coeditor of *South Asian Filmscapes: Transregional Encounters; Interdisciplinary Approaches to Human Rights: History, Politics, Practice;* and *Dissident Friendships: Feminism, Imperialism, and Transnational Solidarity.*